EBRAHIM SOUFIANI

THE LOST KEY

AuthorHouse™
1663 Liberty Drive
Bloomington, IN 47403
www.authorhouse.com
Phone: 1-800-839-8640

© 2012 by Ebrahim Soufiani. All rights reserved.

No part of this book may be reproduced, stored in a retrieval system, or transmitted by any means without the written permission of the author.

Published by AuthorHouse   11/29/2012

ISBN: 978-1-4772-3926-1 (sc)
ISBN: 978-1-4772-3927-8 (e)

Any people depicted in stock imagery provided by Thinkstock are models, and such images are being used for illustrative purposes only.

Certain stock imagery © Thinkstock.

Because of the dynamic nature of the Internet, any web addresses or links contained in this book may have changed since publication and may no longer be valid. The views expressed in this work are solely those of the author and do not necessarily reflect the views of the publisher, and the publisher hereby disclaims any responsibility for them.

SIMORGH—سیمرغ

A painting by one of my best friends, Dr Farshid Pajavand, prepared specifically for this book. Image description to follow.

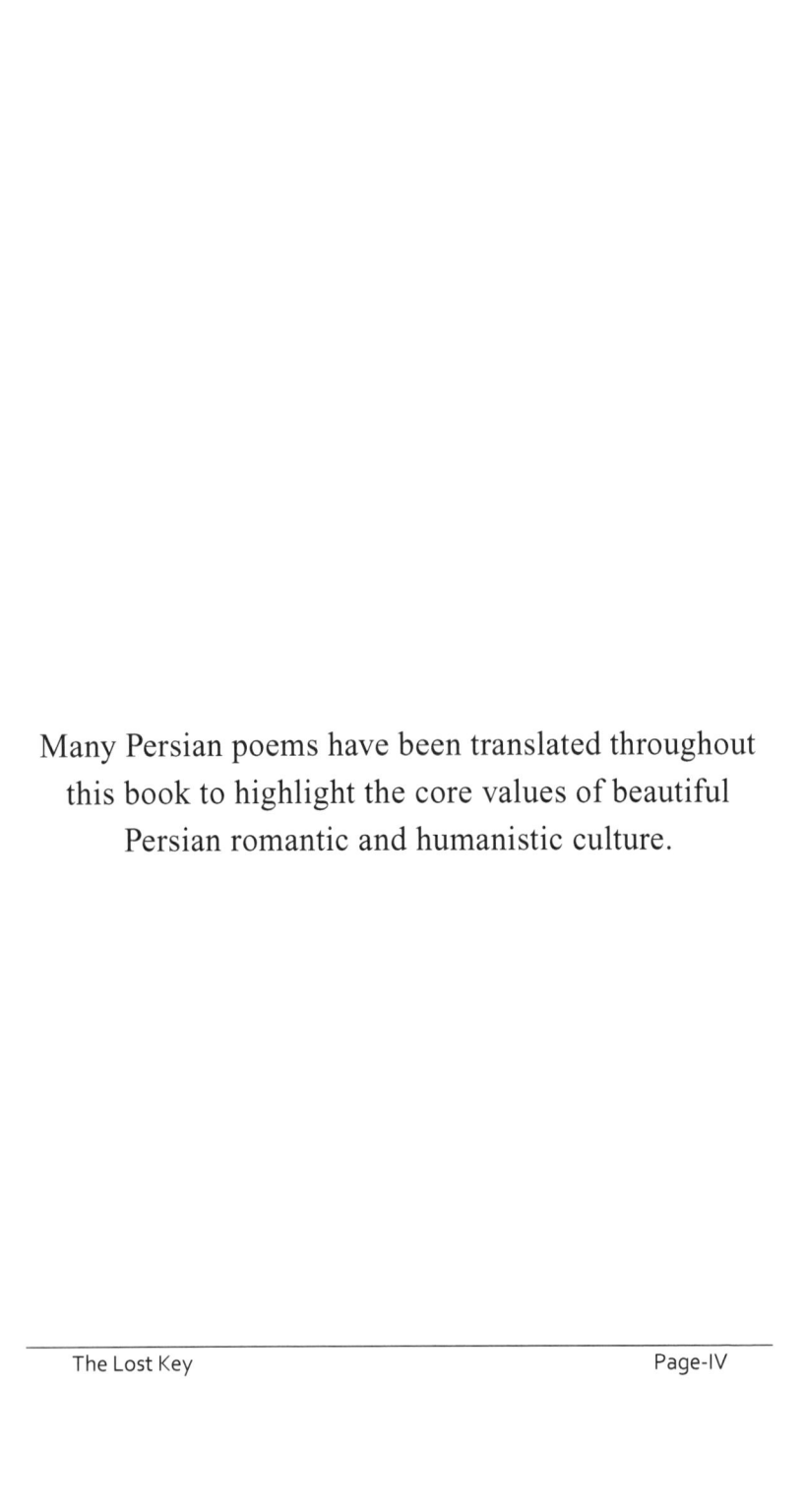

Many Persian poems have been translated throughout this book to highlight the core values of beautiful Persian romantic and humanistic culture.

An exploration into Persian literature in comparison with Western civilization and the lack of democracy in the Middle East

A helpful INDEX is added towards the end of this book for quick references to the interesting verses in this book.

Please use the INDEX for a quick glance.

The ultimate truth is life
Life is divine and beautiful
Every being in this life is divine
I pray to this life
Life is sanctity
Believing in this life is the true meaning of secularism
The best way of rejecting god is to believe every 'being' is god
I explore, therefore, I am

July 2012

این نکته رمز اگر بدانی، دانی
هر چه که در جستن آنی، آنی

—Rumi

Know this secret, you will adore
You are what you explore

ترا هرکس ، بسوی خویش خواند
ترا من، جز بسوی تو، نخوانم

—Rumi

Everyone calls you to their own affiliation
I call you to nobody, but to your own aspiration

Professor Manuchehr Jamali

Dedication

This book is solely devoted to Persian thinker and philosopher Professor Manuchehr Jamali—Jamali is my true spiritual instructor. He has published over 150 books on Persian literature in the Persian language. This book is the result of over ten years of study that touched only upon a fraction on the fifty years of research work of this great man, without whom I couldn't have written this book.

Tragic, shocking, and unbelievable news arrived to me as I made my final preparations of this book—we have lost this great man (5 July

2012—aged: 84), an event that I wholly did not expect. I had found him very healthy in a meeting I had with him just a month before regarding this book. My deepest condolences go to his family and his followers for such a massive loss.

This book is also dedicated to people who are nice to others, who love their pets, and who are excited by the prospect of exchanging new and intellectual ideas. You're a rare and special group.

Acknowledgements

Many thanks to Dr Farshid Pajavand for the paintings he has contributed for this book. Many thanks to the people at AuthorHouse publishing company for keeping this project under control and making sure that my words make sense!

Most of all, thanks to you, the reader, for being interested in this book, *The Lost Key*! You are about to venture into one of the most exciting, rewarding, and creative vision in the chain of the exploration into humanity that has remained lost to most of us for over a thousand years.

I want to hear from you!

As the reader of this book, you are my most important critic. I value your opinion and want to know what I am doing right, what I could do better, what areas you'd like to see me publish in, and any other words of wisdom you're willing to pass in my way.

You can e-mail me to let me know what you did or didn't like about this book, as well as what I can do to make my future books stronger.

Please note that, due to the high volume of e-mails I receive, I might not be able to reply to every message.

When you write, please be sure to include this book's title as well as your name. I will carefully review your comments.

E-mail   feedback@simorghian.com

Reader Services

Visit my website at www.simorghian.com/errata for convenient access to any updates, downloads, or errata that might be available for this book.

THE ABOVE IMAGE/PAINTING DESCRIPTION

Simorgh

The above painting is Persian Simorgh (Phoenix)—from a silver plate that shows the birth of Raam (goddess or Eizad-Banoo[1]) from Simorgh. The naked lady is Raam, Venus, or Aphrodite, the goddess of love, music, happiness, dance, and freedom. This is exactly the Persian version of Venus and the goddess. This beautifully crafted goddess of ideal humanness is made to be touched and to be dressed up an idol. God, to our ancestors, who, by the way, had great humanness and philosophical awareness, was the essence, the mind, and the ethics of every man and woman. God was imminent in every being—this is not hallucination or superstitious… god is beauty and beauty hits us in a moment or a flash and goes away. These momentary events are the most valuable part of our life. Moreover, god was the actual human being and equal to the human. God wasn't an external power separated from humanity; god *was* the humanity. God was an internal strength in every being.

In her work, archaeologist Marija Gimbutas (discussed in chapter 13) revealed the existence of the European goddess culture. I find that this culture has amazing similarities with the culture that comes from the Persian bird, Simorgh. Gimbutas's discoveries show that goddess cultures in Europe achieved amazing and remarkable unity and peace, as did the goddess cultures in the Middle East. In these cultures, people

---

[1] *Eizad-Banoo(Persian word): god woman, goddess*

could feel god, touch god, and smell god. However, these cultures went through very rough times and were deliberately and intentionally concealed from us. Their history has been suppressed for hundreds of years. The complaints over such cover-ups are plentiful in Persian literature; especially Rumi has written many poems in this regard. He said he wants to touch, feel, kiss, and hug the divine. This is the god who is the essence of humanity, a power within, but not an external power.

It was only later in the span of human life that 'god' becomes separated from humanity and was made, bigger, larger, and eventually superior. In fact, god was made unreachable and finally transformed to the almighty God of the Zoroastrian and Abrahamic religions. It is at this period that humanity started losing its own purity and essence to a super god. This led to the separation between the values (essences) and humanity to a large extent. Rumi complained of this exact separation of humanity from the essence of humanity:

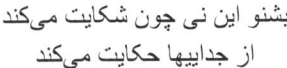

Listen to the tale of this reed
Of the separation pain, it read

Description of this poem: Rumi asks us to listen to the sad sounds or tale of this reed—or flute—which sings the song of the separation pain. The reed or flute here is the message from the book of Rumi and also the divine. What separation pain is this? It is the separation between us and our essence, or from the divine within us.

Through these religious doctrines, our essence, our values, and the true meaning of humanity has been stolen from us and given to an almighty God. Such a huge and supernatural God is unreachable and out of touch with humanity, and therefore we can no longer reach our values. Such an almighty God and such unreachable thoughts are at the base of many of the most critical problems facing humanity today.

The image is from a plate that is kept in the Saint Petersburg Museum in Russia—more than 1,600 years old, which comes from the Sassanian Dynasty (the Persian Empire before Islam). The plate contains the image of a bird that represents Simorgh (also called Sanam, San or Sun). There is also a naked woman, who is Raam or Zohreh, the equivalent of Aphrodite or Venus. The plate represents a culture that lasted over six thousand years and advocated love and friendship. For example, the name of the Persian dynasty of Hakhamaneshian, 500 BCE, means the dynasty of love and friendship. It was a belief that a dynasty could last only through musical and harmonic control, not by force. Such humanitarian views are plenty in Persian literature: As Ferdowsi (940-1020) said:

ستم نامهٔ عزل شاهان بود
چو درد دل بیگناهان بود

Oppression is a letter to the leader, to be deposed
When the grief of innocents is exposed

Description of this poem: Ferdowsi said that, if any ruler or leader takes the path of oppression or tyranny on his own people, the tyranny causes the grief of the innocents. Therefore, if a leader practices oppression, he will automatically receive a letter from the people indicating he should be deposed. If the leader remains in power, then he has to rule by force.

This culture reached many parts of the world—even as far as Europe and Africa. For example, the word *sun* in English, *Sonne* in German and *san* in Turkish derive from the name of this bird Simorgh or Sanam: Reference Indo-European (Sanskrit) and Rumi, the believer of Sanam (Venus)—Manuchehr Jamali.

Mithraism is a split branch of this ethical view; in fact, the Temple of Mithras was discovered accidentally during construction work beside the Walbrook, a street in London.

Sanam or Simorgh represents our capacity for vision with its great beauty creating intense excitement, flow, and deathless inspiration. Simorgh is our soul representing purity, humanity, love, music, and imagination that flies and gives us passionate freedom of the mind. This is the origin of human thinking and philosophy that gives meaning to our lives and worries the powers who desire to be in control over people. The religious ideas that originated from this bird have been manipulated to the advantage of leaders of society, who have caged the bird. Of course, a caged bird is no longer a free bird.

The phrase 'Simorgh rising from the ashes' means that, although humanity, purity, and love may burn or die and turn into ashes, one day it will rise again from its ashes. This means that humanity won't die, and there is always hope for a better world.

Although the painting shows a mythical story, it also represents mankind's ethical past of love and ultimate freedom, helping others, helping the weakest, and admiring the ultimate freedom. The woman is under the total protection of the bird, and the bird is being fed by the woman—a kind of give-and-take philosophy. This proves that our ancestors were very conscious about protecting the weakest, women and children, and helping each other in the process.

Another name of this woman is Al, Elah, or Elaheh in the Arabic language. Even the word for the Muslim God, Allah, is from the name of this woman. Allah is the confined version of Elah. In the Quran, there is a clear message (La Elah Ela Allah) of praying to Allah but not Elah, but there is no clear note explaining of who Elah is. The word *haram* (not permissible by Islamic law) in Islam is *hu-ram* or *khoram*[2] (خرَم) in the Persian language, which means happiness, which again means this goddess. As mentioned earlier, the name of this goddess is Ram. The original meaning of haram was anything that comes from Ram, the land where people used to believe in happiness or used to believe into this goddess.

In fact, religions are a part of mankind's ethical evolution that has been snatched out of the history of human culture and kept in a cage or an enclosed frame of mind and manipulated by authorities to suit their own agendas in ruling or controlling over people. This means: *the values of humanity also have been stolen from us and given to the God of these religions*. For this reason, when we lose our religion we lose the values with it, if we are not conscious enough. Our challenge is to take these stolen values from God, or these religions, and offer it back to humanity—to its true and real owner.

---

[2] *Khoram (Persian word): happiness*

Aside from the Persian versions, there are Chinese, Japanese, Russian, Egyptian, and Native American counterparts of the phoenix (Feng-Huang, Ho-oo, Firebird, Benu, and Yel respectively).

The findings of the goddess culture shows and give us hope that we do not have to go too far in finding solution to our problems. We need only to explore our roots, which we have tragically forgotten. The goddesses were not like the gods that we know today; they weren't super gods or goddesses asking for our obedience. This was a thought, principles and a philosophy where every woman used to be respected as goddess.

As I reference the goddess throughout this book, I will refer to her as the divine or deity rather than god.

TABLE OF CONTENTS

Dedication IX
Acknowledgements X
I want to hear from you! XI
Reader Services XI
THE ABOVE IMAGE/PAINTING DESCRIPTION XII
Simorgh XII

CHAPTER ONE 1

INTRODUCTION 1
   Persian Civilization 1
   The philosophy behind Persian thinkers 4
   What makes this book contemporary? 7
   Humanity, our heritage 12

CHAPTER TWO 17

PERSIAN VIEW OF THE DIVINE 17
   Introduction 17
   The Early Persian view of God 18
   Alternative ideas to present divine, religious thoughts 24
   Creationism 32
   Continuity of life as a dynamic world 36
   The need for a stronger sense of logic 37
   Obedience to God is an insult to God 41
   What is the Persian view of spirituality? 43
   God is meaning 45

    God is image 45
    God is meaning and image 45
    Why should a true belief or religion need our faith? 47
    Faith and love 48
    I explore, therefore I am 49
    Culture 50
    Mythology and myth 51

CHAPTER THREE 55

PLATO AND ROSTAM: TWO DIFFERENT ALLEGORIES OF THE CAVE 55
    Two opposite experiences of thinking 55
    Plato 55
    Rostam 56
    Plato's allegory of the cave 56
    Rostam's allegory of the cave 57
    Enlightenment 63

CHAPTER FOUR 71

HUMANITY AND ETHICAL EVOLUTION 71
    Humanity 71
    What is civilization? 79

CHAPTER FIVE 87

ATHEISM 87
    Introduction 87
    How can an unseen god be real? 88
    Our past heritage and divinity 89

    An alternative to atheism 91

CHAPTER SIX 101

PERSIAN POETS AND THINKERS 101
    Early, true Persian culture 101
    Omar Khayyam (Part One) 108
    Nihilism and Abrahamic religions 118
    The story of Jamshid in Shahnameh 121

CHAPTER SEVEN 131

OMAR KHAYYAM 131
    Omar Khayyam (Part Two) 131
    The power of 'me' 141
    What is fate? 142
    Rend: a character of Omar Khayyam 148
    Obedience to God is humiliation to human intellectual capability . 153

CHAPTER EIGHT 155

WHERE ARE THE ISLAMIC SCIENTISTS? 155
    Abstract 155
    Anti-Semitic and homophobic principles 155
    Muslim mistreatment of their own thinkers and philosophers 156
    The interruption of science and philosophy in Persia 157
    Muhammad Zakariya Razi 159
    Mansur Hallaj 160
    Who is a scientist? 162
    Sharia law in the eye of Attar of Nishapur 169
    Revulsion of Attar at the Sharia law on thieving 169

Attar's indirect sharp criticism of the torture chamber
of god (hell) 171
Emphasis by Attar that execution is murder 171
Attar's story of the potter and the prophet Noah 176

CHAPTER NINE 183

WHY THE LONDON BOMBING? 183
Abstract 183
A brief review of 2005 London bombing 185
The roots of human rights and democracy 186
Philosophy, the solution 191
Conclusion 192

CHAPTER TEN 195

THE DEAN OF HUMANITY 195
Introduction 195
The Divine and Wisdom 197
Dean of humanity—Iraj's dean in *Shahnameh* 206
Religion in the eyes of Ferdowsi as a thinker 209

CHAPTER ELEVEN 215

HUMANITY IN THE EYES OF PERSIANS 215
The root of humanity 215
Wisdom (kharad) is born from the soul of humanity 217
Justice, truth, and law come from wisdom 218

CHAPTER TWELVE 221

SECULARISM AND THE SANCTITY OF LIFE 221
Secularism and the root of Persian culture 221
Introduction of goddess and spiritual values 223
Persian culture is Simorgh—love, beauty, dance, and music 224
Life is sanctity 226
Definition of culture 228
What makes Persian culture so unique? 230

CHAPTER THIRTEEN 233

GODDESS CULTURE 233
Introduction 233
Marija Gimbutas's goddess discoveries in Europe 234
Culture of the goddess 239
The Indo-Europeans invasion of Europe 248
Treatment of Women by Abrahamic Religion 251

CHAPTER FOURTEEN...255

DEMOCRACY 255
Introduction 255
Western democracy or Islamic theocracy 257
Is Western democracy possible for the East? 261
Democracy is one, but there are many ways to it 263
The naïveté of thought in the Islamic world 264
The most precious experience is freedom 266
Systematic teaching to make people socially dumb 268
Morality 270
The responsibilities of the ethnic minorities 273

We are immortal 275
  I doubt, therefore I am 279

APPENDIX 281
List of terms used throughout this book: 281
BOOKS CITED OR RECOMMENDED 288
INDEX 291
THE LOST KEY 311

CHAPTER ONE

INTRODUCTION

Persian Civilization

This book is the result of over ten years of my study and research of the research-work of Persian thinker and professor, Manuchehr Jamali, who, over a period of fifty years, has published over 150 books on Persian literature in the Persian language. This literature is so powerful that it can inspire any free thinker to a much deeper understanding of the path and process of humanity in becoming civilized or enlightened. I personally believe that Persian literature is *the lost key* to many of our humanitarian problems that seem to us to be impossible—or almost impossible—to solve today. As long as we find a correct path to persevere and endure, we can overcome impossibilities and solve any social problems that we face today, no matter how daunting they are. I believe Persian culture can lead the future of humanity.

Many people talk of Persian civilization, but hardly anybody knows what this civilization was and what made Persia so much admired for the legacy of her culture and civilization. Is this legacy due to history or culture? Definitely, history can't be the answer, as history is basically the report of wars and conflicts. The answer must be a humane culture (the early, true Persian culture) that we know little about. This book will unveil the mythology, the culture, and the literature that made the Persian civilization—encouraging brain stimulation along the way.

Persian literature is an asset of all humanity, not just an asset of the Persians. I am in no way trying to represent Persia as a superior nation or the Persian culture as a superior culture; rather, it is my goal to make Persians feel a more responsible nation as they understand their own great literature, and I wish to publicize Persian's great literature for the benefit of mankind. Persian literature is one of the great literatures of mankind, if not the greatest. It contains a multitude of coded messages that are included because of many unfortunate events. I refer to this literature as Persian literature, as it is written in the Persian language. Actually, there were many tribes and nations who lived together and worked together in making this great culture. Because this culture is preserved in the Persian language, Persians have a great responsibility to pass the message of Persian values and culture to our generation and future generations of the world.

Nationalities that contributed to this heritage include Turks, Turkmen, Tajiks, Afghans, Kurds, Arabs, Indians, Balochistan, Indians, and many more. There are many more nations who have contributed greatly, but not in a way that is easy to identify. The Persian culture gave to the West many discoveries in the areas of history and literature. Literature, culture, and humanity know no borders.

This book will investigate Persian literature and its direct effect on humanity and the values that stimulate minds and have made us human today. True Persian literature comes from the thoughts and philosophical view of the Persian civilization of pre-Islamic and pre-

Zoroastrian[3] rule (Sassanian rule). Persian culture has one of the greatest literatures of mankind; however, due to many unfortunate events, it has remained unknown not only to the outsiders but also to many Persians as well for a very long time. It is very common for even educated Persians to find difficulty in understanding their own literature; and any Persians who are not familiar with their culture can become totally confused over the messages and meanings in the ancient texts.

Just as the Persian culture is rich and meaningful, the cultures of other nations that have long histories, such as Egypt, also offer insight for us today. Historians and philosophers in all cultures must have total freedom without prejudice to explore the literature of the past to discover the values that have kept people united. Unfortunately, that freedom does not always exist. It must not be forgotten that foreigners (Westerners, for example) can explore Eastern history, but they won't be able to explore Eastern culture because of the complex nature of culture in relation to history.

One of the saddest thing about the system of education regarding our past is the focus on history, wars and conflicts ... it creates an image that our ancestors had nothing to do but fight each other.

Persian literature can inspire people to understand their own humanity—their consciousness and ethical evolution. It demonstrates that mankind isn't just biologically evolved, but mentally evolved too; our consciousness, values, ethics, and integrity have roots in our past

---

[3] *Zoroastrianism: monotheistic religion and philosophy based on the teachings of prophet Zoroaster, and was the official religion of Iran from 200 CE to 650 CE.*

humanity and have evolved over time. I believe Darwin's theory of biological evolution also applies to ethics. I believe we are the outcome of 'the theory of ethical evolution'.

My strong message to thinkers, intellectuals, and atheists is this: please don't be put off by the word *god* in this book. The meaning of god was entirely different to our ancestors than it is today. God was in no way an outsider, an external force; god in those times was our own self-consciousness.

The philosophy behind Persian thinkers

This book investigates the philosophies of great Persian thinkers such as Omar Khayyam (1048-1131) who was simply a true human, and who is one of the great Persian-thinker who is known well to Westerners. It will also show the astonishing similarity between the thinking of Khayyam and other Persian thinkers who are not as well known to Westerners as Khayyam. It will show the similarity between Persian thought and philosophies and atheist ideology, but at the same time, it will also show the differences. Because of the similarities, many in the West claim that Omar Khayyam was an atheist. Bizarrely, many Muslims try very hard to call him an intoxicated Muslim! Yes, Omar Khayyam is intoxicated with humanity, but not from the image of god that is portrayed in the Muslim religion. We shouldn't forget that Khayyam had his own god and his own interpretation of that god. This book highlights the character of Khayyam's god.

Omar Khayyam was simply a true human and a great person who loved being, who loved exploration and the jubilation of life, and loved people and his surroundings. It is quite natural that people who study his writing today may try hard to persuade readers that he agrees with their way of thinking. It is human nature to connect one's own beliefs to anything that is considered splendid or popular. Muslims claim Omar Khayyam was a Muslim, and atheists claim that he was an atheist.

Moreover, this book will show that Persian thinkers such as Omar Khayyam were explorers who wanted to be free of any belief that claimed to be the only truth. An idea that claims to be the only truth causes division in a society and creates enemies and wars. The core of idea behind Omar Khayyam's rubaiyat[4] is to be free of any belief that divides the society into believers and nonbelievers, wrong and rights. Being free of such believes is the belief. This is the core message of early, true Persian culture, and it is reflected in all Persian literature. The current obsession of the Middle East with religion has created an atmosphere of fear among people who have always loved freedom; they are living in an atmosphere in which they are not free to challenge a belief or a thought. Any person who loves her or his country must work towards building a challenging environment that will encourage the strength in reasoning, the strength in intellectual power, and the strength in mental capacity to safeguard future peace and harmony.

There are many books in the West that define Persian thinkers like Rumi, Hafez, and Khayyam as mystics. This is due to a lack of understanding of the Persian civilization and culture. We have created a problem with this model; we must change the way we see these intellectuals. If the model that we created does not work, then we have

---

[4] *Rubaiyat: Plural of rubai in Persian poetry. This is a group of quatrains in Persian poetry. A quatrain is a stanza or poem of four lines, called a rubai in Persian poetry.*

to change the model rather than simply labelling them as mystics, which is not helpful. A model is only a good model if we can manage to fit everything into it—or at least 99%. If the model keeps giving us the wrong conclusion—mystic in this case—then the model is flawed and must be revised.

There is a lack of nonreligious role models in the Eastern countries. Unless we have strong nonreligious role models, unless we have an intellectual exchange of new and different ideas, there will be no change. Why nonreligious? Because: A role model must be able to embrace everyone—whether a believer or nonbeliever.

I feel very passionate about this book; I believe it is a very important ethical book, especially in these times of growing simplistic and self-serving religious views that seem to be gaining strength in their attempt to control our modern and civilized world.

I am from Persia and from a Muslim background. I have lived in the United Kingdom for over thirty years, and almost every year I have travelled to Persia, the country that is known today as Iran. I have close ties with people in Iran. I know the Western way of life, and I know the Eastern way of life. To a large extent, I know and understand the root cause of the religious terrorism in our world. This book investigates and elaborates many of unknown problems we are facing in our world. This book offers a solution for the future of our world, the Middle East, and, of course mankind.

What makes this book contemporary?

I have made my best effort to make this book contemporary in the areas of ethics and humanity. I have done this by creating a new vision into the exploration of the Eastern goddess culture and its relationship with Western civilization. This book references over fifty years of research done by Professor Manuchehr Jamali, a Persian thinker, who has published over 150 books on Persian literature. This research into Persian literature brings to light the vast extent of the Persian goddess culture; indeed, this culture is well documented and admired in Persian literature. This can be a useful and interesting material to integrate with the discoveries of the goddesses made by a very well-known and well-respected Western archaeologist and researcher, Marija Gimbutas.

Marija Gimbutas has found vast archaeological evidence of the goddess culture in Europe, and she has studied extensively to reveal this European goddess culture. I will discuss her work in more detail in chapter 13. Her amazing and remarkable discoveries show the ability of the goddess culture to achieve unity and peace. All ideologies and religions of the world claim to be peaceful; in fact, those who don't must be mindless and crazy. Claiming to be peaceful is the easy part—anybody can make such claim—but achieving peace by putting the idea into practise is another. Peace requires a real and strong foundation in ideology that can form nexus and create unity among different people. Only then will the idea of peaceful thought pass the test. It is becoming more and more evident that our prehistoric ancestors managed to find the best method for understanding human nature and for putting peace into practise for over thousands of years. There is plenty of evidence in our lively Persian literature that shows this human culture, which I will discuss throughout this book.

Marija Gimbutas's findings about the goddess culture in Europe reveal that people did not believe in a single, universal great goddess; rather, they worshipped a range of female deities. It is important to note that the mother goddess wasn't a super god who asked her followers for obedience or compliance. The principles and the philosophy of the goddess cultures were to respect every woman as a goddess. This is not a strange issue; even today this is more or less is practised to some extent in very culturally based nations whose practice it is to bow to women. Any respect for women that we see in Western civilization must be rooted in such a culture; more research would be required to reveal the extent of this phenomenon.

I don't suggest that we need to go back to a goddess culture; I simply suggest that we need to be able to *think*. For thousands of years, this culture of the goddess has purposely been hidden from us by those who would take over our world—the masters of the religions of light: Zoroastrian, Judaism, Christianity, and Islam. The ideology, thinking, and principles of these religions of light didn't just drop out of the sky. Their roots are in the goddess culture, but they have been manipulated in order to gain control over people. *Zoroastrian and Abrahamic religions broke the chain of continuity of the thoughts of humanity, which was in the process of progressing and reshaping.* For example, from 200CE when Zoroastrian (religious orthodox) took over Persia—Persian struggle for social equality did not stop ... it rather carried on even stronger.

The takeover of Zoroastrian has never been accepted by majority of Persians. Persians continued the struggle for social equality against the rule of Zoroastrian fanaticisms; the struggles such as Kerm-e Haftvad, Bahram-e Choobineh, Sofra, Mazdak, Mani, Salman (Mahyar), Rostam-Farokhzad ... these are only the recorded struggles. *In only one of the recorded struggle—Mazdak—over 12,000 supporters were massacred, including Mazdak himself in one day!* These are only one example of a struggle of our ancestors for social right and human dignity—irrespective of any nationality. It is for this reason that we owe our morality to our ancestors who worked hard and even sacrificed their life for us and shaped the ethics and humanity that we know today.

The continuous, rigorous and tight rule of Zoroastrian has forced Persians for continues struggle for social equality. Adding border conflicts between Persia and Roman Empire—the continual struggle has weakened Persia such that they have lost the war against 'Arab religious ideology' invasion causing a huge setback for humanity.

The takeover of Persian by Arabs has given religious mentality enormous wealth and power—of which—they have used and carried on with many of the wars we know today which took over Northern Africa and many parts of Europe.

However, *the prolonged life of the goddess culture in Persia left a trail of deep philosophical humanistic mythology.* As time went on, and invasions and wars occurred, this mythology was preserved in poetic literature in a coded message. This is how the rich literature of Persia took shape and why Persia remains one of the world's unique and rich cultures.

Amazingly and astonishingly, the culture of the goddess in Persia, as it vanished; it found its way into the rich literature of Persia and gave it the admiring and humanitarian value that we find today. This literature is admired greatly for its messages of love, values, unity, and dignity—by Farsi speaking people and many non-Farsi speaking people—all over the world—even though its message is very difficult to understand.

As mentioned earlier; religions broke the chain of continuity of the thoughts of humanity, which was in the process of progressing and reshaping. This broken chain took humanity into a state of confusion and disarray that continues even today. From this moment, humanity was segregated from the deity, and the deity became an external force instead of internal power. People were taught to believe that, to reach to this separated deity, they had to fight; therefore, bloodshed and war followed, a state of affairs that we seem to have become accustomed to.

In this book I will also investigate the values in Persian literature that can be taken as examples for exploration into the rich literature of the Middle Eastern culture, all of which are rooted in pre-Islamic thought. Persian culture and literature can also be useful in the investigation into the many European goddesses cultures, reflected in the discoveries of Marija Gimbutas.

The goddess culture is our human heritage; it has given us the principles and values that have made us human. A true democracy is possible only through acceptance of these rooted values and thoughts—the root essence of humanity. Without these values, neither democracy nor freedom is possible. We need to explore this heritage in order to initiate the continuity of human thought and wisdom as we search for new ways to address our world problems. Humanity must grow to embrace a new future; we cannot remain in the past. But we must use the lessons of the past if we are to grow in a constructive and productive manner.

It is a lack of ideas that has generated so many problems in our world; it seems as if many people—especially *youngsters have become accustomed to simplicity and naïveté*. Simplicity and naïveté may be good to some extent, but they can bring their own negativity because they do nothing to help us understand the root cause of the problems we face today. Simplicity and naïveté result in humanity allowing itself to be ruled rather than planning their own destiny for a better future.

In this book, I will investigate the limited chance that the Islamic world has for achieving democracy. I explain why there can be neither an Islamic way of democracy nor a Western way of democracy. Democracy must come from values that are very much rooted in the true literature of an area. I will also describe and investigate what I call home-grown democracy. I will show that home-grown democracy is very much possible under the values that can be explored in the literature of Middle Eastern countries. This is the only path to a true democracy and freedom. Democracy doesn't come out of ballet boxes; democracy comes out of our mindset and thinking. True democracy and freedom come out of values and respect. Without these crucial principles of humanity, the establishment of a true and rooted democracy is impossible.

I have taken ample effort to make this book a very important ethical statement. I believe my contribution is important in these times as many of our world problems expand, especially as the growing simplistic and self-serving religious views seem to be gaining strength as 'religious leaders' try to control our modern and civilized world. I have no intension of undermining any ideology or rejecting any faith. My main emphasis is on our heritage, which has made us human, and for which humanity must be proud.

Humanity, our heritage

Our heritage is much more than history. Our heritage comes from our collective ethical values that are rooted in our past and that have evolved for many thousands of years. These values are like pebbles that have travelled for many years over the mountains and through the valleys of nations until they are polished. And these values are preserved in the literature that we have today. These writings are pure treasures that can't be put aside as history. These writings are the result of the effort and struggle of our ancestors who contributed to a legacy for humanity. We owe it to our children and our grandchildren—even to those who will come in the future whom we will never meet—to keep it alive and pass it along. Humanity has always been intelligent. It is an insult to our ancestors to think otherwise. Even though our ancestors lived in ancient times without the benefit of our scientific knowledge, they had true wisdom in a peaceful environment without such chaotic world of science and technology that we have today. We just need to explore our past and recognize our ancestors work and respect it. Our belief in our 'scientific truth' can close our eyes to this ancient intelligence.

In this book, I will show that the research, exploration, and discovery that we are so naturally devoted to are precious passions that can be called the soul or the divine within us. Curiosity is built into humanity; humans are devoted explorers. I believe that we can give spiritual values to this devotion, devotion that has enabled some humans to cure diseases and others to achieve astonishing engineering discoveries that have made living more trouble free, comfortable, and more affordable. We need a philosophical approach to give spiritual[5] values to this world

---

[5] *Spirituality: the ability to define 'life'.*

for the amazing achievements in all areas of science; otherwise *we may destroy our own environment in our quest for supremacy*. In this way, we must be able to lessen the effect of a simplistic view of religion to our society and have greater devotion to our understating of the world, and to the understanding of all of humanity. If we could all unite under the name of humanity, we could eliminate misery, conflict, disease, and starvation.

Early humanity believed in the goddess of beauty—some called her Venus—who had continuity and flow. Humanity has been shaped through the principles of this goddess of beauty. Furthermore, the principles of the same goddess of beauty were adopted by Abrahamic religions, but they were turned into a static god. I will investigate the differences between this adaptable goddess and this static god and point out how the static god has negatively affected our morality, character, and the way we see our environment and our world.

As I was discussing the value and power of humanity during a lecture in my classroom in Iran at the University of Science and Technology, one of my students asked me, 'Don't you think we are just a human, sir?' I responded, 'Well, don't you think being a human is *very important*?'

In many discussions we keep hearing that we are 'just human'! Being a human is tremendously important. We must admire, cherish, and celebrate being human! All the achievements in philosophy, morality, technology, and medicine come from the power of the human mind. Aren't these achievements important? Humanity is what makes us aware of our surroundings and teaches us to avoid misusing the power we possess.

We are only human! What should anyone expect from us? Shouldn't we be proud of being a human? If we aren't proud of being human, if we don't cherish humanity and don't celebrate being a human, then where will our human values lead? Why should anyone be labelled as Muslim, Christian, or Jewish? Isn't such label an insult to humanity? A human is a social, dynamic being and is much more advanced than any label could indicate. The value of humanity is beyond these labels; indeed, these labels can demonize humanity. So, these ideas form the core of the discussions in this book.

With some background knowledge of Persian literature from childhood (schools and universities); I have worked for over ten years studying Persian philosophy with Persian philosopher, Professor Manuchehr Jamali. My goal in this book is to bring to light a tiny fraction of his great body of research. It is my goal to boost the mental capacity of all free men and women in this world who just want to rely on common sense in their service to mankind.

I have included the works of many Persian poems, both *rubai*[6] and *ghazal*[7], in this book. I have translated them directly into English to

---

[6] *Rubai: Persian verse; It is a complete poem that consists of four lines of verses in which the poet puts herself or himself forth as an ideal person or an iconic person for the past, present, and future, representing the path of a person to an ideal world on this earth. Rubaiyat is the Plural of rubai.*

[7] *Ghazal: Persian verse; consists of many lines of verses in which the poet puts herself or himself forth as an ideal person or an iconic person for the past, present, and future; representing the path of a person to an ideal world on this earth. Ghazaliyat is the plural of ghazal.*

highlight the core value of the poetic, humanistic, and ethical world of our beautiful Persian literature. The translations are not taken from any textbook; they are new, with a new vision related directly to this book. It is the beautiful Persian culture, mythology, and literature that have collectively made the characteristic of Persia as being romantic and a poetic nation.

This book provides a new vision into the roots of humanity and ethical identity irrespective of race, religion, ethnicity, or nationality. I will show that Western civilization is largely rooted in Eastern literature. As we know, the Western religions are directly derived from Eastern religions. Western ethical evolution is similarly related.

There are so many lovely messages in Persian literature. If they are translated and explained in depth, I believe Western readers will see them in a very positive light. Omar Khayyam was a philosopher, mathematician, astronomer, and poet. He produced only a fraction of Persian literature, but he is well known in the West. However, there are many more past Persian poets similar or more sophisticated than Omar Khayyam who can teach us through their poems.

The point is, a good understanding of *all* Persian poets can result in many more lovely and interesting poems or humanistic and ethical books for Western culture. To my understanding, living in the west for over thirty years, there is a very good environment for such books.

The reference to 'I' or 'me' in this book is a reflection of each of us as an individual and it is to emphasizes that each of us has the power to make this world a happy world a heavenly world. I can do this. You can do this. We can do this. It is within our power.

Furthermore, the reference to 'I' or 'me' in this book doesn't imply that I am superior to others or I am a divine messenger looking for pride and glory—it is rather accepting the responsibility and tackling the problems of our world. In fact, pride and glory is within each of us as individuals and only needs to be invoked in order to feel responsible and be ashamed of those problems that are embracing our world. These problems seem to be growing every day whether in the areas of moral, ethical, or environmental.

CHAPTER TWO

PERSIAN VIEW OF THE DIVINE

Introduction

In this chapter I will establish an image of god, or the divine, that embraces the rest of the chapters in this book. I introduce this concept purposely at the beginning of the book to show the bond and closeness of humanity and the divine in the original Persian culture. It is important that readers study this chapter thoroughly to obtain an image and understanding of the diverse images and concepts of the divine that existed in the ancient civilized nations that have shaped our current humanity. Although I particularly emphasize Persian culture, similar images and meanings are widespread in many different historical cultures, including those in Europe. Persian literature can elaborate upon and explain many unknowns regarding early human cultures, can address many unanswered questions that arose as a result of the archaeological discoveries of goddesses in Europe, and can elaborate on the findings of researchers in this area, such as Marija Gimbutas, whose main focus of study is Europe.

The Early Persian view of God

The early Persians believed that the divine was an essence that is in all beings. Therefore, their view was quite different to the entity we refer to as 'God' today. The Persian view of god, or the divine, taken from Persian literature, is spirit, values, essence, and morality, but not a ruler or a teacher. Let's look at this vision and this view and see the philosophy that can be derived. The divine was viewed as values and principles that give dignity to humanity rather than a physical and muscular being who inspires fear. The divine was the wisdom and the protector of the souls of all humanity. The purpose of the divine spiritual power was to unify people to make this world beautiful, to make it reflective of Venus or Aphrodite; in fact, *beauty is divinity.* Furthermore, the pursuit of knowledge was religion in the Persian civilization.

Understanding and interpreting such historical thoughts and ideas of humanity may look like an impossible endeavour, but anyone who wants change must find a way to forge a path into impossibilities. Walking into such impossibilities can open the doors for change and can create an atmosphere in which old ideas can flourish and new ideas can grow. When Rumi was advocating beauty and love, he expressed walking into this impossibility. As Rumi said:

مرادم آنکه شود، سایه و آفتاب، یکی
که ا ز عشق، نمایم ، تمام خوشکامی
محال جوی ومحالم ، بدین گناه ، ... مرا
قبول می نکند، هیچ عـالـم وعامی
تو هم، محال ننوشی و معتقد نشوی

برو برو، ... ... که مرید عقول واوهامی

My aim is to make shadow and sun one
To bring happiness and love to everyone
I am after impossibilities, this is my sin
Not acceptable to the world or anyone
You are keeping out of impossibilities like everyone
Go. Go. You are a disciple, smart and full of aptitude one.

Description of this poem: How can we change our world so we may live a better life? Must we walk into impossibilities? It is the impossibility of making shadow and sun as one, and it is the impossibility of making a dark future into shiny future. It is love that makes us move into impossibilities; however, our brains are guided to follow the disciplines and follow our personal interests. Therefore, when we follow the disciplines and our interests, there will be no change for a better future.

The true meaning of the Persian divine (god) can be found in the spiritual values that guide humanity to demonstrate their own purity, essence, consciousness, and the roots of their nature without any fear. The divine, in here, is the protector that prevents any fear; indeed, fearlessness is portrayed in the philosophy of this goddess religion. This is the purity of humanity, this is the purity of spirituality, this is the divine, and this is the true meaning of a healthy society. A submissive society can never progress and can never be productive.

We need to enliven and cherish a divinity that comes from our souls and that cares about others, the others who are among us who are different from us. This divinity emphasizes the divine that is in all of us; we are the divine, we are the world, and we are the key to all our problems.

This is the best way of rising against the image of a fearful, almighty god, not the theory of atheism, which is a negative approach that emphasizes total nonexistence of any kind of divinity. In fact, atheism could bring back the same image of an almighty god in another form or shape; this time, it would seem to be in the name of science or modernism or civilization. The world of materialism, the world of superpowers, the world of the superrich, the world of the super economy are just a few examples of the signs of the new and modern almighty god.

In Persian mythology, the divine encompasses verity, beauty, elegance, happiness, music, dance, and generation/evolution. The names of the weeks and months in Persian calendar and almost every part of our bodies are named after a divine; for example, *Day*[8], *Bahman*[9] and *Farvardin*[10]. Another example is the word *artery*, derived from the name of the god Arta[11]. In Persian mythology, god evolves in the same manor that our thoughts and minds evolve. There isn't such thing as, 'god speaks the truth' or 'god has sent the truth through his or her messengers'. To the Persians, our minds and souls are the divine. It is the divinity within all beings that demonstrates its own purity, harmony and essence on this earth in the form of all nature and in the form of

---

[8] *'Day': The month of December in the Persian calendar, named after the god of love, Khoram.*

[9] *'Bahman: The month of February in the Persian calendar: Bahman is the god of thinking and wisdom that is hidden in every human. It appears during an enlightenment, but otherwise remains hidden. This means, the truth is not obvious in enlightenment but rather hidden and must be explored in the dark or in shadows of the enlightened environment.*

[10] *'Farvardin': The month of March in the Persian calendar. Arta-Farvard is the god of celebration and festivals.*

[11] *'Arta': The god of soul or body, which is also Simorgh (Persian Phoenix). no human—not even an agnostic—would fight his own soul.*

humanity within us. And this divinity is expressed without the necessity of a messenger or a middleman. *The divine is harmony*—divine is the being, and the being is divine. The divine is the world and we are the world. The story of 'the divine' and 'the being' is the same as the story of the chicken and the egg. The divine comes out of her own shell and grows and evolves within us like any one of us. The collective essence of us is divine; the unity between us is divine. The divine is useless without harmony or yoke that combines our energy. Simply, if there is no unity, there is no divinity. The essence of plants was known to be god, the essence of the grape or wine was known to be god. This is why wine has so much divine value in Persian literature and Persian mythology. In this philosophy, the proof of the existence of god or the existence of a messenger of god becomes meaningless. With this philosophy, humans have a direct connection to divine. Under the shadow of this divine, we are the sun … we are the divinity. The divine seeks to create the divine; it is nothing less than its own essence. This is actually the objective of the effort of the divine—the divine wants to make us to be the divine; otherwise the divine would be failing in its effort. This is why there was no need of a messenger or an intermediate being. Rumi has a beautiful poem about this concept:

به فر سایه‌ات چون آفتابیم
همایی تو همایی تو همایی
خمش کردم ولی بهر خدا را
خدایی کن خدایی کن خدایی

Under your shadow, we are the sun
You are the divine. You are the divine. You are the divine
I have preserved for the sake of the divine
Be the divine. Be the divine. Be the divine

Description of this poem: Here, Rumi used the sense of logic and said that, if we are under the shadow of the divine, then we have the essence of the divine ... we *are* the divine. If we come from divine, then we must be divine. This is why Rumi stressed his point: *You are the divine. You are the divine. You are the divine.*

Rumi carried on saying that he has preserved for the sake of the divine and passed the message to those who do not have the necessary confidence and self-belief. Rumi encouraged: *Be the divine. Be the divine. Be the divine.*

Why are we the sun? Because, we are under the shadow of the divine—the shadow of being, and the shadow of humanity. Under this shadow, we are the sun or the divine. We as human are the divine. In early, true Persian culture, the divine wasn't a supernatural god. The early Persian culture encouraged respect for humanity; this was particularly important for leaders who governed others. From this philosophy, we can define the meaning of a true leader. A true leader in Persian mythology didn't own the people over whom she or he ruled. Why? Because, people were the truth if they were free to expose their roots and essence. Since truth comes out of free-minded people, the truth can never have one owner. In fact, truth and freedom can never be captured and owned; they are elusive. As soon as freedom is captured and owned, then it is no longer freedom. This is why freedom and truth are elusive. Responsible people are those who are self-sufficient in defining themselves and do not allow themselves to be defined by an outsider or by a belief or a religion. This is the depth of being a responsible person.

As I mentioned earlier, freedom, apart from a struggle against authority, is also the creation of the right environment in which people are able to illustrate their own purity and capability. In the story of Adam and Eve in the Abrahamic religions, Yahweh and Allah feared such a free and non-submissive people. They didn't want liberated people—especially a liberated women; rather, they wanted submissive people who only listened and obeyed. The minds and thinking of humans can never advance in an environment in which they must be so submissive. In fact, the best way of knowing a god is by being free of that god. If we are not allowed to free ourselves of the god that we believe in, then that god has the full autonomy over us and is our enemy. This is against the nature of the god of love and beauty. God must have a friendly relationship with us, not full authority over us. If we are not allowed to free ourselves from our friends, then those friends are no longer our friends; they are our enemies. Maybe this philosophy can be used to prevent a lot of broken marriages that we see in our world today.

It is human nature that we imitate our god, whether we follow an Abrahamic religion or any other religion. In the Abrahamic religions, a powerful person imitates her or his almighty, fear-inspiring God. A ruler with a strong religious philosophy would rule with fear rather than love, as he would have had no way of learning about love. Similarly, a father would rule over his own family with fear. There are no words of love anywhere in Muslim scripture.

In the view of Abrahamic religions, this world is a game, in that it is unimportant, because the true goal of life in this world is only to prepare for the afterlife. Without their god or their religion, the world is meaningless to followers of these religions. *Basically, religion is not for life; rather, life is for religion!* It is for this reason that the extremists in these religions, when they are experiencing difficulties, have no hesitation in endangering their own lives or the lives of others for sake of their beliefs. The most troublesome idea in Abrahamic religions is the core belief that this life is meaningless without their almighty God;

in other words, it is only God that gives meaning to life. Furthermore, this world must not be taken seriously; it is only the orders of God that must be taken seriously.

Alternative ideas to present divine, religious thoughts

We need new ideas and new thinking. When people lose their belief in an ideology or religion, they find it difficult to find an alternative thought to replace the old idea. It is very important to replace an old idea; otherwise, there is no doubt that we will go back to our old thoughts sooner or later. Atheism has come about due to the simplistic, erroneous, and ridiculous explanation of the 'religious' view of life and afterlife. As atheists exist only in contrast to the presence of these religions; without the existence of these religions, there would be no atheists. This means that atheists could not, in fact, present a core innovative philosophy on which we might build a demanding social life.

To many atheists, the solutions to humanity's problems can be found in science; however, I don't believe science can provide solutions to our problems of morality. For example, science might contribute to the creation of a super-sharp knife; however, the purpose of the knife—whether to skin a cucumber or behead an enemy—is no longer the domain of science, but becomes the domain of philosophy.

A person who becomes an atheist without adopting a replacement ideology or philosophy wonders about the meaning of life. To that person, the future is left in a sort of limbo. That is, atheism will bring back the same image of an almighty God for humans that these religions have done; this time, it will be in the name of science. In the end, they will replace the same ideology that they were fighting against. That is, to rule the world, to rule the life, and to rule the environment in the name of modernism or science. This is why atheists enthusiastically seek a theory that gives power to one human or a small group of humans over others. This can put us into the same trap that religions have done.

Philosophy comes from and explores people's dreams and imaginations; it does not seek to prove the existence or nonexistence of any 'god'. Philosophy wants to know what is in the minds and imaginations of people. Philosophy doesn't want to know whether a god exists or does not exist. If rejection of god is sincere, it is certainly an action that advocates the same god, as rejection of god is basically a counterproductive idea but not an idea that has its own roots. Atheism cannot exist without these religions. The existence of atheism depends on the existence of theism or religions. So can atheism be free thinking? Well, the answer is probably no. We need ideas and philosophies to lead us to the next stages of a fluid and dynamic world.

Philosophies explore the thoughts and beliefs of people even if those thoughts and beliefs seem to be petty or false or superstitious or rejected. It is these thoughts and beliefs, which come from our imaginations that affect our world. Our imagination can't be put aside and forgotten about; it would be rather foolish to do so. Instead of rejecting these beliefs, we need to try and find out what effect they have over people.

We do come across of people who meticulously and faithfully devote all their life, effort, and energy to a supernatural belief and then they suddenly turn away from that belief as a mistaken belief, becoming so indifferent to it that they even hate the idea. It is, of course, a philosophical and humanitarian question—why should anyone believe so strongly and for so long in something supernatural? Or why should anyone adhere to a supernatural belief—whether or not a mistaken idea—and accept this idea and love the idea so much that he or she is willing to live with it for so many years and die for it? These are very serious and deep humanitarian questions. The discipline of anthropology works towards discovering and describing this conflict and what it is that induces this behaviour in human thinking. Instead of simply leaving behind or rejecting these beliefs and behaviours, we should find value in addressing them and studying them and finding alternate solutions for them. It is these strong beliefs that push us to relate our success to a supernatural being such as the Abrahamic God.

A person may give credit for personal success and achievement to a supernatural god because the achievement is too much for that person's confidence and mental ability, or the person may want to relate the idea to god to show its importance. The philosophical question is why should a person want to disclaim all of her or his deeply human values by attributing them to an entity such as a supernatural god? Why would a person say that this god has saved him or her from a mass of rubble following an earthquake? How about an innocent child who dies under the same rubble in the most tragic way? Could the tragic death of a child be blamed on the same god? Does that god torture an innocent child? Human thinking that tries to make a supernatural entity the cause for his success or death is a serious issue, which we need to address.

Why do humans not acknowledge their own precious achievements and continue to say they are the work of a god? Why do humans cheat themselves out of their own value? Why would a person give credit for his or her achievements and success to a god, expressing that god has provided the necessary wisdom? These are the problems. Why would a human try to deny his or her own values? Why are humans so hypocritical to themselves? Why would a person give credit for achievements to god and then make that achievement so incredibly eminent and important that humans can no longer access it? Don't we need solution to these problems? Leaving these problems unsolved will not help us progress. These are philosophical questions that need philosophical answers. Rejecting the existence of a god is not a solution; it may rather cause a believer to fall, as a belief is like a walking stick to a believer.

In Persian mythology, time and truth—or faith—have roots and they grow, accumulate, and evolve. In other words, there is continuity in our world of time. In this continuity, we recognize only one world; believing into two worlds would rupture the continuity and the connections that exist in time. Believing in two worlds removes the possibility of connection and unity. Time and connection are broken. One world is unity and connection; two worlds is division and disconnection—and therefore separation. God should be nothing but morality, values, and unity among members of the human race here on this earth.

In fact, the truth in early Persian philosophy was that god exists in every being. There is no separation between god and all the beings in our world. *This life is the ultimate truth*. Rumi in this regard said:

نه ترسا، نه یهودم من، نه گبرم، نه مسلمانم
نه شرقیم، نه غربیم، نه بریم، نه بحریم
دوئی از خود بدر کردم یکی دیدم دو عالمرا
یکی جویم، یکی دانم، یکی بینم، یکی خانم

I am neither Muslim, nor Jewish, nor Zoroastrian, nor Christian

Neither I am land, nor I am sea, nor Eastern, nor Western
I've seen the two worlds like one, turned away from dualism
Explore as unison, know as unison, see as unison, and call as unison

Description of this poem: Rumi said that he doesn't accept any labels of religion, locality, or nationality. He said, 'I am neither Muslim, nor Jewish, nor Zoroastrian, nor Christian.' Rumi carried on rejecting any location labelling by saying that he is neither from land or sea or East or West. None of these labels is acceptable to him. The two worlds to him are also one, so he also rejects the afterlife and he is free from dualism (two worlds), which is another form of division.

Rumi concludes that *the soul of humanity if free from all these demonizing labels.* Living as one who accepts any of these labels—whether religious or not religious—is, in fact, not being, and is therefore dead. If I accept being Christian, Jewish, or Zoroastrian, I am, in fact, doomed ... I am not 'being'. To be human is to be in flow, to be dynamic, to be an explorer, and to move forward. This is why humanity is like the Phoenix—it is everything, but at the same time free from all these doctrines. Humans can't survive progressively in any one of these doctrines; anyone who claims to be able to stay in any of these doctrines is lying to you and to themselves. Anyone who attempts to stay in these doctrines is doomed and dead. That's why *we have so many dead men walking who are alive only so they can die.*

Humanity is a seed or an egg that grows from its own soul and on its own accord. This is why humans can grow with authenticity and originality free of many boundaries. Humanity is not buildings designed by architects and engineers and built by builders brick by brick to a shape that is already defined.

Our ancestors compared humanity to the Phoenix because they were free to explore in unity. Furthermore, Rumi said knowing is in unity, vision is in unity, and calling is in unity. Now the question is, who is this Rumi who came up with such vision? Rumi is me. Rumi is you. And Rumi is everyone. Rumi's expression in this poem is the essence of humanity that has been born and has grown from the goddess culture. This is why Rumi openly rejects all these labels and disconnects himself from religious labels and any location labels.

Rumi's poems show the meaning of people being and working as one and living as one. This is the portrayal of divine in Persian literature, which is, in fact, the portrayal of a human too—as the divine and the human have one essence. The divine is only divine when she evolves as the being that is the essence of this world—this essence is harmony. We all evolve, time evolves, our world evolves, and our Universe and galaxies also evolve. The divine can never be divine without evolving into the essence of the world. If there was no world, there would have been no gods and no holy wars. It is as simple as that. If there were no humans, there would have been no Mohamed, no Jesus Christ, no Moses, no Quran, no Bible, no Torah and therefore no God. Divine was known to Persians as harmony or Phoenix (the Persian Simorgh)—not unlimited power who can't harmonize with any. As depicted in the accompanying illustrations, this Phoenix is our spirit and soul but is not an external power. The divine comes from beings, and beings come from the divine—a process of harmony. There is no separation between these two. Without being, god or the divine is totally meaningless.

On the following two pages are photos of phoenixes that are allowed to be displayed in Iran. The phoenix depicted at beginning of this book (First image) would be too liberalistic for today's people of Iran.

This Persian Phoenix, known as Simorgh, is located in Simorgh Square in Sarein, a city in north-western Iran. The sculpture is made of fibreglass and is illuminated at night. The characteristics of the Persian Phoenix are its strong wings, claws for defence and protection, and its pride and dignity, which are paramount. This is a philosophy that represents the characteristics of humanity: the spirits of flight, protection, pride, and dignity. The Phoenix and humanity embrace all things, but at the same time are free from all the doctrines such as religion and other beliefs. Anyone who claims to be able to follow only one doctrine is lying.

Here is the illuminated Persian Phoenix—Simorgh, who is rooted in Persian philosophy and represents our capacity for vision, wisdom, and dignity. Simorgh represents humanity, love, music, dance and imagination, all of which give us passionate freedom so our minds can soar. This is the root of human philosophy in defining the meaning of life. Religious ideas also originate from this bird, but religious leaders have caged the bird and have manipulated its message to their own advantage. The phrase 'Simorgh rising from the ashes' means that, although humanity, purity, and love may burn or die and turn into ashes, one day these treasures will rise again from the ashes and fly once more.

Creationism

Creationism goes against formation, flow, and dynamics, and the Phoenix. Creationism contradicts nature. It is the religious belief that humanity, life, the Earth, and the Universe are the creation of a supernatural being, most often referring to the Abrahamic God, and that all creation happened suddenly and quickly. Humans have relentlessly resisted creationism since the Abrahamic religions first put forth these claims. As science progressed, further pressure developed against creationism. Despite this, support for creationism has managed to grow. However, various views developed from the eighteenth century onwards aimed to reconcile science with the Abrahamic creation narrative.

Creationism also does not agree with the nature of the true divine that is the essence of the entire world. Creationism cuts and separates the divine and human. Humanity cannot relate to a god who creates the Universe and the Earth and Adam and Eve in just six days. The existence of such a god has nothing in common with humans; it is too huge … its nature is far too superior. Simply, there can be no relationship between a giant god and a little human being! There are plenty of flaws in creationism; however, the professional cover-up has little room in our today's modern world. The Persian poet Hafez offered an interesting criticism in one of his poems:

پیر ما گفت خطا بر قلم صنع نرفت
آفرین بر نظر پاک خطا پوشش باد

> *Pierre[12] said, nothing went wrong with creationism*
> *Bravo to such a clean cover-up and professionalism!*

Description of the poem: Pierre, the old, wise religious man, claims there are no flaws in creationism—everything has been created perfectly by God. Hafez sarcastically responded back to this claim. He replied that the old wise man has done well to cover up the flaws so skilfully. Well, the same 'skill' would have to be applied in our modern world of today. In fact, Hafez was saying that those who were claiming that creationism had no flaws were deceptive liars and hypocrites.

Creationism supports a phenomenon that goes against nature and against caring and love. In order to create in a particular order and in a short time, one has to cut and slash or a slice the continuity of the world and the continuity of cumulative time. God creates everything, god creates manner, and god creates feeling ... god creates love. Does god really create love? If so, god was without love before creating love!—this is where the cut is: no love ... and immediately there is love! How can this be? What sort of god was this who was without love before creating love ... a vicious god?—criminal god?—cruel god?—a devil god? The same goes with other attributes of god ... this god was without feeling before creating feeling! How can this be? What sort of god was this who had no feeling? These are the basic problems with the idea of creationism. The questions raised; can only be answered logically if god is love (god=love) and philosophically—*love can't go hand in hand with creationism*. The vision of creationism is socially divisive in its roots. This divisive vision has caused much havoc and many disasters in

---

[12] *Pierre: a reference to an old wise man or a man with religious authority as a sarcastic wise man.*

our world. Millions of people have lost their lives, and much poverty and misery have been caused. There seems to be no end to it. So much war, death, and suffering have been caused by this idea of creationism, which has its roots in snobbery and selfishness. Both religion and the philosophies of our 'modern world' are formed from provocative and divisive ideas and thoughts than unity; even our modern world, to some extent, is also based on divisive ideas. Why should we also blame modern world? We must blame the modern world because it is materialistic and has lost its morality to a large degree.

In creationism ideology, power comes from cutting and dividing and eventually separating the divine from humanity. In Abrahamic religions, creation has dictated the separation between god and nature in general. The separation between god and humanity is the cause of almost all of disunities. The big question would be, how can we minimize the separation between divine and humanity without rejecting god? Morality, beauty and happiness are nothing but the divine. Striving for morality, beauty, and happiness is the key to unifying humanity without rejecting divine power; in fact, this effort would *praise* divine power. Until philosophy takes the initiative, our future will be controlled more and more by creationism. As Persian poet Ferdowsi said:

چو شادی بکاهد، بکاهد روان
خرد گردد اندر میان ناتوان

Lessening happiness lessens empathy
The wisdom within becomes unusable, empty

Description of this poem: The word for happiness in the Persian language is *shad*. This word is actually the name of a Persian goddess. Shad is also a divine name in Persian culture. Shad is the name of

Simorgh, the Persian Phoenix. Ferdowsi, in this poem, stressed that, by reducing real happiness. We lose the sense of empathy and understanding for each other, and this can result in the loss of our sense of wisdom.

Building a healthy society is building a happy society. Creating a moral society, a beautiful society, and a happy society is creating a divine and spiritual society where people care for each other; in fact, this caring is the divine power. The lack of vision for creating a divine society in our modern world is giving room for belief in creationism. *We form the divine. The divine forms us.* This is a culture of give and take. There is no separation here between god (the divine) and humanity. If this seems difficult to comprehend, then compare it to the relationship between the chicken and the egg. Which one comes first?

Once, humans and god were one entity—like one bunch of grapes. By insisting on creationism, Zoroastrian and Abrahamic religions have separated the divine from the human soul. This resulted in a supernatural and almighty god—a super god. These religions handed the values of humanity over to this super god and denied humans any further access to them. In this way, our values have been stolen from us and given to the almighty god. Now, the only access to our values is through this god, whom we find difficult to access. In addition, there is nothing in common between this god and us, so we must negotiate for the return of our stolen values. Our connection to this god is only through middlemen—or God's representatives—the mullahs, the priests, and the rabbis. They, in turn must connect us to God through the prophets. This is the problem: we have no direct access to our values or principles. This almighty god is so massive that there can't be any direct contact or direct connection between humans and god. So, this god needs messengers or prophets.

The outcome of creationism is the separation of god from humanity. Moreover, atheists have taken this process one step further and eliminated god from humanity completely. With this elimination, how can we access to our values and principles? This is the dilemma that is facing humanity today.

Continuity of life as a dynamic world

Life is a process, a metamorphosis that maintains some continuity. Life shapes the evolution that we know today, with added values and morality. Life can be defined as a growing or a formation mechanism; everything grows whether biological entities, ideology, thinking, or the divine. Life is dynamic not static, and therefore any static rule or consolidated 'god-given' book has to give in one day and open the way for the dynamic world to take the next step. Our values and principles have been shaped and reshaped by us—humans—on this Earth, and this are a process of growing. Even the divine grows with us in order to be able to be in tune with us and with the world to create the bond and unity among us that we call spirituality. Anything that grows has skin or a veil, and a core inside; therefore, to reach and know the core requires continuous exploration to penetrate into the veil or into the skin. Rumi said:

پوست سخن است آنچه گفتم
از پوست که یافت، مغز آن راز ؟

Skin is speech, a way to the door
From the skin, who found the core?

The core has the secret that is protected in darkness that is created by the skin. *The core is a hidden treasure which invites us for continues research, continuity.* Simplicity and quick solution of ideologies such as religion add more to the skin and pay less attention to the core. Without the core, humanity will lose the power of exploration. The consequence will be disunity, misery, war, and conflict. In any enlightenment, wisdom keeps on searching through the darkness for that enlightenment. This is the exploration that keeps humanity in shape. Furthermore, in any enlightenment, wisdom, in its search, can see only the skin that covers the core. This skin is the attraction that invites further investigation. This is why humanity always is faced with unfinished business and will remain to be unfinished business. Therefore, life is continues exploration: exploration that keeps us wise, united and healthy so we do not create war.

The ultimate truth is that life must be cherished. We must work towards unity and a better future. We have only one world to look after. Only this one world will bring us a better life. One world gives us the truth; two worlds give us segregation, division, and conflicts.

The need for a stronger sense of logic

Our sense of logic has to be strong; it will indeed get stronger through exploration as the human mind evolves throughout the time span of our life on this planet. Our educational establishments are designed to produce good mathematicians, engineers, doctors, and scientists. But they fail to produce scholars who are strong in social logic, philosophy, reasoning, and inspiration. In general, we are brought up very weak in making sense of our lives and the reasons for being on this Earth. We are so weak in the area of common sense that we allow ourselves to be influenced by very obviously illogical ideas, and we can be pushed to supernatural thoughts. In general, our sense of logic and consciousness doesn't seem to have a strong structural frame and bond that will allow us to define a constructive path for the future to stand strong enough against supernatural beliefs. Such weakness in our sense of logic is appalling, and our educational establishment must take a blame for this. Our educational establishments must be encourage to produce strong-minded people who can face up to the world better and distinguish between concepts that make sense and concepts that are really futile nonsense, such as believing in sophisticated and complicated godly torture chambers! We are encouraged to believe in a computer-like god with huge and colossal amount of memory and a hard disk that has all the knowledge of the world and takes every one of our actions into account! Where is our sense of logic? How can we carry on like this? Well, the problems keep mounting every year. It seems that being absurd is a new fashion. We are encouraged not to think and not to develop any kind of philosophy. It is incredible to see so many youngsters trying to believe in supernatural thoughts and remain static rather than advance dynamically in ideological terms. It is amazing to see students studying science and at same time rejecting the principles of science and accepting a supernatural belief in creationism. In doing this, they are denying the complexity of science and all the technological achievements our culture has made. There are students who study science and at the same time advocate the denial of man landing on the moon and the denial that there is a space station above our earth. They even deny that there is a satellite in orbit that runs their mobile phones! How incredible and absurd can a person be? We cannot pass off these absurd ideas by saying these people are dreamers. We have to understand that humanity needs philosophical spiritual values to replace those crippling dreams.

It is almost a common practise to meet a young religious-minded person who calls September 11 a product of a conspiracy of the West and Judaism. If this is so, how about the suicide bombings in Iraq, Afghanistan, and Pakistan and other places by these religious sects? If September 11 is a conspiracy, shouldn't these bombings and brutal killing also be included in a conspiracy theory? The answer you usually get from these people is that September 11 was different from those bombings! Really? Why should there be a difference? Is American blood more important than Pakistani, Afghan, or Iraqi blood? In all cases, innocent people get killed. Additionally, the repercussion of economical disaster and the following poverty is also huge. Therefore, I see no difference between the victims of September 11 and those innocent people who get killed by jihadists in their own countries every day. The bombing that is bringing Pakistan to her knees—the bombing of Shias and Sunnis—is even more disgusting, revolting, and horrible than that of September 11, because it causes division, separation, and hatred. Putting these disgusting killings in the category of conspiracy is being totally irresponsible to what goes on around us. These killings will never stop until we come to terms with our common sense in advocating, admiring, and respecting humanity to its full glory irrespective of any system of belief, including religions.

The human mind is the highway of thought and logic. Free and dynamic people on this highway are travelling at maximum speed. Religions and ideologies are the service stations. We need both—we need the highway and we also need the service stations. It is very comfortable for some to stay at the service station and doze, just watching the cars and time pass by. The religious and ideological people want to keep humanity at this service station for comfort; however, this would result in stagnation, and would eventually weaken our common sense as we tried to make sense of our environment. Only a deep and philosophical path can prevent this. Continuing with the speed along the highway can also be a disaster. We need a better service station where we can rest—one that does not make us sleep forever. And we also need the highway so we can go forward. Therefore, it is important to find and keep the balance—common sense must prevail. Moreover, there is a need for specialists such as mechanics and highway maintenance workers and other skilled workers to keep the highway system functional. There is a need for philosophy to keep the service station in operation. This continuous struggle of mind and soul makes us move forward, makes us like the Phoenix, makes us human, makes us dynamic and able to avoid being static.

In Persian philosophy, there was no obedience to a god; such conduct was beyond the imagination. We have not been created to be obedient to a god. Such thought and such behaviour is the process that can make us hopeless and unproductive. We have been given the mental ability to live our lives peacefully and to manage to sort out all our problems without constantly referring to god. God must be tired of so many demands that we make through these religious prayers. As Ferdowsi said:

ستودن مرو را ندانم همی
از اندیشه جان بر فشانم همی

Praise of the divine isn't something I can do
Thinking from the soul is what I must do

Description of this poem: My job isn't to praise the divine or god; my job is to develop ideas, innovations, and thoughts, such that fires come out of my burning soul so I don't become a beggar knocking on every door. This has inspired me to the following poem:

Fountains of fire come out of my burning core
Avoid being a beggar, knocking on every door

Obedience to God is an insult to God

Ignorance of my mental ability to be obedient to God or any deity is exactly the ignorance and insult to God's creation and formation of this life. Why has God given me such a weak mental power? If my brain isn't powerful enough to run my own life, then why has God given me such a worthless brain—so I can just obey him all the time? Obedience to God is nothing but an insult to God. Obedience to God is nothing but insult to my own mental ability that God has given me. The one who claims to be obedient to God and God only makes a false claim, as that person is obedient only to the hierarchy of his or her faith or religion. If you do manage to free that person from the hierarchy, be sure, she or he will free herself or himself from the god too. *The need for a deity and for obedience to that deity is the ultimate weakness of humanity.*

The early, true Persian culture taught the principle that heaven can be made here on this Earth. Dreaming of a heaven after death was nothing but an irresponsible joke. As Omar Khayyam said:

زان پیش که بر سرت شبیخون آرند
فرمای که تا باده گلگون آرند
تو زر نی ای غافل نادان که ترا
در خاک نهند و باز بیرون آرند

Before death strike you with pain
Ask for colourful wine, joy, gain

You aren't jewels, oh the ignorant insane
To put you in the grave and out again

Description of this poem: Omar Khayyam advised us to ask for colourful wine for happiness and for exhilaration, before death strikes. Happiness, joy, and exhilaration were his main objectives. *Without joyfulness life is meaningless.* He rejected the life after death in this poem and he called those ignorant and insane who believed they'd be pulled out of the grave for judgement day. He then makes this sarcastic remark—*you aren't jewels to be dug out of the ground; oh! the ignorant insane.*

It is very clear from this poem that the main objective of our existence must be *this life*. We have to make this life a happy life—heaven itself. Heaven, or afterlife, is for the unaware, the insane, and the irresponsible. It was the Zoroastrian and Abrahamic religions that took the power of making heaven on Earth out of our hands and then gave it to these super gods (almighty God), and by this tactic they managed to make this life a hell for all of us. Look at the 'very religious' countries in which these doctrines prevail and see the hell in which the people are living. The religious and political leaders of these countries do not feel any shame in seeing their own people living such a miserable life and in such a hell, as to them living this life is not the objective and the purpose of our existence, and therefore this life is not supposed to be made into heaven. These leaders, then, give their people the promise of a glorious heaven as the afterlife while they live in a heavenly like palaces here on this earth. This is hypocrisy at its best! Can anyone be more insane and more irresponsible than this?

Many great people have struggled consciously and mindfully to reinstate the values of humanity for making this life beautiful and sacrificed their life in the process. They have, indeed, been successful even in defeats—otherwise; we would have had an entire different atrocious hell on this earth. *Truth wins ... evens in defeat*.

What is the Persian view of spirituality?

Spirituality in many textbooks is defined as a belief in an ultimate or immaterial reality. However, spirituality also is an inner path one can take to define the essence of being and the values and meanings by which people should live in peace. Spirituality is a source of inspiration or orientation in life. We are not concerned with spiritual practices such a meditation, prayer, and contemplation in this book. Due to its importance, the Persian wording is as follows:

معنویت از معنی می آید، معنویت معنی کردن انسان و زندگی است

Spirituality comes from meaning in Persian language; it is to be able to define life and humanity. There is no one definition for life—leading to continuous clarity and therefore exploration.

In general, there are two different types of spirituality:

- *Defined spirituality*: This is spirituality as defined by religions. As this originated from supernatural belief, it will be subjected to objective discussion here in this book.
- *Procreative spirituality*: This was the spirituality practiced in true early Persian culture and even earlier human cultures as the philosophical mind of human grew through evolution.

Procreative spirituality, in general, is the philosophical definition of our life and the formation (evolution) of the life or beings. The procreative spirituality was the path of early humanity, which was stopped by the introduction of defined spirituality by Zoroastrian and Abrahamic religions.

Procreative spirituality can be divided into the following two sub categories:

- *Philosophical definition of this life:* This defines the purpose of this life as love and unity. Without such understanding, there can be disunity. This definition obviously has a broad meaning, but it can evolve in a cumulative manor over the stages of a human life. This means that our human experiences help us find a deeper understanding and therefore a more unified power in defining and giving meaning to our life.
- *Philosophical definition of the divine, and the divine being the essence of humanity*: This is nothing but the origin and the roots or the essence of humanity. Humanity and the divine are of one essence.

What is god or the divine?

This question can have three answers:

- God is meaning.
- God is image.
- God is meaning and image.

God is meaning

Zoroastrian and Abrahamic religions, especially Islam, say that God has meaning but does not appear as an image. However, this is flawed as every definition and description of a god automatically creates an image in our minds that is unavoidable. Any artist would like to paint such an image, and every human is a natural artist.

One of the important and crucial distinctions of such a god is that his followers must have faith. They must have faith in this god; they must obey him, and believe unequivocally the description of him provided by the religion. And they must never portray him in art, as any portrayal can remove or distort the belief.

God is image

The god of image is an idol … a physical image. Followers of this god worship an idol, a physical object—a cult image, which is also a piece of art. Worshiping an idol is referred to as idolatry. Idolatry is not limited to one idol only; it is also refers to a philosophy, a social phenomenon, and the perceptions behind that image. So, this ideology has the meaning built within but it is not usually dynamic.

God is meaning and image

God as meaning *and* image was the concept of the religions of our ancestors—early humanity before the Zoroastrian or Abrahamic religions came into existence. This ideology progressed further, and at the height of Persian Empire, it had developed to an advanced stage leaving its very interesting footprints in Persian mythology and later in the rich literature of Persia. This ideology is dynamic and automatically moves forward. The shape, image, and concepts of god can change from one generation to another. The process of moving forward is such that, as followers understood the meaning of the divine, they could envision an image of divine. As Obeid Zakan says:

رغبتم سوی بتان است ولیکن دو سه روز
از پی مصلحتی چند مسلمان شده ام

My desire is towards idols ... but for a few days' sake
Converted to Islam ... to pretend being the same

Description of this poem: Obeid Zakan puts himself to be an ideal person or an iconic person for the past, present, and future who want to be free to explore. He therefore represents the path of a free person to an ideal world on this earth who only converted to Islam for a few days' sake to pretend being the same—like others—to escape persecution. Otherwise, Zakan's desire is towards idols which are the portrayal of his own strength, imagination and power.

The image of the divine—idol—could expose the flaws in the ideology, and subsequently the concepts would change to a new portrayal to rectify the flaws. From this process, a new meaning would appear. This evolution of the meaning and the image of the divine was dynamic and was the catalyst that caused art to flourish in Persia and also caused an amazing development in the infrastructure of the country. In fact, when Alexander invaded Persia, he was amazed at the infrastructure and the art he found there. We should not forget that there was some cultural exchange between Persia and Greece; therefore, although the cultures were very different, there was a small Greek influence in the Persian culture and ideology.

One of very important and crucial distinctions of this divine is that there is no requirement of faith to believe in this divine culture. In fact, faith goes against the perception and concept of the ideology. Faith would prevent change and evolution of this ideology.

Why should a true belief or religion need our faith?

It is very important to understand the crucial distinction that requires faith in god in Zoroastrian and Abrahamic religions. Followers must have faith in this god and in his existence. Only then will they obey him and believe in the defined description of him, and never portray him in artwork, as any portrayal can destroy the belief.

As we have seen, in early human cultures—and in the early, true Persian culture—it was quite the opposite. *There was no requirement for faith in order to believe.*

The relationship we share with our divine must be similar, at least to some extent, to the relationship we share with our friends. A true friend will not put forth a condition that I have to have faith in her or him in order to establish our friendship. A person who would demand my faith as a condition for friendship would be my enemy, not a friend. The relationship I share with my god is the same. If god requires my faith in order to be my god, then that god isn't my friend; rather, he is my enemy.

Faith is the mother of fanaticism—the deeper the faith, the more intense the fanaticism. Faith isn't related to religion only. We have faith in capitalism, modernism, and science as well. *Faith is the stagnation of thoughts.*

Faith and love

Faith isn't love, and love isn't faith. *Love and faith are antithetical* because a person who has faith in a belief, such as faith in a religion, will be antagonistic to any other belief and antagonistic to any change in ideology. However, love is open to sacrificing and making changes. Love seeks to meld with others to propagate and spread further and further. Love adores and embraces all thoughts and ideas and cherishes advancement and moving forward.

The product of love is identical to the root in essence but entirely different in character and intellectuality as it takes life into the next stage of formation. This is evolution. This is like a child who is the product of the love between a man and a woman. He is like his parents because he has inherited their traits, but he is quite different in personality and intellectuality.

For humanity, *love is superior to all the beliefs or religions*. Love goes beyond infidelity and religious beliefs. Faith, on the other hand, must be aligned with a structure of belief, such as a religion.

Anyone who does not understand this simple difference between love and faith will have difficulty in thinking freely and understanding the essence of humanity. People who change the world for the better are those who do so through love and affection without expecting any reward. Furthermore, they are persistent and know no limits and no barriers to their success.

I explore, therefore I am

Descartes said, '*I think, therefore I am*'. Rumi said, '*I explore, therefore I am*'. This means 'I think and explore, therefore I am'. If we do not explore or think, then we do not effectively exist. Furthermore, this means our existence is irrelevant to whatever goes on around us if we do not explore.

Our Middle Eastern modern intellectuals and thinkers, in fact, can't stop copying the West or the East, instead of following their own independent minds. The Middle Eastern modern intellectuals can be divided into three categories:

- Middle Eastern modern intellectuals say, 'Westerners think, therefore I am.' Or they say 'Descartes, Hegel, Nietzsche, and Freud think, therefore I am.'
- Middle Eastern leftist intellectuals say, 'Easterners [Karl Marx, Das Kapital] think [or thought], therefore I am.'
- Religious intellectuals thinkers say, 'The Quran, or god, thinks, therefore I am.'

In general, our Middle Eastern intellectuals say the Western philosophers and Eastern philosophers such as Karl Marx thought and cooked the ultimate thoughts in god's kitchen. The ideas of these thinkers define these intellectuals.

Today, there is virtually no one in the Middle East who believes that anybody can think new thoughts and explore new concepts in philosophy. Any new thinker would be accused of either playing with words or restating the same thoughts that are written in their Quran, the Quran of the Western world or the Quran of the Eastern world (Karl Marx's *Das Kapital*). Today, we have three Qurans in our modern Muslim world—the Muslim Quran, the Western Quran (western philosophers), and the Eastern leftist Quran (Karl Marx's *Das Kapital*).

It is these Qurans that are preventing members of the Muslim world from gearing their minds to exploration and free thinking, and this is preventing their ability to explore and cultivate their own identity from their own literature. This is currently crippling our thought process to such an extent that there are hardly any creative minds today in our Muslim nations.

Culture

Our word *culture* is from the Latin word *cultura*, which means 'cultivation' or 'tending'. Thus, our concept of culture derives from the concept of cultivation. Culture grows from the roots. Culture is the process of growing and is part of evolution of humanity. Therefore, culture has self-originality and self-identity; two traits that do not originate from an external force, but come from the roots of humanity.

In this description of culture, there is no room for the behaviour of people, their mental content, or society's norms. These should not be referred to as culture. Furthermore, any system or religious law such as Sharia law—or Islamic law—is nothing to do with culture; rather, they are opposite to culture. Culture is cultivation and needs to grow and change, but Sharia law, or any other established system, wants to remain static in order to maintain control over its own rules and guidelines.

Systems of belief, such as religions, have tried to create and manipulate culture and keep it static, as if imprisoned; however, a system cannot create a culture. Culture, by definition, demands change. A system or static ideology resists changes—preventing creativity.

Culture isn't just the betterment or refinement of the individual through education or the fulfilment of national aspirations or ideals; culture is the fulfilment of human aspirations. Culture is universal human capacity grown from the roots. Culture is a concept central to anthropology, encompassing all human phenomena that are not purely the result of human genetics, but from humanity itself, as creatures of ethics who care for one other and have roots in many thousands of years of history.

Mythology and myth

'Mythology' refers to the study of myths, which are collective narrative explanations of how the world and humanity came to be in its present form. The point of concern in this book regarding myths is the process in which humanity came about, not how the world came into being.

In fact, myth is the product of thousands of years of experience of mankind explained through one character—story. Very deep philosophy and ethical values can be expressed through mythical characters. A mythical character is often wrongly interpreted as a supernatural being when; instead, he or she is simply the result of over a thousand years of human experience defined in one mythical character or *story—tale*. The mythical characters only *appear to be* supernatural—as they are the product of collective experiences. Any historical nations have evolved through time; must have struggled in unifying people to live together—as result of this—they have developed *experiences and the art of living together*. This portrayal of struggle against obstacles and the experiences of living together created culture that is built around characters—called mythical characters. These are the stories that define humanity and life—which would have been much more difficult to be expressed in any other way. Moreover, in some other cases, it would have been more dangerous (danger of being persecuted) to define a problem in any other method than forming a well defined story, as Attar said:

قصه چیست؟ از مشکلی آشفتن است
آنچه نتوان گفت هرگز، گفتن است

What is story? It is being disturbed of a problem
It is to say those that could have never been said

Description of this poem: We may not know the importance of a *story* today and define a story as a childish thought ... but a story can have the origin of a big philosophy for freedom. A man has to speak out when facing with a disturbed social problem to show his truthfulness. The problem of social disturbance of rule and order, and calmness affects the soul of humanity and makes any future progress impossible. It is at this stage that a wise man can ask the question: who has disturbed the essence and the soul of humanity and prevented the calmness of humanity?

However, this disturbance that is forced upon the society by violence and sword has the wise man under control and domination. Hence, a man can never tell of his essence and his nature—on the other hand—being silent makes him deceitful and mendacious. This is where a *story* becomes a vital tool for a wise man to utter his anger and frustration against a society that suffocate any creative and inspired mind. A story can plant the philosophy of freedom in the essence and the spirit of humanity to free people from religious dogma. Why is it that a man is prevented expressing the essence of humanity in a religious dogma environment? It is because; religious dogma … with its guidance of the whole population … makes people to be the enemy of their own freedom.

Moreover on the subject of mythology, we need to correct the definition of myth as it is currently incorrectly understood in almost all areas of study. Popular media such as the BBC continue to translate myth so as to perpetuate a lie. This is completely misleading and wrong. A myth can be much more powerful than the truth or fact; a truth or a fact can originate from one person and from one experience, while a myth involves mankind's experiences through thousands years of cultural history.

Misleading people in the meaning of myth itself can destroy our past heritage and identity, which can result in simplistic and weak minds. It can turn us into simple, materialistic people and encourage the growth of a materialistic world. The materialistic world is doing as much harm to humanity as religions have done. *To come out of religious dogmatic and simplistic thoughts and fall into the trap of a materialistic world is a terrible fate!* No wonder religious doctrines are gaining ground in our modern world.

CHAPTER THREE

PLATO AND ROSTAM: TWO DIFFERENT ALLEGORIES OF THE CAVE

Two opposite experiences of thinking

This chapter will explore the humanistic values of Persian culture in contrast to Greek culture. The humanistic values were far more prevalent in Persian civilization than they were Greek civilization. At the very least, it is important to know there were different classical ways of looking at humanity. I will use Plato's allegory of the cave and the Persian mythological hero, Rostam, to illustrate the differences.

Plato

Plato was student of Socrates. He was a Greek philosopher, mathematician and author of philosophical dialogues. Although we are living in a very modern world, the core of ideology of our modern world is, in fact, based on the theory that Plato presented in his allegory of cave. The word *democracy* is from the Greek *demokratia*; Greece is known to be the cradle of democracy that we know today.

Rostam

Rostam is a Persian national hero and mythological figure who is characterised in famous epic poem by Persian poet Ferdowsi (940-1020) known as the *Shahnameh*. Rostam was born of Roudabeh via caesarean section; in fact, this is the first-ever mention of caesarean section in literature. According to the *Shahnameh*, Rostam was the first person who was born with this method. Rostam is immortalized in the *Shahnameh* because he is a character who can exist in every person. All humans have heroic talent built into them. The pure ideology behind this is that this talent can be explored and invoked in every individual. In fact, we are all Rostam and we, as a whole, are immortal, and, as an individual, we are mortal. In another word, society always can thrive and therefore it is immortal; however, an individual is mortal.

Plato's allegory of the cave

In Plato's allegory of the cave, Plato, as a philosopher, becomes enlightened and runs away from the darkness of his cave. Subsequently, he takes on the role of a preacher or prophet who has seen the light and reality and can preach to others and makes them come out of darkness and see the light. Furthermore, to Plato, succeeding in getting people to come out of darkness and see the light isn't the entire solution. The people must also be taught to see through the light as they are not used to seeing in the light.

This idea of the allegory of the cave, in fact, comes from Persian culture. Plato took this idea from Persian culture, as there was cultural exchange between Persia and Greece. Persians used to see their divine and philosophical ideology through the caves. Where there was no cave, the use of underground chambers created a cave-like atmosphere. This is why adherents of Mithraism, *a mystery religion that began in Persia and expanded to Rome*, used to build their temples underground or in caves. A clear example is the Temple of Mithras found under the ground in Walbrook, a street in London. This is now displayed at Museum of London.

Furthermore, in taking the idea from Persian culture, Plato misunderstood the concept and expressed it totally the opposite way from the way it was intended. *To the Persians, the truth is hidden and is in darkness, such as caves*. Moreover, to the Persians the world—the globe—is full of secrets and therefore the whole world is cave. It is the job of every individual to go through the cave/darkness and find the hidden treasures. We should not look at the world as if all enlightenment is displayed for all to see; rather, we should look at the world as a place that is full of hidden places for us to discover and explore.

Plato's version of enlightenment has made the enlightened individuals superior to others and has created super humans and dictators and almighty gods who have dominated over people for many centuries.

Rostam's allegory of the cave

In Rostam's allegory of the cave, *Rostam goes into the darkness and effortlessly makes his way through—he is able to see through in the darkness with his own eyes*. He does not run away from the darkness; rather, he goes into the darkness and sees through the darkness. This is in contrast to Plato, who, as a philosopher, is enlightened and runs away from darkness. This is why Plato plays the role of preacher and prophet who has been enlightened. Persian ideology was quite the opposite in the sense that nobody can be enlightened; we all move towards enlightenment but can never be fully enlightened. As soon as we are enlightened and find a truth—called sometimes the light—the truth escapes from us and runs farther away, encouraging us to seek even more enlightenment. This is called *Sanam e Gorizpa*[13] (Elusive Sanam) in Persian Literature, As Rumi said:

بروید ای حریفان بکشید یار ما را
به من آورید آخر صنم گریز پا را

Oh, my adversaries depart! Portray us our sweetheart
Fetch me, the elusiveness Sanam[14], at last

Description of this poem: Rumi asks his adversaries to depart and paint the portrayal of our lover in order to bring back the lover, the sweetheart or the ultimate goal. He calls the sweetheart or the ultimate goal an elusive Sanam (goddess). Why is Sanam elusive? Because Sanam is the ultimate goal, and we never reach the ultimate goal; we only move towards her.

Sanam in this ghazal is the idol, the ultimate love, the ultimate lover or the ideal world/place. To the Persians, even the divine is an imminent explorer who exists in every being's soul. Persian ideology was totally against a totally enlightened or almighty god with a massive amount of memory space—a super computer with huge hard disk space that could

---

[13] *Gorizpa: This is a Persian word that means elusive.*
[14] *Sanam: Lover, the beauty; the image given at beginning of this book.*

store all of our private and non-private matters of life and keep track of everything forever! To the Persians, the divine did not create the world. *To the Persians, the divine* was *the world.* The divine is harmony in every being and is imminent and elusive—this is nothing to do with hallucination or superstitious… divine is beauty and beauty hits us in a moment or a flash and goes away. These momentarily events are the most valuable part of our life. Every being is beautiful, and beauty is divine and elusive. *Divine is all of the beauty and colours—divine is multiplicity and exuberance. Divine can't be pinned down or owned by anyone or by any one idea.* If principles of law and order are elusive, they cannot be pinned down or owned by anyone; they are always open for amendment so culture can advance into the future with the changes necessitated by the passage of time.

Therefore, the concept of an almighty god was against the belief of the Persians and not acceptable to any intellectuals. *Belief in the afterlife, such as heaven and hell, was only for the uneducated.* Such a belief would have been a joke to Persian intellectuals. The belief in heaven and hell is an insult to humans who are intellectual explorers. There can never be a relationship between an almighty god (a god of great size) and a human (so little in comparison). There is no tune and no harmony between two things of such different sizes, and that's why belief in an almighty god goes against nature and against human values. No soft or delicate preaching can ever bring an almighty god in tune with humanity.

To the Persians, exploration and discovery were divine. They are always there in our minds and thoughts, and they evolve as we evolve. When we explore, we awaken the divine in our souls and in every part of our bodies; that's why exploration gives us happiness.

Evolution gives true meaning to life; it comes from exploration and therefore the divine. *I explore, therefore I am. I doubt, therefore I am.* Darwin only expanded on the theory of evolution, but the original idea and the philosophy of evolution was there for thousands of years. We cannot exist without evolving and without exploration. Therefore, we cannot exist without the divine, which is exploration. The divine had such beautiful meaning to the early Persians—the meaning of unity, the meaning of love. The divine evolves like every being on this Earth. As Rumi said:

تا در طلب گوهر کانی، کانی
تا در هوس لقمه نانی، نانی
این نکته رمز اگر بدانی، دانی
هر چه که در جستن آنی آنی

Seeking the essence of the globe? You are the globe
Looking for a morsel of bread? You are the bread
Know this secret, you will adore
You are what you explore

Description of this poem: The message in this poem is that you are what you explore. If you seek for the essence of the globe, you are the globe. If you are after a morsel of bread, you are the bread. And, finally, Rumi concludes that you should know a secret from him: *You are what you explore.*

The vision of Plato escaping from darkness and his view of enlightenment has created super humans and dictators who dominate over people. The vision of Plato escaping from darkness has created many ideologies and religions whose core idea is enlightenment and fighting against darkness. Do we really want to fight against darkness, the place we come from? This is a fight against our own roots and identity. This ideology has given the perception and insight to the general public that there is a core ideology that can enlighten us to all the complexities and phenomena of life. Such an ideology is being claimed by many factions, religions, and ideologists, and this is causing havoc in our world—so many deaths and so much destruction in the name of enlightenment! Aren't we going crazy?

There are so many people, even intellectuals from eastern countries, who support freedom and democracy, but the unfortunate thing is that they believe that the West has cooked for us in their god-given kitchen a pure democratic system and kept it on a shelf waiting to be applied! Where does this kind of vision come from? This vision is exactly the philosophy of enlightenment. This kind of philosophy about the West is very dangerous and can make the East fall into another trap—another dictator who can be worse than the first dictator.

Darkness is where we all come from. We come from our mother's womb, which is a dark place ... dark in a sense that no one can know what kind of human and intellectual the unborn child is going to be. Everything about that child is hidden to us.

Additionally, the existence of all the trees and plants springs from their roots, which dwell in a dark place. Furthermore, all of our new findings come from darkness. *Darkness gives birth to our findings.* If there is no darkness, then there is no birth and no light. Dark and light are complementary to each other; one can't exist without other.

In Rostam's allegory of the cave, the world is cave, and the world is dark and mysterious. It's down to all individuals to be like Rostam and open our eyes and ears and see through darkness. We should not emulate Plato and run away from the darkness towards enlightenment or brightness and then preach to everyone to escape from the darkness. Every nook and cranny that we see in our surroundings contains hidden treasures that need our innovation—a breakthrough to the darkness. The reflection of such thoughts comes in a variety of ways in Persian literature. As Rumi said:

تو هرگوهر که می بینی، بجو درّی دگر، در وی
که هر ذرّه همی گوید که درباطن، دفین دارم
تراهرگوهری گوید، مشو قانع به‌حسن من
که از «شمع ضمیر» است آن، که نوری درجبین دارم
چه دانی تو که درباطن، چه شاهی، همنشین دارم
رخ زرین من منگر که پای آهنین دارم

Whatever essence you see, explore for more quintessence within
Every bit of a matter tells you it has something hidden within
Every essence's message is that there is no satisfaction with my beauty within
Beauty is my nature, look for hidden treasures within
In me, how do you know there isn't a treasure within?
Don't see my paled face; see my strength as an iron man within

Description of this poem: This poems show the values of exploring to find the quintessence of any 'bit of matter'. That quintessence is divine. The quintessence or essence isn't just *like* the divine; it *is* the divine to Persians. This is why wine is valued and admired in Persian literature, as wine is representative of essence and purity.

Enlightenment

There is no separation between good and evil, and there is no separation between darkness and brightness. There is nothing in the world that just enlightens us, and there is nothing in the world that just darkens. *Any brightness creates a shadow and a darkness area; that is unavoidable.* Darkness and brightness are the two sides of one coin, complementary to one other. Seeing something as purely dark or purely bright is an incorrect perception; and seeing two things alike is a product of our imagination. There are no two things in the world that are alike.

The most falsified thinking in today's modern world is a belief in a thought that just enlightens us. A thought that enlightens a matter also casts a shadow on the other side of the matter and darkens the other side that we don't see. The problem is, we forget about this darkened side of the matter and see only the lightened side.

Persia's native culture was in love with discoveries and exploration, as these were directly related to the phenomena of knowing the world, knowing a stranger, knowing an outsider, knowing ourselves, or seeing through different eyes and different visions which are unknown to us.

Rostam, who is the symbol of the Persian way of thinking, did not escape from darkness but enlightened himself through the darkness with his own insight. *His story of 'Haft Khan-e Rostam' shows that darkness and clarity are complementary to each other rather than being against each other.* Seeing through the darkness is an art. We have seen in recent years discoveries that even a blind person can really see. This phenomenon of seeing into our world does not divide the world into believers and nonbelievers, into brightened and darkened, and into friend and enemy. We are capable of seeing through the darkness; we should not escape from darkness and divide humanity into good and evil. We need to explore darkness, not put it aside. It is important to find out why something that is labelled 'evil' has been so labelled; maybe it isn't bad after all; maybe it has been given the label for the benefit of an ideology so that it can gain supremacy.

Another very important point that makes the mythological Rostam superior to the historical Plato is that Rostam is a humanised figurehead who has been created from a collective knowledge over thousands of years. He is a symbolised character of humanity rather than a historical character who become an idolized figurehead. Furthermore, Plato borrowed the root of his allegory of the cave from Persian Mithraism, which he did not understand correctly.

The figureheads in the *Shahnameh*, such as Rostam and others in different stories, were selected deliberately and intentionally to document Persian philosophy and wisdom that were forbidden at the time of religious domination under Islamic and Zoroastrianism rule. The Persian way of thinking and philosophy was forbidden; followers were called infidels and unbelievers. They were said to be against almighty God and a threat to religious theocracy and also a threat to any oppressive rulers.

Ferdowsi used his artistic talent and his skilful poetry in the *Shahnameh* and characterised Persian philosophy in many characters. He did this very skilfully and with great care so that his book would be published and would not be banned and burnt. He used his skill to avoid the punishment by the establishment and religious figureheads. Ferdowsi somehow managed to publish the book at the last minute before his death. Regarding the evolution of the world and humanity Ferdowsi said:

چو زین بگذری، **مردم** آمد پدید
شد این بندها راسراسر، **کلید**
سرش راست بر شد، چو سرو بلند
به گفتار خوب و خرد کاربند

Passing this stage, humanity has been shaped
The key to all the locked matters is reshaped
Head high as cedar tree, so much gratified
Due to fine speeches and wisdom beatified

Description of this poem: After the stage in which the Earth was shaped, humanity was shaped, and humanity was given the key to all the locked matter, humans have been shaped to hold their heads as high as the cedar tree. The reason for such confidence in humanity is fine speeches and working-wisdom[15] (beautiful wisdom).

Why does Ferdowsi compare humans to the cedar tree? There are two reasons for this:

- The cedar tree is straight and tall, and it is green all year round. Humans are vibrant and active all the year round.
- The cedar tree is tall and straight; therefore it symbolizes humans holding their heads high. Ferdowsi's philosophy is that humans can make a difference only when they are full of confidence; therefore, their heads should be as high as a cedar tree.

---

[15] *Working-wisdom: The wisdom that listens and finds the mistakes and corrects them and therefore moves forward.*

In this poem, Ferdowsi confirms that humans are the key to all difficulties and to all the locked matters. We are our own saviours; we are the only solution to our problems. There is no supernatural saver; there are only us humans on this Earth. The solution to our problems is not in the Quran or in Bible or in any other 'god-given' book. *We are the solution to all of our problems.*

This is why almost all Persians recognize Ferdowsi as the greatest man in Persian culture. However, due to the current and past domination of ideological religious theocracy over the Iranian population, there are only a few Iranians who really understand the core message that is presented in the *Shahnameh*. Iranians are allowed to have the *Shahnameh*, they are allowed to read the *Shahnameh*, but they are not allowed to truly understand this great work. This is the problem facing Iranians, not only with regard to this book, but with all Persian literature.

Iranians are not allowed to understand their literature. Their understanding quickly becomes a threat to Islam, to the rulers, and to the establishment. I am sure such problems exist in all Arabic countries too. Are Egyptians allowed to explore their rich culture? They can explore the history but not the philosophy of their culture. Can Jordanians explore their rich culture? The Islamic view in all Islamic countries has been so simplified that any real explorations into humanistic values and cultural values become a threat to religious figureheads. Without these cultural values, there will never be a real path to democracy, and the vicious cycle of violence will carry on. Democracy and freedom are rooted in the values and respect within these cultures. Values and respect must come from the core of society, which is rooted in a culture that can be many thousands of years old. This is why the research and exploration into the morality aspect of any culture is very vital. Values cannot be imported from the West in a jumbo jet; neither can it be dropped from the sky through religious dogma. We also can't be beggars for democracy and freedom forever. As Rumi said:

گدا رو مباش و مزن هر دری
که هرچیزرا که بجوئی ، تو آنی
دلا خیمه خود براین آسمان زن
مگو که نتانم ، بلی میتوانی

Don't be a beggar, knocking on every door
Be an explorer, you are what you explore
Come home! Your key to success is here
Don't say you can't. You can, if you adhere

Description of this poem: Rumi said we shouldn't knock on every door begging for what we want. He encourages us to explore: *you are what you explore.* If we don't explore, we are nobody and don't have any productive skill. The exploration shouldn't take place in a faraway location; it should be done at home, as our key to success is at home, inside of us. Our key to success is not an external power such as a god. Finally, Rumi said; don't say you aren't capable of this exploration— you *are* capable if you adhere to your roots.

Democracy must be cultivated from the roots of the society, not imported from an outside country or from a religious belief. Values are the results of the process of the evolution of our ancestor's minds and thoughts over thousands of years of effort. The foundation of a democratic system has to be built from these values; without such a root base, any democratic system would be shaky. *There is one freedom or democracy, but there are many ways to it ... each way has its own philosophy*

Theocracies took over Arab countries and remained in power. For many years, dictators have governed over the area with no political infrastructure. Will there be democracy after theocracy? The answer to this may again be pessimistic. There will be a few more dictatorships under the name of Western democracy. Many more demonstrations like the one at Tahrir Square will be needed! The cycles of taking the wrong path to democracy must carry on until the area wakes up to its own self-consciousness. These paths are well classified and explained in many characters in Persian literature and Persian mythology.

The characters in the *Shahnameh* show the essence of the Persian view of humanity, which is in everyone; that is, everyone is Rostam or Fereydoun, who is another famous character in the *Shahnameh*. In other words, the value of humanity is within every individual. It only needs to be invoked within us using human artistic talent. As Ferdowsi said:

فریدون فرّخ، فرشته نبود
ز مشک و ز عنبر، سرشته نبود
بداد و دهش یافت آن نیکوئی
تو داد و دهش کن، فریدون توئی

Fereydoun wasn't a cherished angel
Neither was he covered with a heavenly principle
He was a true character of integrity, a visionary
You can do it too; you are Fereydoun, the principle

Description of this poem: Fereydoun in this poem is an ideal and an iconic person who has saved Persia from one thousand years of dictatorship. Fereydoun is a mythological character who is from the goddess culture. Anybody from the goddess culture is also a goddess. This is the principle of the goddess culture. Ferdowsi said that Fereydoun was neither a cherished angel nor covered with heavenly principles. He was rather like you and me ... like every one of us. However, he was a true character of integrity and he was a visionary. Ferdowsi carried on to say that we can do it too ... we can also be Fereydoun.

The goal of the *Shahnameh* is to portray this message to every individual human being: *you can do it too; you are Fereydoun*. In fact, the message tells us to get up and make the effort because we are our own idols; we are the Kabah (the Muslim holy shrine); we are the divine or we are the Jesus Christ. All of this goddess is in you and within you. These are not fictional stories. As Ferdowsi in another poem said:

تو این را دروغ و فسانه مدان
به یکسان روش در زمانه مدان
از او هر چه اندر خورد با خرد
دگر بر ره رمز معنی برد

These aren't fictional stories or lies
Don't accept them as one way over the times
Read and weigh them with your sense
The messages are tied, open up the ties

Description of this poem: Ferdowsi points out that the mythological characters and the stories in the *Shahnameh* aren't fiction or lies; neither should we accept them as one method or one way over the times. He then stresses that; we should read them and weigh them with our own sense of logic. The messages are tied within the mythological characters and the stories, and we should have the skill to open the ties.

The characters in the *Shahnameh* portray the ethical values and wisdom that made us human. Without these cultural ethical values, we wouldn't be human today. This is why Ferdowsi said that the stories in the *Shahnameh* aren't fictional stories, but rather tools for us to use to discover human values. Leaving the ethical values to history and fictional stories would be harmful to the ethics of our modern world.

The ethical value that makes us human exists in us and all around us. The negativity of human values also exists in us. Humans have the artistic talent to invoke the positive aspect of human values and to explore the ethics that make us human, not animal. Humanity is the key to all of our problems on this earth. We have to create that belief among us and move forward. Without such confidence, we can have disastrous setbacks, and it will take generations to overcome the difficulties.

Our heritage is much more than history. Our heritage as humans comes from our collective ethical values that are pure treasures hidden in our history. These invaluable treasures have been built for us through the evolution of humanity over many thousands of years. We can't just forget these or leave them aside. We owe it to our children, our grandchildren, and to generations we will never meet to keep it alive and pass it along.

CHAPTER FOUR

HUMANITY AND ETHICAL EVOLUTION

Humanity

Humanity isn't only the product of the modern life. Humanity has been with us through the span of human life on this Earth. Our historical records may reach back for over 10,000 years or less. In the span of human life on this Earth, there have been many good times and some difficult ones, but through it all, humanity has persevered and has risen from the ashes in difficult times and has been productive in good times.

Why does this matter to us? Because it is important that we understand the path and the process of hard work and sacrifices that our ancestors had to go through to hand over the values of humanity to us. Understanding our past can create a belief that it is all in our hands; we can make the difference. We can make a better world. We are the world. It is this confidence that can make us work together, care for each other, and help ideas to go forward for a better life and to turn our ambitions to achievements. This is the process of humanity evolving and gaining confidence to make heaven here on this Earth.

This has in no way been an easy process; rather, it has been a painstaking process, which we must admire. Humanity needs confidence to continue this evolution so that we do not buckle under the pressure of many challenges and difficulties in a dynamic world where population is increasing. Humanity has evolved not only biologically but morally and mentally as well. The path of evolution of the mind must reopen for the future of mankind. Darwin's theory of biological evolution can also be applied to the moral evolution. Our moral evolution has been shaped from our past heritage.

Ignoring our past heritage is ignoring the ethics that our ancestors have worked hard and sacrificed so much for. Our ethical past has been shaped to a large extent by the Middle East. By elaborating on these values, the East can contribute to humanity and challenge world terrorism from its roots. In this book, I will elaborate on the roots of the ethics from the perspective of Persian mythology. I will show that Persian values do not match what we usually hear in news. The exploration of Persian mythology in this book is a good example; such values with a different approach can be found also in the early literature of India, China, Egypt, Greece, and many other nations. We, as humans on this Earth, are like one body. So, when one part becomes hurt, the whole body suffers. As Saadi, the Persian poet, said:

بنی آدم اعضای یک پیکرند
که در آفرینش ز یک گوهرند
چو عضوی به درد آورد روزگار
دگر عضوها را نماند قرار
تو کز محنت دیگران بیغمی
نشاید که نامت نهند آدمی

Humanity is of one body, all as one
The root of its formation is of one essence
If a part of a body receives pain,

The rest of the body follows in accordance
If you are indifferent to people's pain
How can you be addressed as a human?

Description of this poem: Saadi described humanity in this poem in its full glory. He described humanity as one body; its root of formation is of one essence, like organs in one body. So if a part of the body receives agony, the rest of the body feel the pain and agony. If we are indifferent to people's pain and agony, then how can we be called human? *Being able to feel other people's pain is one of the most important principles of the culture of humanity.*

The Persian civilization has always been looked at through the eyes of Greek culture and Greek historians, and Greece was the sworn enemy of Persia. The majority of books published in the West regarding Persia's past take a very negative approach. However, the fact of the matter is quite opposite. In this book, I will present a Persian view of the Persian civilization with deep background knowledge of the Persian culture that has one of greatest literatures of mankind. It is very important to know this, as our values come from our ancestors, and Persia has played a great role in our ancestral heritage. Our ancestors paved the way for today's concept of equality. It is important to understand the time span and the way these glories of human values have been shaped. Our apathy about these values has made us lose the valuable material that has been left for us.

Very deep philosophy and ethical value can be found in mythology. How can we say myth is a lie? A myth, as a story created from the people and experiences of an entire civilization over thousands years of cultural history, can be much more powerful than a truth created about a single person and his or her experiences.

For a long time, religious leaders have done all they can to discredit myth, and this hampers the advancement of civilization. When we lose the myths, we lose who we are. Now some people are following the simplistic teachings of religion and materialism, which are equally harmful to humanity. Mythologies preserve humanity's past experiences by explaining them through a character and a story. Myths are powerful and should not be underestimated. Mythology needs to be explored as it serves as a guidepost for the future of mankind.

Freedom and Simorgh, a benevolent, Persian mythical flying creature, are one, but there are many paths to freedom. Any nation can achieve freedom, but freedom can't be achieved through force or dictatorship. Freedom has to come from thinkers, philosophers who are rooted in the culture and know the culture through their philosophical minds. *Because each country has a different cultural background, these thinkers must achieve freedom and democracy by following different paths.*

Cultural heritage is rooted deep in history and in ancient religious beliefs, not in the more modern Abrahamic religions. These religions have stolen an uncountable amount of human values and principles and have manipulated them to their own needs and even called them god-given values and principles. Religion, in principle, is against evolution and against these rooted historical values. A religion is like a cage. Any phoenix, bird, or broad-minded person confined in a cage will never have the opportunity to grow because progress in a cage of religion is always limited to the framework of the cage. Even though this cage of religion is an environment that feels safe to some people, it is not a free environment in which free-thinking minds can grow to their full potential. In actual fact, *religion is a thorn in the flesh of every wise person.*

This 'cage of religion' is the basic and the fundamental problem that stops Muslim nations from evolving out of their current status as third-world nations. Muslim nations will never be able to pull their heads higher until they get back to their roots and rise from their ashes like a tall proud tree ... like a cedar tree as expressed in Persian literature. Is this expectation too much? Is this a fantasy? Rumi said:

تو ز خاک سر برآور که درخت سربلندی
تو بپر به قاف قربت که شریفتر همایی

Grow from the soil (soul) as you are a tall tree, a black pine
Jump over divinity; you are the most honourable divine

Description of this poem: Rumi was saying that we must hold our heads as high as a tall, black pine tree, so that we go over the divine. Why? Because, all people have in their roots the most honourable divine.

Is humanity the most honourable divine? This is the respect for humanity we find in Persian literature—humanity is honoured as having divine quality. Here Rumi tried to steal the values from God and give them back to humans. This is similar to the Greek myth in which Prometheus stole the fire from God and gave it back to the people. Is this supernatural? Is this paranormal? If so, then, morality should also be paranormal! There are such precious values in Eastern mythology that need to be explored and shown to the outside world. Then the world would recognize the Eastern values of freedom and humanity—leading to publicity and the right encouragements needed for the Eastern Nations.

An identity and value taken from early, true Persian historical cultural background can boost morale and self-confidence in the history of mankind. This self-confidence in the moral evolution of mankind could take away that simplistic tenets and self-serving purpose of today's religions, which are trying to degrade humanity. *Any 'god-given' script is an insult to humanity, and to god too.* The values of humanity are rooted in almost all historical nations; they can be found in the historical artwork and literature of that nation. However, this book focuses on only one nation—Persia. As we look at Persian mythology, we keep only one thing in mind: to improve self-confidence in mankind. As Rumi said:

ترا هرکس ، بسوی خویش خواند
ترا من، جز بسوی تو، نخوانم

Everyone calls you to his or her own affiliation
I call you to nobody but to your own aspiration

Description of this poem: Rumi sent a powerful message here. He didn't want us to be drawn without thinking into the ideas and philosophies of others who try to lure us. Rather, he wanted us to explore our own essence, to be our own boss. This is the only way we can reach our own aspirations.

To extrapolate, Rumi did not want us to be drawn into Westernization, Easternization, Arabization, creationism, or evolutionism. He wanted us to be drawn towards our own self-consciousness, so we can stand up on our own feet without a walking stick. *Religion is nothing but a walking stick; you take it away from a believer, then, see how vulnerable that person will become.* So, we can live full and cherished lives that derive from our own consciousness that can benefit us as well as others.

Conversely, an external thought framework such as a religious ideology wants to impose its restrictions and beliefs on us and will endeavour to take our own identity and self-conciseness away in order to take us over.

Religious believes are static ideas—prevents creative talent. Humanity is and must be dynamic and open to change. This is exactly the reason that we see Muslim nations being much less productive than Western countries and other countries that have democratic systems. Any religious country that does manage to become successful for a period of time does so only because they were able to turn their belief into dynamic activity for a short period of time. Any of these religions can be dynamic, but only for a short period of time because being dynamic goes against the essence of their beliefs. The democratic system isn't just the product of West; far from that. Democratic systems are the product of our ancestral heritage … from our forbearers who sacrificed so much for humanity and for the values that make us human. The modern democratic system is the product of shaping and systemizing our ancestral achievements in humanity and values; and of course new good and bad ideas have been added. We underestimate the people of the past, and we do so at our peril.

Our ancestral heritage is the eyes and ears and the path for our future. *To not explore our valuable ancestral heritage is like blinding people and giving them walking sticks.* This is exactly what religion has done to the poor and innocent people of this world, including those of the Muslim nations. Not allowing people to openly explore their ancestral heritage is an insult to the heritage and to the dignity of the people of that nation. None of these Arab nations can achieve democracy unless they wake up to their pre-religion identity.

In this book, I will elaborate on the ethical values from Persian literature, which are is rooted in freedom, the Persian phoenix, and Simorgh or Peri. Again as Rumi said:

آنها که طلبکار خدائید، خدائید
بیرون ز شما نیست، شمائید، شمائید
چیزی که نکردید گم، از بهر چه جوئید؟
و اندر طلب گم نشده، بهر چرائید؟
تا دامنتان پر دُر و پر زر کند آن شاه (سیمرغ)
ای بیخبران از کرم شاه بیائید

Those who seek the divine, you are the divinity
Not outside you, in you, in you, is the trinity
What's the gain in searching far for your own deity?
When the ultimate divinity is in your vicinity?
To shower you, your own deity, with dignity
Come to your essence, to your own affinity

Description of this poem: Rumi wrote so many similar poems in which he told us that the divine (god) is in inside of us, and therefore we don't have to go too far—as on a pilgrimage—to find our divine. The deity is inside us, and showers us with pride and dignity and therefore becomes part of our essence and our own dignity.

Essence in this poem is Simorgh, the Persian phoenix. Simorgh is the soul of humanity; in other words, ourselves and the power of our consciousness. In this ghazal, there is mention of a different god to what we know in the Abrahamic religions. This is a god—the divine—that is inside us, lives with us, and makes us all to be the real divine in unity. Why? *Because our purity and awareness are possible only through unity. Without unity we are blind. This unity and togetherness is inside us, and that is the divine or the deity or god.*

We are misguided into searching for an external deity when our own divine is separated from our essence. However, when we recognize that the deity *is* our essence and is within us, then there will be no need for an external deity. Religions have taken away the essence of humanity and replaced it with an external force. Religion forces humans to beg this force for their own essence. *The need for an external deity is the ultimate weakness of humanity.*

In fact, to an extent, Abrahamic religions are rooted from the same divine that was the essence of humanity, but it has been captivated like a phoenix and caged. *Religion is nothing more than a piece of dynamic ethical evolution that has been cut off from our past heritage. It is then caged until it becomes static and manipulated to suit a certain objective.* Religions have nothing to do with civilization. Here I will provide a definition of civilization in order to make the point clearer.

What is civilization?

The word *civilization* comes from the Latin *civilis*, meaning civil, related to the Latin *civis*, meaning citizen, and *civitas*, meaning city or city-state. The closest Persian word for civilization is *farhang*[16] (فرهنگ) and if you say to a Persian: "without farhang", it means he or she is uncivilized—it would be an insult.

[16.] *Farhang: The Persian word for civilization and culture; it is also the name for the Persian Phoenix, Simorgh.*

However, civilization can have several controversial meanings. Primarily, the term has been used to refer to urbanization related to the material and instrumental side of human cultures that are complex in terms of technology and science. Meanwhile, in a classical context, people are called civilized to set them apart from barbarians.

Unfortunately, in a modern-day context, people are also called civilized to set the modern people of today from primitive peoples. The use of this term in these ways is incorrect—it is an insult to our ancestors who have worked relentlessly for humanity.

There is also a tendency, in the modern age, to use the term 'civilization' as a synonym for culture or human society that has attained a particular level of advancement, especially in the founding of cities, which is not the subject of this book.

The roots of civilization—called farhang (فرهنگ) in Persian literature—are always 'making bouquet of flowers' of thoughts that can live in harmony … collected from different nations that have grown far away from each other. Every struggle gives a gift to a culture—from which a civilization grows. The only reason for a struggle having a historical value in a civilization is due to one great thought. This great thought gives birth to a great new experience; only that one thought from the whole struggle is collected into a 'bouquet of flowers' of culture or civilization, although the final result of the struggle may produce a negative effect. Therefore—briefly: *Civilization is harmony of the flowers of thoughts—collected from different nations—that have grown far away from each other.*

Culture or civilization is natural product of humanity—has roots in humanity—it is not and can't be a supernatural (god given) product.

In light of this definition, we seriously need to avoid using phrases such as 'bad civilization'. Bad things can't be called civilization. Civilization is the art of living together in peace and harmony gained and experienced through thousands of years of human experience of living this life together, irrespective of any religions factions or sects.

Civilization comes from our actions in relationship to others ... to others who are different from us, who think different, whose attitude is different, and who are from different races and come from different backgrounds. *Civilization is the path of understanding and acceptance of others despite—or because of—their divergence. It is being able to understand the divergence and finding a common ground to work together to live together and learn from each other.* Civilization is a maturity of thinking ... that encourages us to understand the divergence of cultures and finding a common ground that people can work together. The divergence of cultures should be used to find a common ground for the advance of humanity to a better life on this earth. In contrast, religions fight against the divergences and achievements in humanity in order to focus on the belief and the afterlife. Therefore, with this description of civilization, can we call a religion a civilization? Does religion cherish differences and divergences?

The term 'clash of civilization' that has become popular these days is misleading. Civilized nations do not clash; this term is meaningless nonsense. Clash is an action of the uncivilized, either one or all parties involved.

Civilization is born out of humanity; humanity is born out of the evolution of human thinking. Humanity is basically our inheritance from our ancestors. Humanity is the wisdom that has gone through evolution, shaped in the course of the process of many thousands of the years. Without this growth in humanity, no civilization would have ever been possible.

In earlier times, as there was not much population on this Earth, there wasn't much contact between different tribes; however, as the population grew, contact also grew, and conflict between different peoples grew too. So, people who were different from one another had to find a way to live their lives side by side. The philosophy with which people managed to live together and solve their differences is called humanity. *This understanding of how to live together in peace and harmony and build an infrastructure for a better society is called civilization.*

There is still a great deal of work that must be done to safeguard our world from predictable and unpredictable disasters, both ethical and environmental. To do this, we must find a way to fall in love with our environment and cherish our ethical values. As Rumi said:

هفت شهر عشق را عطار گشت
ما هنوز اندر خم یک کوچه ایم

Seven cities of love Attar roamed
On turning of a pathway: we loom

Description of this poem: Rumi set Attar as an ideal person. He said that Attar has roamed the seven cities of love, but we are looming on the turning of a pathway.

Attar was another Persian thinker and philosopher and poet. Well, we are probably looming on a turning point of an alleyway of humanity today—in order to unite, to bond, to come together and love each other and to love the very environment that enables us to exist.

I want to emphasize the essence and value of humanity, which is rooted deep in the history. We must see humanity as the core idea or seed that must be cultivated and grown again and adapted into our new environment. Otherwise, we may lose our sense of humanity to a large extent. As Rumi said:

به سر درخت مانم که ز اصل دور گشتم
به میانه قشورم همه از لباب گویم

I am like the top of a tree, far from the roots
I am amid the branches, but all I say is from the roots

Description of this poem: This poem is a reference to us. We have roots, and those roots are our existence. We are proud; our heads are high like the top of a cedar tree, and we are among the branches right at the top but all our values and being are from the roots. We are civilized and glorified, but at same time, we must not forget our existence is from the roots. We *are* the roots; we depend on the roots; and if the roots are destroyed, we are destroyed also—through wars and conflicts.

Finally, there is hope. As we say, the Phoenix is rising from the ashes. Although humanity and ethical values can be burnt and turned into ashes, with our powerful morality within us the ethicality will not only rise again from its ashes, but it will also fly to existence. As Ferdowsi, poet and author of the *Shahnameh*, said:

نمیرم از این پس که من زنده ام

که تخم سخن را پراکنده ام

No death. From now, I'll remain alive
Due to planting of the seeds of communication; I've arrived

Description of this poem: Ferdowsi in this poem sent a message that, in his book, the *Shahnameh*, he has planted the seed of communication. There is no death for someone who plants seeds of communication and unity, he said. The messages in the *Shahnameh*, as Ferdowsi said, aren't advice but rather seeds of communication, which need to be planted and cultivated.

We need a coherent and harmonic society. A single ideology or religious dogma can be detrimental to a harmonic society. Today, many people say to others: 'If you don't believe in my god, you are not part of our community!' or 'If you do not believe in my book, you are not part of our community!'

These comments are detrimental to our modern society and a civilized world. We as humans have to show our superiority through our dignity and humanity as we address these simplistic and dogmatic ideas that are demolishing our ethical values.

We have a big responsibility to raise the standard of ethics among the intellectuals as we endeavour to influence the current and future of our wrongdoers in our political and economical systems. If we don't sort out the ethics among us, someone will come and use the opportunity to sort it out for us in a dangerous way—violence way or terrorism way.

Life is happiness—without it life is meaningless. Without happiness life may lead us to a territory that no one likes. We are the key to all the problems; bad and good are within us. Happiness and sadness are luck also from us. As Omar Khayyam said:

نیکی و بدی که در نهاد بشر است
شادی و غمی که در قضا و قدرست
با چرخ مکن حواله کاندر ره عقل
چرخ از تو هزار بار بیچاره تر است

Good and evil that are within the roots of us!
Joy and sorrow that is also a luck, within us!
Don't blame this to the wheels of the globe
It is a thousand times weaker than you, this space probe

Description of this poem: Khayyam sarcastically brings in the religious comments saying—Ok: both; bad and good are the roots of us—happiness and sadness are also luck within us! If so, then we have no role for our destiny and therefore the wheel of the globe has to be blamed for all our problems! This is why Omar Khayyam caries on saying—do not blame the wheel of the globe, a god, or a defined destiny for our problems as the wheel of the globe is thousands times weaker than us and our will.

Persian literature is very rich and very powerful, if you understand it. Unfortunately, the world is unaware of this deeply philosophical and rich literature, because of the clouds of religious doctrine that have been laid over it. This is very unfortunate and very sad. This is the core of my reason for writing this book. I want to tell the world about the assets that exist in my culture. I hope that this book will be sufficient to make others understand the flavour and beauty of our stunning Persian literature. Hopefully, with encouragement from my readers, I will be able to write additional interesting books to follow this one.

Many bright and modern religious people I have met keep telling me that this life is not an ideal life. They stress that the ideal life is the afterlife, which is only accessible to us when we are dead! Is this not being irresponsible? Don't we have a sense of responsibility to make this life a heaven? Religion is irresponsible to the problems of this world. Religion is irresponsible to the welfare of our own people. Religion concentrates our own individual selfish imagination in its vision of an afterlife. Religion focuses on the afterlife, which has nothing to do with our lives here on this Earth. Religion entirely rejects the changes and evolution that have been taking place for thousands of years. Religion opposes the true meaning of culture, which comes from cultivation, which is the mother of all evolution. Religion has changed the meaning of our beautiful words—culture, humanity, spirituality, and ethics—and turned them into faith, fanaticism and supernatural beliefs ... thoughts that are valuable only to the naive and inexperienced. Religion has stolen the values of humanity and passed them to an almighty god, and they have taken away our direct access to this god.

This life that is keeping us alive is very sacred and very precious. This life deserves to be viewed as holy and worshiped. We should not focus on worshiping an external force that we cannot even see. Human must unite in the name of humanity to cherish this life and the values that keep us alive. In the name of humanity, we can become united and reclaim our values. This unity is the core answer to our world problems. We must work hard together to make this life a happy life. Our heaven is here, on this Earth. If this Earth is not the heaven we want, then it is our responsibility to work together and change into the heaven that we deserve.

CHAPTER FIVE

ATHEISM

Introduction

Atheism can be either the rejection of theism or the position that deities such as the Abrahamic God do not exist. Atheism is a very brave and admirable campaign against the static ideas of religion, but it is a reactionary thought and a negative campaign. Atheism rejects the existence of any god and advocates the fact that humans are merely another type of animal. This negative approach is the basic problem with the great thoughts of atheism. Atheism is reactionary because its very existence relies on the existence of religion; without religion there is no need for atheism. Basically, there seems to be no independent core ideology in atheism. Nevertheless, as a believer, one can ask these very important questions:

- How can a god be real when it can't be seen?
- Does a god exist?
- Is there truth in religions?

How can an unseen god be real?

Nature can be seen, so it is real. How about humanity, ethics, and morality, which can't be seen? We know from experience that they are real. We can't honestly say they are fictitious. It would be a misfortune and a disaster for the future of humanity if we delegated the values of humanity to history or fiction.

For the same reasons, one can argue that a god, although he or she can't be seen, is also real. In fact, in Persian literature, the divine (god) is ethics and morality. These are both intangible and can't be caught and owned. This implies that values of humanity are elusive and therefore no one can claim ownership. The divine soul—ethics and morality—has been built into everyone's personality. Can we live without ethics and morality?

Furthermore, a god exists because he or she dwells in the minds of our nations and our people; we cannot make him or her go away through rejection. We need to deal with the problems that are in the minds and souls of our society. The phenomenon of god can't simply be forgotten and put aside. This is a problem that must be addressed and looked at philosophically. Our invaluable past heritage with all its values is well connected with the divine (god), so by putting aside the divine we will put aside our past heritage too. The self-serving teachings of religion should not put us off from the concept of a god completely; however, we would do well to discover and embrace more traditional interpretations and explanations of a god, as these have changed throughout the span of human life on Earth.

It is therefore important to understand god rather than question whether she or he exists or doesn't exist … whether she or he is real or not real.

Is there truth in religion? Even though we do not favour religion, we must answer this question in the affirmative, because many basic truths were stolen by current religions from past cultures. These religions added these truths to their scriptures and claimed ownership. They now manipulate these truths to full fill their agendas, but a trace of the origin is still there. We must reclaim these truths and present them to the real owner: humanity.

Our past heritage and divinity

Our past heritage is well connected to divine power; throwing the divine out of the door could seriously endanger our invaluable heritage. Throwing the divine out of the door means throwing Greek, Persian, Indian, and Egyptian heritage out of the door. This means throwing away literature and mythology. Wouldn't this be a disaster? To a certain degree, this disaster is happening now and causing real but hidden distress in many nations that are deeply rooted in culture such as Egypt and Persia. By throwing the divine away, we throw our roots away, our culture away, then we start throwing our entire past heritage out of the door instead of adoring it. As an example, there is an interesting poem from Ferdowsi:

به نام خداوند جان و خرد
کزین برتر اندیشه برنگذرد

In the name of the divine of soul and wisdom
No thought can be greater than this notion

Description of this poem: In this poem. Ferdowsi invoked the name of the divine of soul (the body) and the name of divine wisdom. This is the god of wisdom and god of soul. Ferdowsi carried on saying that there is no thought that can be greater than this conception. This is different with reference to the god of this religion or the god of that religion. The god of wisdom and the god of soul are the protectors of wisdom and soul irrespective of any religion, beliefs, race, or nationality. Any one has wisdom and soul and therefore no one should be allowed to harm another person's wisdom or soul. This is a true meaning of secularity.

This divine that Ferdowsi is talking about is the divinity of soul and wisdom—a culture that does not support harm or violence. Can we throw this away? If we throw away this vision of the divine, then we have to forget about the whole rich and invaluable world of culture and literature. The divine has had an entire different meaning at different times and at different places. If we throw divine out of the door, we may throw our values, morality, and ethics out of the door too.

Many people think that, if we prove the non-existence of God (in this case, the Abrahamic God) and thoughtfully reject God, the problem of God will go away, as they think that God has influence and power on us only if he exists. However, these assumptions in general have the reverse effect, which can be seen around us. There are imaginings and dreams that can be far more powerful than an actual fact or thing that exists. Dreams are reality and fact because we really and factually have dreams. Our civilization and all the success of mankind come from dreams. Nothing important happens in life before it is first experienced in a dream state. This is a very important subject; we should not take it too lightly. A dream can be more powerful than a fact. The majority of our writers and thinkers make this basic mistake about rejecting a god. We should be more worried about how we imagine god in our minds and thoughts than we are about the actual existence of a god. Rejecting god and proving he or she doesn't exist do not diminish the dreams of god in people's minds; in fact, it could actually increase the delusion of god. The more we persist in the non-existence of a god, the more the delusion of god will increase in people's minds. So, the rejection of god will only increase the power of the god in our minds. One lively dream can be a thousand times more powerful than a fact.

The rejection of a super god or an almighty god is a basic, fundamental right and the natural instinct of any free-minded human being. *The supernatural god is a thorn in the flesh of any free-minded person.* In fact, rejection of such a god doesn't even require high intellect. *The intellectual's job isn't to prove or disprove the existence of such a god; rather, it is to help people think about how to make a better life on this Earth.* The intellectual's job is to see what role deities have played in the minds of people throughout the span of human life. We need to find the meaning of the gods and to figure out the good and bad sides to following them. We should not be scared of deities. There are bad gods, lovely gods, and beautiful gods. No one should have a problem with a vision of a god that is beautiful and lovely. It is with this vision that we can overcome the problems of an almighty god.

An alternative to atheism

As an alternative to atheism, we must come up with a way of replacing dogmatic religions ideas. New meaning can be given to religion; we need to paint a new portrait of a god that fulfils our dreams and expectations. This was done to a large extent in Persian literature, four hundred years after Islamic invasion of Persia in the middle of the seventh century AD. Persian literature is full of finely crafted and well-structured poems on these subjects. However, the hopes of Persian poets and philosophers were dashed by so many events during and after the Mongolian attacks of Persia. The modernists in Iran thrived on the poems and literature that were left over from this period. Extensive work has been done to change the image of the Abrahamic God and to change the image of humans from submissive to glorified humans. This change of the image of God also happened by Western philosophers during the Renaissance in Europe when many people became nonbelievers; in fact, they were accepted in the Western world and were afforded equal rights without question. However, the power of these nonbelievers seems to have been losing momentum over the last few decades. To a certain extent, humanity is beginning to lose ground on morality and ethics to the materialistic world, and the extremists are benefiting from this environment. The extremists are becoming so confident that they are shamelessly advocating the most brutal methods of enforcing their ideology in some parts of the world. Brutality such as slashing people, amputating body parts, stoning and beheading people are growing in some parts of the world without any remorse in this twenty-first century. How can we stop this without a hard work on ethics and morality?

Many people think we can relieve ourselves from an ideology by simply putting it aside. However, an ideology or religion that a person has been brought up with and lived with can't be put aside with ease and forever. Even if a person manages to put it aside, he or she will most probably go back to the same ideology one day, thinking that the original belief is far better and simpler to comprehend than any other belief. Moreover, it can also be dangerous to leave an ideology that we have lived with, as it is that ideology that has given us discipline and good manners. Completely disregarding an ideology can cause chaos and can destabilize our social lives. Well, what would be the solution? *An ideology has to be replaced by a new, rooted philosophy that dwarfs the original ideology.* A rooted philosophy is a philosophy that has its beginning and identity in a true culture of society. Let's see an example: Richard Dawkins, in his book *The God Delusion*, writes, 'Isn't it enough to see that a garden is beautiful without having to believe that there are fairies at the bottom of it too?'

The answer to this would be yes. But, wouldn't it be even nicer to believe that all the being that make the garden beautiful are fairies, including the person who works in the garden? Well, wouldn't this give more value to the garden as well as the gardener? The problem comes when we are after an exterior power or just after commercialization of the flowers in the garden. Each individual of us has—and is—a fairy, an angel, or a guardian angel. We are the angels of each other; we can look after each other and make this world a beautiful world ... a heavenly world. We need to give each other these heavenly values that have been taken away from us and given to an almighty god. Caring for each other, looking after each other, makes us into guardian angels. It is this value that is missing in our world to a large extent and allowing us to destroy virtually everything as we seek short-sighted advantage and comfort. It is these values that persuade us to love our neighbours, to love our environment. In fact, the gardener in Richard Dawkins' comment is the real fairy. The gardener should be valued and praised as god of the garden. Why not?

Persian literature is based on god being equated with nature (God = Nature). Every being is god. You are god, I am god, every being, including plants and every member of the animal world, is god and therefore nature *is* god. Every being contains the essence of god. The true meaning of god comes to the surface when people come together in the true meaning of wisdom and intelligence. This is divine power; this is morality and ethics at the same time.

As Rumi said: 'As the light said to Moses, "I am God. I am God. I am God"', you are that light. You, as a human, are that divine.

تو آن نوری که با موسی همیگفت
خدایم من خدایم من خدایم
بگفتم شمس تبریزی کیی گفت
شمایم من شمایم من شمایم

> *You are that light that gave Moses the sign*
> *The divine, I am. The divine, I am. The divine, I am*
> *I've asked. Shams-Tabrizi[17]! 'Who are you?'*
> *He replied, 'You I am. You I am. You I am.'*

Description of this poem: You are that light that told Moses loud and clear, I am the divine, I am the divine, and I am the divine. Rumi asked the question from Shams-Tabrizi, 'Who are you?' The reason for this is that Shams-Tabrizi was the ultimate, the divine to Rumi. In fact, Rumi was asking this basic question, 'Oh, Divine! Who are you?' Shams-Tabrizi (the divine) replied, 'I am you. I am you. I am you.' This clearly says that the divine (god) is you; the divine is me and all of us in harmony. We, as a whole, are responsible for our harmony, fate and destiny. We are the key to all the unlocked matters. We are the divine. This is also about ultimate respect for nature, because every being is god.

---

[17] *Shams Tabrizi: The spiritual instructor of Rumi. Rumi was such a total devotee to Shams that Rumi called him God.*

Maybe we have to take nature one step higher in respect and call it divine in order to convince people to treat it with the respect it deserves. Modern technology, unfortunately, is trying to conquer nature rather than respect and cherish it. Why? It is due to lack of ethics and morality and to rivalry for political and economic supremacy.

We really need to replace rather than reject the image of an almighty god. Rejecting the image calls for supremacy of one set of beliefs over others. The best way to be free of the image of an almighty god is to craft and promote an every-being god. This is exactly what has been done extensively in beautifully crafted Persian literature.

Farid ud-din Attar (1145-1146), another famous Persian poet, has an interesting story about the Simorgh. In his book of poems, *The Conference of the Birds*, he tells how these birds set off on a journey to find their king (the divine) because they have none. They pass through seven valleys and endure many difficulties. At the end, they find out that they are the divine (Simorgh); they are their own divine (god). This story tells us that we are responsible for our own well-being and for our own ill-being as well. This is it; we are our own destiny and our own divine—there is no super-natural power. It is all down to us, whether we like it or not. *We must sit together and solve our own problems; there is no one out there who will do it for us*. This is the only solution to our economical, environmental, and social problems.

However, the atheists believe that the truth is the science and intelligence that gives power to humans over others. This thinking will take us right back to exactly those scenarios that religion has given us. In religious ideology, we are controlled by a god. In the atheist ideology, we are controlled by science.

In fact, truth is an illusion ... a phoenix; that is, as soon as you get close to the truth, the truth escapes from you. This can be explained further by referring to Persian mythology in Ferdowsi's writings. First of all, let's remember that myth is not a lie; myth has quite the opposite meaning. Myth is born of the cumulative knowledge of humanistic values over hundreds or thousands of years explained in one character. This process is very close to idea of evolution.

In Persian mythology, freedom has two meanings or two steps:

- The first meaning of freedom is political; in a free society, people do not live under a dominant and unjust power ... they are free from tyrants.
- The second meaning of freedom is personal; all individuals must have the opportunity to demonstrate their purity, essence, consciousness, talent, and roots of their nature. People must have self-confidence and must not be encouraged to follow a pre-defined goal or belief—people must be rather encouraged to refrain from a pre-defined goal or belief. Giving people a pre-defined goals or beliefs is an insult to their wisdom and capability, and removes their freedom.

The second type (step) of freedom is the most crucial and the most important. It is vital in the prevention or repetition of the first stage—the creation of another political dictator. This second step is usually disregarded by any revolution that gets rid of a dictator. A repeat dictatorship can be prevented if individuals are given the freedom to explore their potential and stop being submissive. Those who have personal freedom cannot allow dictatorship. This is a vital and the most important stage of freedom, which can lead us on a path to an ideal world. With this major step, we can look for a better future, a peaceful future.

Throughout history, people have revolted against powers of authority. Powers of authority were the barriers that kept members of the general public from becoming awakened to their own consciousness. People in Europe rose not only against the state, not only against church, not only against the power of the economy, but they rose also against the power of their God too. The God that is known to moderate Europe today is entirely different from the God that was known then. The changes in Europe happened only because of this power struggle as God changed from an almighty deity to a softer and friendlier one who did not interfere in all aspect of life.

What is the problem with an almighty god? The almighty god has the knowledge of the past and the future. With this unlimited knowledge and power, this god can do anything. With this perspective, a god could do anything to knowledge and science. With the presence of such a powerful god, people could not take credit for discoveries or findings. This is why we have atheists, and quite rightly so. Atheists reject an almighty god, as the essence of such a god is power. Freedom cannot exist in the face of such power. In fact, getting rid of a human dictator is much easier than getting rid of an all-mighty and powerful god. With an almighty power in our minds (the most important part of the power), there can be no freedom. *If there is no freedom, there can be no going forward.* There is only one freedom and there is only one democracy, but there are different ways of getting to each of these. Each nation has its own unique paths, which depend on the root of their identity and culture, which must be explored and identified by the philosophers of that nation.

As I have stated, freedom is not just victory over power; it also involves finding the opportunity to illustrate the capability of each individual in a supportive environment. In Persian mythology, the divine just does this for each individual; it is called the Persian Phoenix (Simorgh or Sanam). This is the truth—verity. No one can own a truth or catch truth, as truth is always elusive. As soon as you try to catch the truth, it will escape from you. This is why Sanam in the Persian language is called *gorizpa* (elusive). This is the positive meaning of the divine. No one can have ownership of such divinity and no one can claim to be her or his messenger. At the same time, this divine is inside every individual's soul which can be invoked in harmony. We must invoke this divine, not reject it. By invoking this divine, we encourage individuals in harmony. As Rumi said:

اینجا، کسیست پنهان، چون جان و خوشتر از جان
باغی به من نموده، ایوان من گرفته
چون گلشکر من و او، در همدگر سرشته
من، خوی او گرفته، او آن من گرفته

Within me, one hidden, sweeter than my soul
Given me a garden, taken a porch as a goal
Like sugar and cane, we are merged as a whole
I have her temper; she has mine; that's our role

Description of this poem: Rumi was referring to what is within us that is sweeter than our soul. This is the divinity (goddess) within us that keeps us alive and happy. She has a culture of give and take—take a porch from me, but instead give me a garden. This divine within is tightly bonded with us—as sugar is to cane.

The Persian belief was that, within the dark root of humanity, there are five deities; *Soroosh, Rashn, Farvardin, Bahram*, and *Raam*. These five deities, as well as being individual, also work in unity. The unity of these five deities turns them into one egg or seed, which is the Persian Phoenix, or Simorgh. This unity gives human the power of wisdom, wealth, and enrichment. Such honour of humanity can't be found anywhere else in the world. The five exclusive attributes of the divine can combine together in many different ways and provide dynamic ideas with a wide range of options in thinking, philosophy, and defining both beings and life, spirituality, and the purpose of life. A separate book would have to be written to clearly define the purpose and the pluralism behind these Persian deities and their role in shaping ethics and humanity. I shall write such book at my earliest opportunity.

The Persian civilization was in a very advanced dynamic path before they were influenced by Abrahamic and Zoroastrian rule. They were on a path of evolution that would have taken them to further stages of advancement. Of course, there were difficulties as there are in every civilization, but, before the introduction of these religions, humanity and ethics had been shaped by the hard work of our ancestors through their minds and thoughts. This very dynamic path of evolution was suddenly disturbed and, to a large extent, overthrown and turned to static ideas first by the Zoroastrian religion and then by the Abrahamic religions. These religions have a lot to answer for, as they have caused many of the problems that humanity has been facing for over 2,000 years. Civilization was on a positive, progressive path before these religions came to be; in fact, all the values and the foundation on which these religions are based come from the civilizations that preceded them. This is well explained in the works of well-known America archaeologist Marija Gimbutas.

A long-running prejudice among historical scholars holds that 'civilization' and the written language were born together in the ancient Middle East amid an orgy of empire building. However, Marija Gimbutas challenged this view by showing three things:

- The urban settlements of Neolithic (Stone Age) pre-dated the 'first cities' of the patriarchal (men domination) tradition.
- Neolithic urban settlements, at least some, had no defensive walls, no military burials, and no artwork recording warfare.
- The cultures were prime objective, as the decorative designs and the artwork of pre-patriarchal were found to be sophisticated system of symbols through which ideas and values could be recorded and transmitted rather than warfare.

Surprisingly and astonishingly, Marija Gimbutas's great independent archaeological work in Europe proves that the similar philosophical views we know existed in the early, true Persian culture were widespread.

CHAPTER SIX

PERSIAN POETS AND THINKERS

Early, true Persian culture

The Persian way of thinking, wisdom, and philosophy, which I call the early, true Persian culture goes back over 6,000 years. This is beautifully and skilfully crafted and characterised in the Persian mythology, the *Shahnameh*[18] by Ferdowsi. This is the most famous and admired Persian book in Iran.

The expression and analysis of the true nature of Persian culture has been restricted for over 1,800 years. This restriction was started in 224 CE by the Sassanid Persian Empire[19], a Zoroastrian religious theocracy, and was perpetuated by Islamic religious theocracy after the Arab invasion of Iran. Alteration of Persian mythology or scripts has been also quiet common throughout the religious theocracy in order to change the heroic nature of Persian icons or figureheads; however, any person knowledgeable in Persian literature can easily trace these alterations. Persia's culture and philosophy, which was rooted in

---

[18] *Shahnameh: The Persian mythology book, national epic of Iran and related societies; it consists of some 60,000 verses.*
[19] *Sassanid Persian Empire: The last pre-Islamic Persian Empire. ruled by the Sasanian Dynasty from 224 to 651 CE.*

Persian civilization, was strictly controlled by the rulers through teaching methods and taught to people from childhood as a way of getting into the minds and thoughts of people. As Hafez said:

گفت آن یار کز او گشت سر دار بلند
جرمش این بود که اسرار هویدا می‌کرد

Said the friend whose head went to the gallows
Blunder of revealing secrets brought him deathly hallows

Description of the poem: Mansur Hallaj (c. 858-922) was a Persian Sufi poet who was hanged. His crime was revealing the secrets … the secrets of his own identity and nature. He believed that the divine—God—was within him. This happens even today in Muslim countries. Anyone who reveal secrets must live in fear—the fear of execution … the fear of being ambushed and murdered.

Despite of all the enforcement in preventing the spread of the early, true Persian culture, it remained as the true soul of Persians through the stories and the romantic poems left behind by Persian thinkers, found plentiful in Persian literature in a sort of coded messages. It is these poems that stimulate, although vaguely, the mind of today's Persians. To prove this, let's look at a very famous Persian poem from Hafez. It is claimed by many that Hafez was a devoted Muslim!

در خرابات مغان گر گذر افتد بازم
حاصل خرقه و سجاده روان دربازم

If I encounter my native ideal world one more time
I'll lose the harvest of religious teachings swiftly, in no time

Description of this poem: Hafez set himself as an iconic Persian who represented all Persians. He said that, if he got a chance to meet his origin—his native ideal world—once more, he would swiftly lose all of the religious teachings he had received.

We should remember that all the teaching in Persia after the invasion of Islam was religious teaching. Hafez set himself, here, as a model of a Persian individual who has lived in Iran for thousands of years and passed through different times—times of native Persian culture and times of religious theocracies. He clearly shows *the only way to be a 'religious person' is to be hypocrite*. It is only the force of fear—fear of God or fear of hell—that makes a person a devoted religious person.

To understand Persian literature and comprehend the thinking and the philosophy behind the messages, we must undertake an overall study and exploration of the writings of many poets. Concentrating on one poem or one poet doesn't give us a good, wide, and helpful view that can make clear sense. Without this broad view, we will encounter contradictory views that can't be made sense of. For example, reading only Omar Khayyam will make us wonder who Khayyam was as did Edward Fitzgerald, who translated many of Khayyam's poems and included them in his book, *The Rubaiyat of Omar Khayyam*.

During times of difficulty, Persians—who are called Iranians inside Iran—always try to identify themselves through poems and Persian literature. However, as mentioned earlier, there are many coded messages in Persian literature, which can make a comprehensible interpretation difficult and confusing. To strengthen their control over the populace, authorities often purposely tried to add to this confusion. However, to a person who has a deep enough study of Persian literature and no religious prejudice, the messages are very clear. The messages are free of any influence from any religion; they address the most aspects of humanity.

There are difficulties in categorizing Persian thinkers as believers of Islam or religious figureheads, despite of all the propaganda spread by believers of Islam to support this. On the other hand, there are also difficulties in categorizing Persian thinkers as nonbelievers. Due to the confusion and the purposely hidden identities of Persian thinkers, they are often labelled mystics, and their works, mysticisms. Such labels are truly unsupported and an insult to the great work of these thinkers who have given their entire lives for humanity and for a better life. How many Western writers, scientists, or thinkers do we call mystics? I really don't know of any; definitely, Shakespeare is not called a mystic.

Due to long domination by religious theocracy, the identity and way of life of the Persian people have been tarnished or taken away to a large extent, but the core messages have been passed though the plentiful stories, poetry, art, dance, and music that can be found in Persian's very rich heritage. This is why Persians try to identify themselves through their culture rather than through religion. Moreover, like Persian poetry, Persian music and art contains many coded messages about early, true Persian culture, because direct publication or display of this information was not allowed under authoritarian rule. Unfortunately, today, these coded, but very clear invaluable, messages are labelled as mysticism by many, which is disappointing and wrong.

The Persian way of thinking and philosophy has been forbidden in recent history, and it is still forbidden, as it is believed to be the way of infidels and unbelievers and, of course, a threat to authoritarian dictators and religious theocracies.

Persian thinkers and poets had to use their artistic talent and skills to enliven Persian philosophy with many characters in order to avoid punishment by the political and religious establishments. As Ferdowsi said regarding the evolution of world:

چوزین بگذری، مردم آمد پدید
شد این بندها راسراسر، کلید
سرش راست بر شد، چو سرو بلند
به گفتار خوب و خرد کاربند

> *Passing this stage, human has been shaped*
> *The key, to all the locked matters, reshaped*
> *Head high as cedar tree, so much gratified*
> *Due to fine speeches and wisdom, beatified*

Description of this poem: In this poem Ferdowsi described the formation of the world. It is important to realize that Ferdowsi used the word *formation* rather than *creation* in his description of the origin of the world. Ferdowsi said that after the *formation* of the world, humanity was shaped, and humanity became the key to all the locked matters. He carried on admiring humanity further for their language and wisdom and self-assurance. This is a very powerful message from Ferdowsi: Humanity holds the key to all locked mater—not scriptures from any god. Until we understand and accept this confidence in Islamic nations, there will never be a real solution to the problems of the Islamic countries.

In fact, the true heroes of Persian intellectuals are their poets and thinkers—not religious figureheads. These intellectuals get their inspiration from Khayyam, Ferdowsi, Hafez, Rumi, Attar, Abolkhayr, Obeid Zakani, Saadi, and many more.

Persian festivals also have the same characteristics among Persians. Persian native festivals that are practised and admired dearly such as Norooz[20], Sizdah-Bedar[21], Charshanbe-Soori[22] and Yalda[23] have no relationship with any religious event. An important question immediately appears here: if these celebrations are not rooted in religions, then from where do they derive? Many Persians don't have a clear answer to this question because the truth has been covered up for so long. We may be able to say that Persians are the most confused nation in the world as a result of the ideological religious theocracy domination over the Persian population for over 1,800 years.

One of the very famous Persian scientists and poets known well to the Western world is Omar Khayyam (1048-1131). The famous Persian love poet, Rumi (1207-1273), is also known to many Westerners as a great poet. Many people totally misunderstand the messages of Khayyam and Rumi and other Persian poets. It is generally understood that Rumi wrote love messages and Khayyam wrote atheistic messages. Both opinions are somehow true; however, there is much deeper meaning in their poems and thoughts than what is being understood in the West. The truth of the matter is that the messages from both are loud and clear if you understand the early, true Persian culture. All Persian poets talk about human dignity, ethics, and humanity that are rooted in Persian literature. In fact, all Persian poets and thinkers wrote one

---

[20] *Norooz: Persian new year.*
[21] *Sizdah-Bedar: An outdoor—picnic like—festival that is held thirteen days after the new year.*
[22] *Charshanbe-Soori: A festival of fireworks held on the last Tuesday evening of the year.*
[23] *Yalda: The first night of the winter—celebration of the longest night—or winter solstice.*

message—a message of love and dignity and not being dominated by dogmatic ideas or religious views.

I will include a few examples here that will illustrate the messages of dignity and humanity presented by Persian thinkers. These examples will show that Persian thinkers were largely inspired by early Persian cultural values—values that originated far into pre-historical culture, the goddesses' culture. This common source gave them unity to a large extent in their thoughts as they endeavoured to explore their past and raise the awareness of human values and the beauty of living this life to its fullest. The point is—the messages of all the poets are similar—each poet use different artistic and creative approach to expresses themselves.

Omar Khayyam (Part One)

Omar Khayyam (1048-1131) was a Persian poet, philosopher, mathematician, and astronomer. He also wrote treatises on mechanics, mineralogy, climatology, music, geography, and theology.

Outside of Iran and other Persian-speaking countries, Khayyam has had an impact on literature and societies through the translation of his works and popularization by other scholars. The most such impact was in English-speaking countries. Thomas Hyde (1636-1703), the English scholar, who was the first non-Persian to study him. However, it was Edward FitzGerald (1809-83), who made Khayyam the most famous poet of the East through his translation and adaptations of Khayyam's quatrains (*rubaiyat*) in *The Rubaiyat of Omar Khayyam*—with this, Omar Khayyam became famous around the world ... almost overnight.

Edward FitzGerald's translation of Khayyam's poetry wasn't a direct translation, but rather what I choose to call 'inspired interpretation'. FitzGerald's famous verses, though inspired by Khayyam's quatrains, had little in common with the original verses. However, the verses express the views that originated in the Western world in the eighteenth century—the age of enlightenment, which are still prevalent today.

Why was FitzGerald so inspired by Khayyam? They were divided by thousands of miles, totally different cultures, and many generations, but still the answer to this question is very simple: humanity is one essence and is the same entity in all parts of the world. In the name of humanity, we are very close to each other and very close to our past culture too, which is not necessarily history. The difference between culture and history is clearly discussed in many places in this book, particularly in chapter 9. Omar Khayyam wrote his rubaiyat in the name of the early, true Persian culture, which is, in fact, in the name of humanity. Omar Khayyam was neither a devoted Muslim nor a devoted Sufi. He was simply a devoted human—a true human being.

A contemporary view of Khayyam's rubaiyat indicates a different view of his thinking ... a much wider and deeper meaning and a stronger relationship to humanity and past Persian heritage. He was an astonishingly free thinking and confident despite the many claims that he was a man of God.

Let's begin with this *rubai*[24] from Omar Khayyam:

می خوردن و شاد بودن آیین من است
فارغ بودن ز کفر و دین دین من است
گفتم به ((عروسِ دهر)) ، کابین توچیست ؟
گفتا : دل خـرّم تو ، کابین منست

Drinking and happiness is my dedication
Free of believer and nonbeliever is my conviction
Asked the bride of the globe, what's your dowry?
Replied, your cheerful heart is my dowry

---

[24] *Rubaiyat: Is a group of quatrains. A quatrain is a stanza or poem of four lines, called a rubai in Persian poetry.*

Description of the poem: In this rubai, Khayyam said that drinking and happiness were his ethic. Happiness wasn't achievable for him unless he was free from believers and nonbelievers. He called life a bride and he wanted to wed this bride. He asked the bride of the globe to describe her dowry. She—life—answered back that her dowry was his cheerful heart. This poem shows how valuable and important this earthly life is. *This life is the ultimate truth.*

Khayyam's faith was the essence of happiness in humanity—the happiness of everyone everywhere … a true happiness. Khayyam was saying that drinking, being joyful, cheerful, and happy was his faith. The natural essence of humanity was freshness and happiness. This is the faith or the religion that Khayyam was advocating throughout his rubaiyat. This is also the message of almost all Persian poets. This is, in fact, the essence of the early, true Persian culture—a culture of beauty, ethics, dignity, and happiness. *Being cheerful is the full meaning of life.* All of the very well-known Persian poets wrote about the same message of love, unity, and happiness, but each did so in his or her own way. This message of happiness originates from the soul of humanity; it comes from the rooted values of humanity; that's why these messages are so popular and so affectionate. Secularism and freedom are possible only through these rooted values.

The core ideas of Islam, Christianity, and Judaism oppose secularism, unless the roots of their philosophies can be updated. Secularism gives priority to the essence of humanity rather than to a god. This is not opposing god; it is opposing the idea of a god who takes our freedom away and takes human dignity away. Under the present description of an almighty god in all of these religions, followers must pray to power instead of to a god, as everything about an almighty god is power. Praying to power has its own consequences.

People who pray to an almighty god aren't really praying to a god; they are praying to power ... to supremacy and the commands of a god. These people greatly fear the sophisticated torture chamber they might encounter in the hell! In fact, they are praying in the name of power, not in the name of a god. We may think we can disregard these thoughts easily, but such thoughts haunt us in all aspects of our lives, such as our relationships with any authority figures—parents, bosses, or political and religious leaders. Our thoughts regarding an almighty god interfere with our character and weaken our social sense of self-confidence.

We have to strengthen the character of humanity among us, encouraging attitudes of friendship in its true meaning, which will increase our self-confidence. It is our own attitude that sends the idea to our superiors and leaders that they are better than we are. We send them signals about how they should treat us. *None of the leaders is dropped from the sky; at the end of the day, we have put them in power with our own collective approval, directly or indirectly.* We should work hard towards humanity-based objectives to decrease our sense of living this life as inferior to others.

Omar Khayyam was not tired of this world; he rather cherished the life and saw the beauty in this life. As we have seen, he even saw this beauty in himself.

Khayyam's religion was to be free of believers and nonbelievers. Nonbelievers at that time were also those who believed in Christianity or Judaism—this is being advocated even today by some Muslim scholars. Khayyam said that his own religion was to be free of these religions. Was Khayyam a true atheist?

Khayyam was definitely a believer in his past heritage, the early, true Persian culture, which is humanity. Therefore, his 'religion' was very similar to atheistic thinking, which is closely parallels humanism. Due to this similarity, many in the West claim that Omar Khayyam was a true atheist. Strangely, many in the East describe him as true religious man, which isn't true at all. Omar Khayyam saw the world of beauty and freshness through the eyes of Persian culture, a culture of being happy and being fresh and being lively.

The culture of being fresh, being happy, and being cheerful doesn't reflect only a momentary event; instead, it is an insight into the essence of human life that gets born from a human soul that must be cherished and applauded. This was the belief of Omar Khayyam, which made him free of those religions that claimed to be the only truth. Khayyam wanted to free himself from such religious belief. Khayyam called the world a bride, and he wanted to wed this bride. The view of love, the view of beauty—this was the view Omar Khayyam.

In his beautiful rubaiyat, Khayyam searched for the meaning of life, but not after making people feel insecure or doubtful of their beliefs or ideology, although this may be the end result. Khayyam wanted to be free of any belief that claimed to be the *only* truth. He wanted to be free of any belief that caused division in society and divided people into believers and nonbelievers, as such thing was against the core idea of the early, true Persian culture and against humanity.

To the early, true Persian culture, the world was a bride who was ready to conceive, bear a child, and give birth to the unknown. The whole philosophy behind Persian literature was to be a bride and to be new and to be fresh and to be beautiful and to be open to the unknown. It was this philosophy that could bring real change and transform the world to colours and varieties and therefore happiness. *If there is no happiness, then, there is no life.* In the past, the dress of a bride wasn't just all white as it is today. The white of today's bridal dresses comes from the influence of Zoroastrian and Abrahamic religions. This is not the case, for example, in India. The success of brightness over darkness is the principle of all Abrahamic religions including Zoroastrianism, which gives supremacy to the colour white.

The core of our being in this world is directly related to changes; without change we would not be able to move forward. There has to be change in our morality for the better to equal the changes that are causing progression in technology and the economical aspects of our lives.

Omar Khayyam said that being free from certain religions didn't make him a nonbeliever, but rather a believer. What kind of believer is this? He was a believer of not believing in these religions. Instead, he believed only in his own native cultural belief, which is the root of humanity, *khoramdean* (dean of happiness).

Khayyam had problem with these religions because they instilled fear into the hearts of humanity—fear of God, fear of the fires of hell and the many sophisticated modern and advanced torture chambers in the hell, which is against humanity. The modern and sophisticated technology seems to be only for torture in the heart of these religions. This fear has caused humanity to be divided right in the middle—one half of humanity wants to be devoted thinkers and explorers, and the other half wants to be subdued and controlled because of these troublesome fears.

Let's see what Omar Khayyam said of such world:

گر بر فلکم دست بُدی چون یزدان
برداشتمی ، من این فلک را ز میان
از نــو، فلکی دگر، چنان ساختمی
کآزاده، به کام دل رسیدی، آسان

Like God, if this world, I could control
Elimination of the world, would be my role
I would create such a world anew, whole
Freedom lovers could easily attain their desired goal

Description of this poem: Khayyam said, if he were in God's shoes (this is the God of these religions that he wants to be free of), he would change the world entirely and create a new world in which freedom lovers could easily and happily build a better life. Humans can think only in a free environment; fear is the biggest enemy of thought, and it is an insult to human dignity. Khayyam desired to make this world a better place; he was basically seeking a better life here on this Earth.

Omar Khayyam wasn't apathetic about this world; he simply wanted a different world—a world of happiness and cheerfulness. Which world was Omar Khayyam talking about? He was talking about the world that has domination and control over his life. He was actually questioning the existence of such an almighty god who has such power over everyone's life. He was complaining about the god who had created an undesirable world of fear. He was for a harmonic and peaceful world. He had the confidence that we could create such world. In his writing, he set himself up an example of me and you and all of us. We can create such world; Omar Khayyam was confident that this new creation was possible. He saw in himself the power he needed to change the world to another entirely different world in which people could be free and enjoy the beauty and the happiness that is in the heart of this true world. Simply by envisioning this new world, he was questioning the very existence of an almighty god. He was not just complaining of an intolerable world around him. *Omar Khayyam was on a mission to change the world to his ideal world for the entire span of human life, not just his own life.* These are the points that make a thinker a great thinker.

Omar Khayyam was purposely interfering with the power of the almighty god in order to show his criticism of the world of unearthly view and religious law (*Sharia* law[25]) that has no roots in humanity. He advocated a world in which people could live happily and freely. He wasn't complaining about a painful world, but rather about the pains that prevented the freedom and exploration, the pain of interfering and medalling in the lives of individuals in the name of Sharia law.

Omar Khayyam knew that government, law, and thoughts must enable people to choose their destiny in freedom and happiness in this world rather than the world of the afterlife. He saw the ideal world with ideal rule and regulation inside himself—not far away, not in another country, not even in a different neighbourhood. He found the beauty and the divine painter inside himself as the essence of humanity. Let's look at the most beautiful and the most wonderful rubai in Persian literature. It was written by Khayyam:

هرچند که رنگ و بوی زیباست مرا
چون لاله رخ و، چو سرو، بالاست مرا

[25.] *Sharia law: The moral code and religious law of Islam (eye for eye, blood for blood …).*

معلوم نشد که در طربخانه خاک
نقاش ازل، از بهر چه؟ آراست مرا

The beautiful colours of my face and the smell of me
Like a tulip my face, my stature is up like a cedar tree
It is unclear, in the pleasure dome of dust
For what gain the divine painter has adorned me?

Description of the poem: Khayyam wondered, although he had a beautiful smell and a colourful face and a stature like a cedar tree, it still wasn't clear, in the 'cherished musical Earth' or 'pleasure dome of dust', for what gain the divine painter had adorned him. It is important to know that he called this earth a pleasure dome.

This is a very important rubai. As we can see, Khayyam, as a human, was bravely, without any hesitation, expressing his own beauty. This philosophical view comes from the early, true Persian culture. The core of the idea is to be able to see our own beauty and to be proud of what we are. It is to be proud of our own beauty, which is in every person. *Every being is beautiful*. This beauty has to be looked for and discovered. When we find this beauty within ourselves, then we can go forward ... we can be successful. Finding this beauty in ourselves helps us see the beauty around us and in others. Finding the beauty in ourselves creates self-respect, self-belief, and an assurance that we can change the world. Beauty is very powerful, beauty is divinity, and beauty is the essence of humanity that exists in all of us. The world can become united under the name of beauty—we can change our world for the better life. Our world is greatly lacking this true self-confidence and respect, which is needed to glorify our surroundings and our beautiful environment. Without these we will not glorify this precious life. We can create the happiness that our world is so desperately lacking. The extremists have created an ugly god that has put off so many people from the name of god.

Omar Khayyam, then, asked this question: why has the divine adorned him—crafted him in the cherished musical Earth (pleasure dome). It is very important to note that he was talking of adornment and cherished musical earth. There is no mention of immortal Earth. He is not even saying that he was created; he is rather saying that he was adorned to be beautiful. He doesn't believe in a less-than-heavenly Earth, but rather in a cherished musical Earth for everyone. In fact this world is a place of music, cheerfulness, and happiness. *Everything should flow through music and harmony rather than be forced and threatened by punishment.* This is the core of the message: the Earth is a place in which everyone should work towards happiness. Then he asked a rather sarcastic question—why has the divine painter adorned him? Surely Khayyam knew the answer to this question. He was only stressing the point to the religious people or blocked-minded believers who kept denying happiness. He was passing the message to those who prevented others from achieving happiness through music, cheerfulness, and harmonic life.

Omar Khayyam's message in this rubai is clear—this Earth is a place of happiness for all of us, and we are capable of choosing our destiny. There is a strong message here that we are capable and no one should be allowed to take this power of humanity away from us. This is the root of secularism—respecting everyone whether believers or nonbelievers. In general, this is the core of the message in any true artwork, be it poem, prose, sculpture, or painting.

Nihilism and Abrahamic religions

Furthermore, regarding Khayyam's view on beauty of this life he stresses that without this cherished musical Earth, we lose our objective in life, and our lives are nihilistic—senseless and without meaning. This is exactly what religions are doing to all of these devoted countries, especially to the Muslim nations. This is why none of the Muslim nations is very productive in the areas of science and exploration. Nihilism is encouraged when a religion removes all possibility of achievement from humans and gives it instead to an almighty god. *The Abrahamic religions are the roots and seeds of nihilism.* Nihilism is the essence of devoted believers in religions that support an external entity. People who trust in an external entity for all their fortune become nihilistic. These people feel life on Earth is meaningless, so they must have full hope for an afterlife. This causes them to lose concentration for this life and keep working for an afterlife. They do not expect to experience pleasure of happiness here on this Earth; they believe they will only experience these things in the afterlife. How can we trust people like this with any power—here in this life—whose priority is afterlife?

Unfortunately, these same nihilistic beliefs are flourishing among our pro-democracy movements in the Middle East in the name of Western democracy. Democracy comes from values, self-belief, and confidence. The more we rely on the West (as an outsider), the more we lose our self-belief and confidence and encourage nihilism. There are many routes to the achievement of democracy, and many can be very positive and enriching. In the Middle East we have very rich literature; we have ethics, values, and respect from which we can establish the seed and roots of our own democracy. Without rooted value and respect there will be only nihilism, and therefore no foundation for a true democracy. We can import factories and machinery, but we cannot import ethics, values, respect, and true democracy. True democracy and freedom can come *only* from our own ethics, values, and respect.

So, why did Khayyam talk about beauty? Why did he talk about beauty in himself? Because of the values of self-belief and confidence, traits that made Omar Khayyam one of the greatest thinkers whoever searched for the beauty of this world. He was not a selfish thinker who was concerned only about his own life or his own afterlife. His views of the world were not indifferent, atheistic, agnostic, or non-believing. He was, rather, a believer; he just did not believe in any other faith but his own. So, he had a faith. What was his faith? His faith was a universal faith, the dean of humanity. What is the difference between the Zoroastrian and Abrahamic faiths and Omar Khayyam's faith? His faith was derived from the natural human values and ethics that make us human. His faith was his identity and culture, which is the dean of humanity, a universal religion.

The beauty of life and humanity is portrayed by almost all Persian poets; for example: Abusaeid Abolkhayr (967-1049) said:

گفتم که کرایی تو بدین زیبایی
گفتا خود را که من خودم یکتایی
هم عشقم و هم عاشق و هم معشوقم
هم آینه جمال و هم بینایی

I've asked who has given you such beauty!
Answered; it's me! And all these on me, uniquely
I'm lover, also beloved, also beautiful; and
The mirror of beautiful faces and vision

Description of this poem: In this rubai, Abolkhayr said he has asked someone: Who has given that beauty? The person responds that he or she *is* the beauty. In one person are combined the lover, the beloved, the beautiful, and the mirror of beautiful vision. This is the character of a true and beautiful human, whether woman or a man. This is the glory of humanity who can be so beautiful and see the beauty in herself or himself.

This rubai is about this life here on this Earth. It is simply about humans being self-confident and living in harmony. It is the nature of humans to be attracted to beauty and kindness. This is the essence of humanity. Humanity is only real and true when this essence of humanity, which is beauty, is searched for, discovered, and displayed. The essence of humanity is in harmony, in music, in dance, and in flow; not in fear and obedience. *Fear of a god, which is advocated in religions, is an insult to humanity.* It degrades the value and respect of humanity.

In this rubai, we can see the similarity of Abolkhayr's thoughts with those of Khayyam. There are amazing similarities and extraordinary connections in Persian poems, which haven't been noted up to now.

Let's go back to Omar Khayyam's rubai again, in which he asks these questions:

- What is being?
- Why I am beautiful?
- What is thinking?

Khayyam has answers to these questions. Being is the exploration for and finding of the reasoning behind his beauties. We are beautiful because we exist. *Thinking is love of reasoning*. That also means, love of those who are after reasoning. Thinking starts in finding the beauty in ourselves. *One who thinks is from his own essence, and the essence is beautiful.* Wine is praised throughout Persian literature because of its pure essence. People are pure like wine when they do not hide their true faces ... when they do not follow hidden agendas. Wine makes a person be more frank. In Persian literature, there is a famous phrase, '*masti-o-rasti*'—there is truth in wine. There is also a famous Roman saying, which means the same thing: *In vino veritas*. When Persian kings gathered for a summit of decision making, they met a day in advance to drink and socialize. The decision making took place the next day when everyone was sober. The one who had a hidden agenda had to try to avoiding drinking, but also not get caught doing so; therefore, he had to pretend to drink a lot by mixing water with his wine. In many Persian stories, there are scenes in which a hero catches the opponent pouring water into his wine, a sign of deception.

Omar Khayyam was a great thinker who thrived from the early, true Persian culture. He extolled the beauty of his own life. He taught that we all can find our own beauty. This is the meaning of life—finding the beauty. Khayyam didn't want to make us doubt our ideology or faith; he was rather exploring the meaning of his own life. He was an example of humanity in his own poems.

The story of Jamshid in Shahnameh

I will tell the story of Jamshid here to show the similarity of Omar Khayyam's philosophy to that of the philosophy expressed in the *Shahnameh* and the true culture of Persia.

The *Shahnameh* contains Persian past heritage in many mythological stories that show the similarity between Omar Khayyam's philosophy and that of Persian mythological characters. In Persian culture, life begins with the word *why*? And every human should find the answer to these whys, the answer to her/his own essence—beauty. By asking why, we are seeking the meaning of life. In fact, as mentioned earlier, Omar Khayyam wasn't trying to shake people's beliefs or question people's beliefs. He was on a mission to explore his own life.

In Persian literature, the word *me* is 'man' (من) has the meaning of thinking. Therefore: Me (man) = thinking, or god of thinking

The first iconic man in Persian mythology is Jamshid, and we find his story in the *Shahnameh*. He ruled Persia for over three hundred years and is named after the god of thinking and reasoning. Why is it so? In Persian mythology, Jamshid is an icon for all of humanity on Earth; he is the key to humanity. This is the reason that he is the king of the world; he is not a historical figure. Jamshid sends a strong message to humanity: *The one who thinks exists from his own essence.* This was very important in Persian literature. He explored the beauty of life, found and crafted beauty, disciplined life, developed the art of building homes and baths, found a way to safeguard the environment, developed measures of security, made beautiful jewellery, manufactured perfumes, wine, medicines, and discovered methods of healing. He produced goods that helped make life easy and enjoyable. He made the life beautiful. Basically, humanity rose to a great civilization in Jamshid's time. During this time, longevity increased, sickness was banished, and peace and prosperity reigned. *Jamshid made heaven here on this Earth.* These accomplishments Jamshid gave to be the world. Such thinking, obviously, is against any authoritarian system and against any religious theocracy. So, someone who seeks power must fight against such rooted humanitarian ideology.

Moreover, with these achievements, Jamshid said, 'I am the world.' This means, of course, that I am the world and you are the world; we all are the world. Westerners Michael Jackson and Lionel Richie wrote a famous song called 'We are the world'. The idea must have come from the story of Jamshid. Nevertheless, would an Islamic country allow their singers or artists to claim 'We are the world'? Well, before they allow such freedom, they have to send a sincere apology to the great thinker and philosopher, Hallaj, who was hanged for saying, 'I am the truth'. Even today, we are not allowed to say 'We are the world' in a religion-dominated country.

Finally, Jamshid made ships and navigated around the world, and at the end he made a palanquin fly! It is here that he talks about himself as iconic person who represents all humanity. As Ferdowsi said in the *Shahnameh*:

چنین گفت با سالخورده مهان
که جز خویشتن را ندانم جهان
هنر در جهان از من آمد پدید
چو من نامور تخت شاهی ندید
جهان را به خوبی من آراستم
چنان گشت گیتی که من خواستم

Jamshid spoke to the wise man, old,
No one but I am the world
I have crafted the splendid world
As legendary a man as I, hasn't seen the globe
Such fabulous world, I have beautified

The globe become such that I glorified

Description of this poem: Jamshid described his achievements to an old wise man. He explained that he managed to achieve … what he was supposed to do. He therefore said, 'I am the world'. Jamshid created the arts in the world and then he proudly said, '*As legendary a man as I, hasn't seen the globe*'. He carries on saying; '*Such fabulous world, I have beautified. The globe become such that I glorified.*' According to today's religious views, such confidence must not be allowed—is this not outrageous?

We must not forget that Jamshid is a mythical character; this means he was not an individual in the real historical sense at a defined time and place. Due to this mythological characteristic, Jamshid is representative of every individual ideal person who wants to make this world a better place.

As I mentioned in the introduction of this book, the reference to 'I' or 'me' in this book is to each individual of us, as 'I' or 'me' emphasises that I can make this world a happy world a heavenly world. I can do this. You can do this. We can do this. It is within our power. The reference to 'I' or 'me' in this book isn't that I am superior to others or I am a divine messenger looking for pride and glory. In fact, pride and glory are within each of us as 'I' or 'me' which must be invoked. The true pride and glory is when a society is glorified—not an individual achievement.

In another poem Jamshid said:

ندید از هنر، بر خرد، بسته چیز
هنر درجهان از من آمد پدید

No mystery is closed to my wisdom
The articulated world is of my system

Description of this poem: There is no mystery in the globe that is closed to me, to you, and to the wisdom of all people. The wisdom of people is the key that opens the doors to all the mysteries of the globe.

We shouldn't forget that Jamshid is the first person—the iconic person—in Persian mythology. He is the symbol of every individual of us on this Earth, he is the philosophy of humanity, he is the symbol of humanity, he is the essence of humanity. He is named after the god of thinking and reasoning; this means, the essence of each of us is also the god of thinking and reasoning. Having such pride can glorify our world to a path that can lead humanity to an ideal world. It is this philosophy that paved the way for so many Persian poets and thinkers. Poems are very good vehicles for passing coded messages. Through poetry, great thinkers can undermine the foundation or roots of dictators and only the initiated will be able to understand the hidden meaning.

Furthermore, Jamshid promotes science for the betterment of the world As Ferdowsi wrote:

پزشکی و درمان هر دردمند
در تندرستی و راه گزند
همان رازها کرد نیز آشکار
جهان را نیامد چو او خواستار

For the medical treatment of pain sufferers
For the well-being and prevention of harms
Revealed all the secrets for the treatments

No one gives to the world such respectfulness.

Description of the poem: Jamshid worked to find medical treatment for the pain suffers and for the general well-being of people. He worked at protecting them from harm. He succeeded in finding the secrets in doing so. Finally, there is a description of the character of Jamshid: *There is no one like Jamshid who has such respect for this world.* This is a very lucid and important sentence. It means that respecting this world, respecting this life, is the ultimate meaning of being secular. This is a true meaning of secularity. There are no borders that should separate people because of their beliefs or their racial background.

There is a painting of depiction of Jamshid being sawn in half before Zahhak in Wikipedia. Jamshid was an inspiration to humanity and great philosophical character.

Jamshid, who is such great mythological character, such a great philosophical character, and an inspiration to humanity, is finally cut by a saw right through the middle. He is basically killed in this brutal way to be a lesson to every human who wants to make this world a heaven. In fact, from this moment, humanity is halved right in the middle into two different type characters: First are the subdued people who are obedient to an almighty god. Second are the free-thinking humans who have the self-confidence to be able to change the world to a heaven.

This philosophy represents that every person—every human in the world—is divided right in the middle into two—a subdued character and a free character in each person. These characters keep on fighting each other for supremacy.

Now, there is a real and interesting question here. Who killed Jamshid in such brutal way, cutting him with a saw right down the middle? Of course Zahhak did this. Who is Zahhak? He is a mythological character and the symbol of all dictators and injustices who ruled Persia for 1,000 years. Why did he kill Jamshid? He did so to teach a lesson to everyone who intends to change the world with such confidence, which would interfere with the business of an almighty god or Zahhak himself, who is also an almighty god. Having such confidence is having god's power. Therefore, such confidence that 'I am the truth' or 'I am the world' is infidelity to someone like Zahhak. It is blasphemous, it is offensive, and it is irreligious!

We shouldn't miss the point of mythological characters here. As mentioned, Zahhak is an almighty god, and Jamshid is the god of thinking and reasoning. Both of these characters are gods; that's why they lived for over 1,000 years.

So, therefore, Jamshid should be the ideal and real symbolic character for every human who wants to be free and change the world to a heavenly world. Well, this is the reason we are here—to be confidant, to be able to find our way, to explore, and to change the world. However, this is not the case. The end of the story of Jamshid in Ferdowsi's *Shahnameh* suddenly becomes very confusing and difficult to comprehend. Obviously there has been interference with this story during Sassanian Empire, the time of Zoroastrian power (224 CE to 651 CE). The Zoroastrians were eager to take the symbolic and iconic character of Jamshid away from the public.

At the end of the story of Jamshid in the *Shahnameh*, it is claimed that Jamshid's pride grew with his power! But there was no mention of any wrongdoing by Jamshid. It is also claimed that he began to forget that all the blessings of his reign had come from God! He boasted to his people that all of the good things were from Jamshid's power alone, and demanded that he should be accorded as divine honours, as if he were the creator! Aren't these preposterous and ridiculous reasons? Jamshid is the symbol of all humanity, and of course humanity is divine and was the divine. We are the key to all our problems.

Many explain that the mythology of Jamshid is proof that any rise has a fall. This is totally false because, in the *Shahnameh*, Jamshid makes a palanquin fly, using only his own wisdom and wish. He even lands it safely. Such claim that any rise has a fall is preposterous and against the essence of humanity. Humans are here on this earth to explore, to find, to fly, and also to land safely. We live with this philosophy today; otherwise, we wouldn't have been able to see the safe landing of our aircrafts.

So, what does the end of the story of Jamshid in the *Shahnameh* tell us? The answer to this question is very sarcastic and probably very true. The answer is; if you make heaven here on this Earth, you will be brutally killed … you will be cut right in the middle!

Another claim is that, by making this world a heaven and free of all disease, Jamshid rose against 'god'. The question would be, against which god? Definitely not! Not against Jamshid's god. Now, the answer becomes tricky! Can the answer be the almighty God that we know today?

This mythological character of Jamshid appears in many stories; the final destiny of Jamshid is seen as evidence now in our Middle Eastern countries that religion has the final say. Any devoted scientists must live in fear of being halved right down the middle. Anyone who attempts to be an advocate for humanity and make this life heaven also must live in fear of being halved right down the middle.

The story of Jamshid is the genesis of 'me', the true meaning of 'me'. I am responsible for all the well-being and none ill-being of the world. The problems we see in the world are from me and you and all of us. We have to take responsibility. No leader just falls from the sky and sits on the throne. At the end of the day, we elect our leaders either through ballet boxes or by paving the way for them in one way or other by not believing in the word of 'I' or 'me'. We are somehow responsible for disease and starvation anywhere in this world. None of us can just totally disregard responsibility for these humanitarian or environmental problems.

In this poem, Jamshid isn't a historical character or a historical king who wants to teach us humanity. Jamshid is a mythological character. He is the thought and the philosophy of the strength and divinity of humanity. It is very important to know this, so we can distinguish between a historical character and a mythological character. A mythological character is a collective idea and therefore a philosophy, while a historical character is limited to her/his own span of life only.

The loss of the meaning of 'me', the loss of the meaning of 'self-confidence' through the fear of selfishness has caused humanity, to a large extent, to have apathy about themselves and the world.

The story of Jamshid is one of many stories in the *Shahnameh* that show the essence of humanity irrespective of nationality or belief or race. The emphasis is that we must believe in our own power and work for the heaven on this earth for all. This is the true meaning of secularism.

There is no need for Eastern nations to beg for the philosophy of secularity from the West, which can never be comprehended.

There is much similarity between the story of Jamshid and the messages of Omar Khayyam. Furthermore, Khayyam drew his philosophy from early, true Persian culture. This is proof that Omar Khayyam wasn't born in the wrong place; he was a true son of his own culture. Without the beautiful Persian past mythology and culture, there would have never been great thinkers such as Omar Khayyam.

CHAPTER SEVEN

OMAR KHAYYAM

Omar Khayyam (Part Two)

In this section, I will highlight further similarities between the thoughts of Omar Khayyam and early, true Persian culture.

One of the most important messages from early, true Persian culture is the message of love and unity. When a society claims to have and know the total truth, Persian culture refers to that society as diseased and in need of treatment. The claim of having the total truth is the cause of all the conflicts of the world. Such an idea makes people forget to love each other and is the cause of the creation of seventy-two[26] nations. The number seventy-two or seventy+ was used by Ferdowsi, before Omar Khayyam. The claim of each of these seventy-two nations in having the only truth is an illness and therefore false, which tore people apart, causing anger and war, which is against the basis of humanity.

In Persian literature, there are many references to the number seventy-two; for example, calling for unity of seventy-two nations or factions.

---

[26] *Sseventy-two or 70+ : The symbol of unity of many different nations. It is also the unity of Arta (goddesses), the principles of human unity and dignity in true Persian culture*

Where does this number of seventy-two come from? It comes from a few sources deep in early, true Persian culture. Four of these sources are listed as follows:

- The number seventy-two in early, true Persian culture is the symbol of unity and bond and continuity.
- *Zunnar* is a belt worn round the waist. It is made with thirty-three or seventy-two threads of a variety of colours and is a symbol for unity among nations.
- Time, existence, and the globe are the bond of seventy-two gods (Arta[27]) in Persian true culture. The unity of seventy-two parts of human body was also Arta.
- There are seventy-two verses of Zoroaster.

To rupture seventy-two in early, true Persian culture is to annihilate love and eliminate the truth and honesty. Therefore, the number seventy-two used by different religious factions is nothing to do with either historical events or religious events.

It is important to know that the meaning of the word 'Zunnar' (Zonnar or Zonar) was later changed and turned upside down by 180 degree by Muslims. This beautiful word has later been used as reference to demonize people: A reference to a distinctive cloth forced upon the Dhimmi, Christians and Jews, to signify their inferior and submissive status to Muslims as required by Sharia Law.

The poems of many poets in Persian literature applaud love and friendships and happiness even if one must drink wine to make it

---

[27] *Arta was a Persian god. The word arteries in the English language is believed to have come from this name.*

happen. The message is that drinking wine for happiness, although forbidden in religion, is many hundred times more worthwhile than the belief that segregates the societies.

As Hafez said:

در مذهب ما باده حلال است ولیکن
بی روی تو ای سرو گل اندام حرام است

In my religion wine is halal, but
Without you my dear, it is haram

Description of this poem: Drinking wine was part of socializing and togetherness and, of course, happiness. Because of such benefits, Hafez said that in his religion (religion of humanity) the wine is *halal* (permissible by Islamic law), but drinking it alone is against the objective and that's why he called it *haram* (not permissible by Islamic law).

Hafez clearly defined that happiness and social gathering were the objectives, which is a similar message to that in Omar Khayyam's poems. And, of course, Khayyam's message is much more articulated and much more open.

Omar Khayyam's articulated message is to create a peaceful world. He is tired of the beliefs of these seventy-two nations, each of which claims to have the only truth. He is tired of the fighting over these truths. This claim of having the only truth was the biggest and the most painful disease of humanity; it was torture to the human soul. To Persians, the divisions between these seventy-two nations were the core of all the problems; it was impossible for each nation to have the absolute truth.

The division of seventy-two nations tore love apart, tore friendships apart, tore the truth apart, and finally tore dignity apart. The most horrific illness in these seventy-two religions was that each claimed to have the only truth. This is the cause of almost all segregation and war. This is the reason for the encouragement of social gathering and then the need for wine to create bonds and bring the nations together so that they can see the real truth within and in their own essence.

An example from Khayyam:

می خور که ز دل ، کثرت وقلت ببرد
واندیشه هفتاد و دوملت ببرد
پرهیز مکن زکیمیائی که از او
یک جرعه خوری، هزار علت ببرد

Drink wine, take exuberance and deficiency away
And the thoughts that takes seventy-two nations away
No abstinence to alchemy of which
One sip can purge a thousand pains away

Description of this poem: Khayyam advocated the drinking of wine to take exuberance and deficiency away and to take away thoughts, ideas, beliefs, and judgments that segregate nations (seventy-two is the symbol for multiple nations). He further advocated no abstinence to alchemy, to exploration, and to discoveries, as these can purge great pain, quarrels, fighting, and illnesses.

The encouragement to explore and make discoveries is fascinating in Persian culture; to Persians, science and discoveries were like a religion. This poem is an arrow hitting the heart of all the problems in the Middle East, in our Muslim nations. Discoveries can be made only by those totally devoted to science and exploration. A devotee of god can never be a real explorer; therefore, no real discoveries can ever be made in a society that has to be devoted to an almighty.

Rumi also has a similar poem regarding seventy-two nations:

جمله هفتاد و دو ملت در تو هست
وَه که روزی ، آن برآرد از تو دست

Outright seventy-two nations are as one nation in you
Oh, of the day, when they segregated from you

Description of this poem: Rumi complained about segregated nations in this poem. He talked of seventy-two nations that are one in you if you are the person who you should be; you have to have that bond of unity. If you have this sense of humanity, the seventy-two nations are you and just you. He regrets of the day that you do not have this sense of humanity, the sense of unity and bonding. If you don't have this sense, then the outcome can be war, blood, and misery.

When the seventy-two nations are as one, and there is no segregation ... that is love in you. If you segregate and divide the love, then you have hate. After the segregation, the more you dig into each segregated love the more hate you create ... the more you enlighten these segregated loves the more you tear them apart, creating hate out of love, creating bad out of good, making them all enemies of each other. Therefore, you are creating war with your own enlightenment ... with your own hard work and effort, which was supposed to initiate and create love.

There is also a very interesting poem from Attar on this subject:

ای تعصب ، بند بندت کرده بند
چند گونی چند ، از هفتاد واند
در « سلامت » ، هفتصد ملت زتو
لیک هفتاد و دو ، پرعلت زتو

Oh fanaticism, every little bit of you strangles
How many? How many? Seventy and more pain and tangles
In heath, 700 nations, all, as you to your joys
Or else, seventy-two nations, the reasons of your stings and entanglements

Description of this poem: Fanaticism strangles a nation and suffocates it as many times as there are factions or nations—seventy-two. In a healthy society, 700 nations live side by side with joy and love, but in a sickened, divided society, even seventy-two nations can't live together, and every single of these seventy-two nations is the cause for pain and suffering.

This thought of digging into my own belief or religion and trying to define unbelievers is prejudice and the worst illness. People who have a healthy consciousness see the truth and a spectrum of beautiful colours in different intellectual ideas and beliefs; however, people who have a distorted consciousness experience a lessening of their enlightenment power and they see the colours as working against each other. Now, these people will sicken any idea or religion that they come in contact with.

There is another interesting poem from Baba Taher[28] on this subject:

اگر جز مهر تو اندر دلم بود
به هفتاد و دو ملت ، کافرستم

If not yours, but any other love in my heart
Swear to seventy-two nations, I am an infidel cult

It is quite clear that the line of thoughts in Persian poets, to a significant extent, is interconnected; they are all entirely positive about life, and they all encourage the unity of nations and the unity of the world. The Persian poems highlight the negativity of the world of fanaticism and the world of segregation that eventually have led us to so much hatred. Omar Khayyam knew the source; he knew the very roots of this hatred and also had experienced it during his own life span.

Khayyam's complaints, in his rubaiyat, weren't due to being negative or being lost or unhopeful about life, but rather quite the opposite. Omar Khayyam was very hopeful of this life:

اسرار ازل را نه تو دانی و نه من
وین حرف معما نه تو خوانی و نه من
هست از پس پرده گفتگوی من و تو
چون پرده در افتد نه تو مانی و نه من

The eternal secrets, neither you know nor I
Answers to the riddles, neither you know nor I
Behind the veil is the conversation of me and you
When the veil falls, neither you remain nor I

---

[28]. Baba Tahir: An eleventh-century poet in Persian literature/Kurdish literature.

Description of this poem: Neither you nor I have known the eternal secrets. We don't know the answers, as we are all explorers. Knowing needs no exploration. Neither do we know the answers to the riddles of the world. Khayyam then carried on and said that behind the veil, behind the façade, and behind the falsehood were the conversation and communication between you and me. We, in fact, don't know each other except through the veil, which is a façade of lies. We communicate through this veil. We exist only if we communicate; if we do not communicate, we cease to exist. Now, when this veil of lies and falsehoods falls, neither you nor I will be left. Why? The fact is, when the veil falls, our true faces will show, and with the true faces we are strangers and we won't be able to converse.

This brilliant rubai is for the believers who have answers to all the problems and complexities of the Universe and are also aware of our destiny! Omar Khayyam referred to their exaggerated or simplistic claims that they know the answers to the mysteries of life. The basic questions of science remain to be answered, yet religions claim to have the answers of the eternal secrets now! The whole objective of these writings was to become free of this simplistic view and become free of simplistic solutions to the secrets of our lives and the Universe. Khayyam had a problem with a believer who couldn't find a solution to the simple problems of being together and working together; yet claimed to have the knowledge of the eternal world.

Khayyam's rubaiyat is to free humanity from those 'god given definitions' that takes our freedom away. This is a very interesting poem by Omar Khayyam in this regard:

دریاب که از روح جدا خواهی رفت
در پرده اسرار فنا خواهی رفت
می نوش ندانی از کجا آمده‌ای
خوش باش ندانی به کجا خواهی رفت

Sense—your soul will part away
Drift behind curtain to a mystery way
Drink wine, the origin of life—no one knows
Be happy, the end of life—no one knows

Description of this poem: Khayyam rejects a defined source of origin of life … he is happy to announce that we will drift away behind the curtain of mystery that no one knows the answer. This poem of Khayyam is not pessimism—in fact, it's quite the opposite. It is an excitement and a loud announcement of being free—free of that god given definitions that are taking our creative mind away. Khayyam celebrates this by drinking wine and being happy for such a freedom. Khayyam is rejecting the religions definition of life—he says humanity is undefined by god. He says that, those who call themselves representative of god are liars—a very big proverb by Khayyam in a very religious environment. Again, this is not pessimism—but actually quite the opposite—it is rather freedom—freedom from those definitions that defines us and take our freedom away.

Persian literature points out that no one has the ultimate truth—the whole solution of the Universe or the afterlife. We cannot find solutions to the mysteries unless we reduce the mysteries to problems. Humanity has always been a mystery and remains a mystery. The mystery of humanity can't be reduced to a problem. The inadequacy in most religious beliefs is that they try to find quick solutions to mysteries by reducing the mystery to a problem. Some mysteries—humanity, for example—cannot be reduced to a problem. Once a mystery is perceived as a problem, then a quick solution can be found such as cutting off a hand or easily eliminating a person from the society! This is disrespect for humanity and disrespect for the power of our wisdom.

Humanity remains a mystery: There is a famous ghazal from Hafez:

حدیث از مطرب و می گو و راز دهر کمتر
که کس نگشود و نگشاید به حکمت این معما را

Tell me of harmony, music, wine, but less of eternity
Nobody has or will doctrine to open up this mystery

Description of this poem: Hafez complained about the simplicity of the religious theories about the afterlife and the Universe. He was very much bothered by enforcement of such simplistic views on young people as well as on the public in general. He favoured wine, harmony, music, and happiness, as these know no borders and encourage people to get together, which can foster understanding.

Religion has turned the mysteries of humanity into a problem. And, they say they have found a quick solution for the ills of humanity— these include cutting hands, slashing bodies, and other capital punishments. But humans are mysterious creatures, and should remain so. Therefore, there is a need for a much more clever solution to humanity than the false one supplied by religion. We can change only a fraction of human mystery to a problem, and only for a short period of time. So we can solve only small problems. There is no ultimate solution to the problem of humanity and nature; this is why human exploration has to be continuous. This is why exploration is divine and should be regarded as a religion. This is the core of the messages from Persian literature.

The power of 'me'

Taking a simplistic attitude towards finding a quick solution to the problem of humanity is the fault of an image of an almighty god in our minds and thoughts. This applies to almost all believers and also nonbelievers. Why nonbelievers? Many nonbelievers have inherited the image of an almighty god in their thoughts, though to them, this god is science, ideology, or philosophy. Yesterday, 'god' had the responsibility to solve our problems in a religious type of view; today it is the responsibility of science to solve our problems. We have forgotten about 'me' and the power being 'me'. We are shy of being 'me'. To be 'me' is shameful! Also in our modern time, 'me' has become meaningless. To be modern, we have to forget about being 'me' and therefore just follow an outsider such as a Western power, or Western technology or science. We have forgotten that *me* are the key to our own bad and good. We have forgotten that *me* are the key to our entire set of locked problems. Omar Khayyam was very familiar with this power of 'me' in Persian literature. This is why he said:

بر من قلم قضا چو بی من رانند
پس نیک و بدش ز من چرا میدانند؟
دی بی من و، امروز چو دی، بی من و تو
فردا به چه حجتم به داور خوانند؟

When my fate is scripted without the presence of me
Then why should the outcome of bad and good be me?
Yesterday without me, today also without you and me
Tomorrow, for judgement day, why should the deity call me?

Description of this poem: This rubai is exceptionally important. Khayyam portrayed a very important message of 'me'—a 'me' who is rising against fate. He asked, if his fate is already scripted by these religions, how can he be responsible for his own actions, bad or good? Due to the impotence of the meaning of the word 'fate', I would like to discuss it further in detail in the flowing separate section.

What is fate?

Fate is an order and warrant. Fate is an inescapable measure. Fate is inescapable death. As an intellectual and as a thinker, I reject fate. Fate is arbitration without you and me. Fate exists without the presence of you and me. Omar Khayyam argued that, if fate exists, then judgement day is meaningless. If fate exists, what is there to judge? These yardsticks of bad and good are not from me and I wasn't the decision maker to set things that are bad or good. 'I' am the yardstick of things that are bad and good; and 'I' can't accept the bad and good that have been decided for me without my presence. I am the key to the bad and good, yet I don't know about the bad and good that is already defined for me without my presence. This yardstick of bad and good has been forced upon me from an oppressor, and this is not acceptable to 'me'.

We have been measured, you and me. And we are being measured and judged today. With this order and warrant, they are making our inescapable fate. If fate is inescapable, for what reason should we be called for judgement day tomorrow? Even in this world, for what reason should we be judged on the basis of religious, or Sharia, laws, which we have had no say in writing? We humans haven't made these laws …

these laws of haram or halal; therefore, we should not have to accept them or be judged by them.

The essence of all discussion is about the word of 'me' who has come about to be intellectuals, thoughtful thinker, scientists, and philosophers in order to explore, make this world a beautiful place, make life worth living. This is why Omar Khayyam said that this world of 'me' does not believe in fate, because we are capable of planning our future.

Omar Khayyam, truly, had little respect for religious figureheads and great respect for the word *me.* He complained about these religious figureheads or rulers who were not their own person ... who did not have a sense of their own self-consciousness. In a way, they were without this word of 'me' as a thinker. I do not mean an egotist with an exaggerated sense of self. I mean the 'me' who wants to explore the essence of humanity to its full potential. This is why Omar Khayyam said:

یک نان به دو روز اگر بود حاصل مرد
از کوزه شکسته‌ای دمی آبی سرد
مامور کم از خودی چرا باید بود؟
یا خدمت چون خودی چرا باید کرد؟

If a morsel of bread, two days, owns a man of me
A bit of cold water in a broken jar, if happen to be
Why should he be the envoy of the one less of being 'me'?
Or why should he serve anybody but worthy of 'me'?

Description of this poem: If for two days a person of 'me' has only a morsel of bread and a bit of cold water in a broken jar, then, it is not worth it to serve anyone who is less than being 'me' or less than being her or his own person—the one that is not his own person is a beggar. Don't serve a person who is a beggar, and not a person of his own. The reference to be 'me' is to be a person who has self-confidence, who is not mentally a beggar, knocking on every door and knowing nothing of her or his own capabilities.

This Rubai elaborates the ultimate freedom. Khayyam pointed out that all the religious devotees lacked the word 'me'. They do not come from their own souls ... from their own essence. If I am not from my own essence and self-consciousness, then what hope is there for me to make a difference to my surroundings? Therefore, life will become stagnated. There will be no change and no hope. This is what we see in almost all religion-dominated societies, especially Muslim nations.

Submission to religious laws and denying our true selves goes totally against the meaning and essence of life. No entity has permission to rule my life except 'me'. Therefore, we can see that it is only the consciousness of 'me' that makes our world beautiful, makes all being beautiful. This is not just a classified thought of Omar Khayyam; it is rather reflected throughout the Persian literature. As Rumi said:

اندیشه جز زیبا مکن، کو تار و پود صورت است
ز اندیشه‌های احسن، تند، هر صورتی احسن شده

Think nothing but beauty, the essence of the face
The pretty thoughts carve beauties on every face

Description of this poem: Rumi said that thinking was also beautiful; it was the essence of the face. Furthermore, it was the pretty thoughts that carved beauty on every face. Rumi believed that the root—the first image—of thought, or the divinity, of humanity was the beautiful face of a woman—a goddess. It was on this image that people saw the beauty of god. The essence of divinity was beauty, not the order of, obedience to, prohibition of, or torture and hell of a god.

In this ghazal, Rumi said that beautiful thoughts give us beautiful faces. In fact, the essence of the original thoughts of humanity comes from beautiful images, from the portrayal of the beautiful faces. This view of the beauty of the world existed in almost in all ancient cultures. This is the reason for the popularity of the beautiful images and statues that came from the minds and thoughts of our ancestors—images of Venus, Aphrodite, and Zohreh or Raam (as seen at the beginning of this book, the first image—painting). *In the minds of our ancestors who worked hard for humanity, god was equal to beauty and exploration, the essence of humanity.* We shouldn't forget this; rather, we should try to make sense of it, otherwise we will not be able to take advantage of our heritage—our ancestors' experiences and thoughts. If we don't do so, then we have to go through the same painful experiences again and go through all the sacrifices again and reinvent the wheel—learn humanity the hard way. To some extent, today we are learning humanity the hard way. However, humans are very smart; hopefully they will use humanity's experience as a tool. I will discuss this further in relation to Persian literature in the relevant chapters.

Our ancestors who worked for humanity used to see the meaning of life and the beauty of life in the faces of people, not in beliefs, nationality, or race. This is the true meaning of secularism. The importance of the meaning of face is explained in this poem by Rumi:

هر صورتی پروردهای معنی است، لیک افسردهای
صورت چو معنی شد، کنون آغاز را روشن شده
یخ را اگر بیند کسی و آن کس نداند اصل یخ

چون دید کآخر آب شد در اصل یخ بی‌ظن شده

Face is a meaning, crafted, except the gloominess
Decode the face; see the origin and the quintessence
Ice, you see, you can't know its origin
When melted, eventually, emerge its essence

Description of this poem: Rumi said that every face has meaning to tell except the sad and gloomy faces. The gloomy faces are like ice, frozen. Once the gloomy face is decoded (melted) the origin appears. You will not know the origin, or essence, of ice until it melts and flows.

When you study a face, you can see its source and its essence; however, this is not possible with a sad and gloomy face, which is like ice—frozen with no motion, hard and solid. Only when a gloomy face melts does the origin, essence, quintessence emerges and flow. *You will never know a face unless it is happy.* Rumi is showing the relationship between beautiful faces and the meaning. A sad and gloomy face is like ice; has no meaning and no beauty. *A gloomy and sad face has to be melted to flow, to give out meaning in order to see its essence and its beauty.* This is a very powerful message regarding the unhappiness in a society. There should be no sad faces; we must find the sad faces and make them flow to give out meaning and beauty. *Faces are idle and fixed, but meaning must flow.* It is in this philosophy that we can see and understand the true meaning of secularism.

Meaning isn't solid like ice. Meaning is flow—a stream in motion and harmony. Meaning is fresh because of its motion. Rumi seeks fresh faces. Even an ideology or a faith has face that should flow in order to provide meaning. Meaning can't be caught or owned because it flows like water or like a cloud. In the flow and motion we can find meaning.

Beauty is divinity, incentive, stimulant, and motivation to the meaning of life, and the meaning of humanity and the reason or purpose for our being. We have to understand the meaning of humanity, and it must flow from us. We have to *be* the meaning and work so that it will evolve into the meaning—not own it. Meaning cannot be caught or owned; in other words, the phoenix can't be caught. As soon as you catch the phoenix, it is no longer the phoenix. The phoenix is a phoenix as long as it is free and as long as it can fly. An ideology that accepts no change and is solid, frozen, and rigid is no more a phoenix.

What is the beauty that can be seen but can't be caught? Beauty is an elusive concept; in one instant it is in front of our eyes, and then it disappears. We are what we explore; *when we explore beauty, we are the beauty; when we explore meaning, we are the meaning.*

Moreover, the eyes of our ancestors for humanity were Venus, Aphrodite, and Zohreh or Raam. Our ancestors loved beauty. However, we as modern humans today, in the first instance, seek financial profit rather than beauty. Why? Because, humans feel that monetary abundance can protect them from the dangers they see around them. In fact, humans are living in fear of the future; for protection they must go after profit as a safeguard. For this reason, they see everything as a tool to make profit. We try to make everything we encounter into a tool for success. This is why we store huge amounts of profit without a need for it. Even then, the fear doesn't leave us alone. In such an environment, we strive to protect ourselves against fear, but where there is fear there is no truth. Where there is no truth, eyes can't see, everything become misty, blurry, uneven, and vague. This is why we have so many bumpy roads in our world today.

Our fears began with stories of our magical creation by an almighty God. He is the source of all our fears—fear of god and fear of his treacherous and complex torturous chambers in hell. These fears are reflected into all other parts of our lives: leaders must create fear to rule, the judge must create fear to prevent the repeat of the crime, and the father must create fear to have the authority over his family and so on. The ideal society is a society that can be ruled without any fear. This may be called a utopian world, but it is not an impossible world. Well, at least we have to seek a society that can be ruled with the least amount of fear possible in order to allow human consciousness to grow.

Rend: a character of Omar Khayyam

Finally, another characteristic of Omar Khayyam is being a rend[29]. Let's look at this beautiful rubai of Khayyam about being a rend. In this Rubai Khayyam is actually the rend:

رندی دیدم ، نشسته برخنگ (اسب) زمین
نه کفر و نه اسلام و نه دنیا و نه دین
نه حق ، نه حقیقت ، نه شریعت ، نه یقین
اندر دو جهان ، کرا بود ، زَهره این ؟

I have seen a rend sitting on the horse of Earth
Neither Kaffir, nor Muslim, nor vale, nor faith

---

[29] Rend: Character of humanity aappearing in a mystery manor who can't openly show her/his character; therefore he or she sends indirect messages and hides behind a mask. It is much secure to be rend in poems than being a philosopher that we know today

Neither God nor Sharia nor certainty nor truth
The only shame of the two worlds is lack of faith

Description of this poem: Khayyam has seen a rend sitting on the horse of Earth. He was Neither Kaffir, nor Muslim, nor vale and nor faith. He believed to neither God nor Sharia nor certainty nor truth. The only shame of the two worlds was having no faith.

Omar Khayyam's cultural or philosophical desire was a world of no fear, no harassment, and no religious persecution. This is the world of humanity, the core of early, true Persian culture that sees and views the beauty inside human, sees and views Zohreh (Venus, Aphrodite) inside every human, sees and views the divine inside every human. This is the humanitarian character in Persian literature.

Omar Khayyam wasn't totally free to express this beloved humanitarian character; therefore, he expressed himself behind a mystery character called a rend. The rend is the general character of almost all Persian poets but varies in intensity and description. In this poem, in fact, the rend is Omar Khayyam himself. *Khayyam is a well-articulated rend who knows no boundaries, knows no submissive character, and is free of any such believes.* He is on the Earth sitting on a horse, holding his head high; he is not Kaffir, nor Muslim, nor vale, nor faith; he doesn't know God or truth or Sharia or certainty. Consequently, in the two worlds the only stigma that would be attached to him is not being any of these characters. He said that he was a rend and free of causing any harm or causing anyone fear. This is his absolute goal and he doesn't care about being called Kaffir, infidel, non-Muslim or without faith.

Who is as bold or brave as to turn his back on religion and all the truth and certainties that are known to humanity? This would have been a crime punishable by death penalty. Such a bold person has to be a rend; otherwise, if a poet were to directly express his view, his past, identity, culture and thoughts would be banished from the history. There are many Persian philosophers and thinkers in general who have been vanished throughout history.

Why were Persian thinkers in contrast with the beliefs of their time? Because, these beliefs were in contrast with science and in contrast to the bases of human values that were left for them from their past literature, from their ancestors. It was in contrast to the roots of humanity or the essence of humanity that they had studied in past literature. It was in contrast with many of the Khoday-nameh [30] and many other articles that were survived of burning books by Muslims— left from their ancestors from which the *Shahnameh* was written. Persians used to see the divine as the essence of humanity, boiling from life and the spirit of humans that is beauty and love. Such persons have the essence of divine in them. In fact, humans have the same essence as the divine. The divine are the origin of love and peace and friendship in every soul in this world and the roots of continued rebirth, evolution, and freshness. *This is the beautiful divine face in human soul which is the rend in Persian poetry.* We all evolve with the divine being inside us; we evolve towards the utopian world, which is in our thoughts, our minds, and our souls. This is the essence of humanity and divinity. This is the shining divine in Persian literature that was in the minds of Omar Khayyam, Hafez, Attar, Ferdowsi, Rumi, and many other Persian poets. Persian poets shine from these thoughts and philosophy. It is from this philosophy and it is from this freedom that Persians used to see their

---

[30] *Khoday-nameh: Aarticles that were left over in the hand of farmers, inherited by Persian ancestors from which Shahnameh is written.*

divine directly and the beautiful faces again and again and get intoxicated and become legendary.

By seeing the rend as such a beautiful divine face, humans come out of their own purity and essence unable to harm anyone, whether believer, nonbeliever, or idol worshiper—Arab, Turkish, American, European, or any other nationality. It is in such a view that even harming an enemy is not acceptable. This is the true meaning of secularity. As Ferdowsi said this 1,100 year ago:

هرآن چیز، کانت (که آنت) نیاید پسند
دل ودست دشمن ، بدان در مبند

Whatever isn't your characteristic wish
Don't accept for your enemy, such wish

Description of this poem: If you do not admire or adore a possession for yourself, you shouldn't force it upon your enemies. Therefore, the same right of humanity goes even for your enemy too. Harming others can only be stopped if harming is not admired, for whatever reason.

These poems clearly show the extent of the values, admiration, and the universal values of humanity throughout Persian literature. As Omar Khayyam said:

تا چند زنم بروی دریاها خشت؟
بیزار شدم ز بت‌پرستان کنشت
خیام که گفت دوزخی خواهد بود؟
که رفت بدوزخ و که آمد ز بهشت؟

Brickwork over oceans, how many times I shall?

Exhausted of the worshipers of shrine idol
Khayyam! Who said there'll be afterlife or hell?
Who is back from paradise? Who went to hell?

Description of this poem: Omar Khayyam asked how many times he must build the brickwork over the ocean. It was a useless effort. Likewise, building the infrastructure of a society on shaky ground is hopeless. He was tired and exhausted of all the hard work that yielded no result, exhausted of these religious environment and figurehead worshipers who he calls them idol worshipers—solid and frozen-faced worshipers. He then categorically rejected any religious view of afterlife: heaven and hell. This is the ultimate and the most obvious message of Omar Khayyam, who finds no other world but this world. This is why he set about making the most of this life on this Earth. Our heaven and hell are here on this Earth; if this Earth isn't heaven, then it is our duty to make it heaven.

This rubai of Omar Khayyam points out the exact problems facing the Muslim world or any religion-dominated nation: the problem of building infrastructures over an unstable foundation. The building blocks of a free mind (not a submissive mind) must be gathered together and stimulated in childhood. We should not applaud submissive and obedient characters, we should rather abstain submissive and obedient characters—even those who are submissive and obedient to God. God doesn't need our submissive thoughts. I reiterate this: *God doesn't need our submissive thoughts and obedience.*

Obedience to God is humiliation to human intellectual capability

Why should God need my obedience? God has created such powerful brain in us, a brain that enables us to run our own affairs, to be needless of him, to be independent, and to be able to explore our way through life. This is why God has given us exploring mind. *Diminution of my intellectual capacity in obedience to God is exactly the diminution of God in its formation or creation of humanity*. If my intellectual capacity isn't good enough to run my own affairs, then why in the world has God created such worthless intellectual capability in me? *Obedience to God is humiliation to human intellectual capability*.

CHAPTER EIGHT

WHERE ARE THE ISLAMIC SCIENTISTS?

Abstract

Muslims today have found themselves asking where are the Muslim shining beams—the philosophers, mathematicians, astronomers, thinkers, and scientists who had the upper hand at the beginning of Islamic power? Why have achievements in these areas dwindled gradually throughout the centuries? The answers to these questions are at home. The lost key is in the homeland, not in United Kingdom or USA or in any other part of the world. The straight answer includes these points: anti-Semitic and homophobic principles, and the Muslim mistreatment of their own thinkers and philosophers. Furthermore, I would like to add that, through my own experience; over 99% of my Muslim brothers don't even reads their book (Quran) and yet claim that they have read it—it seems to me they are only Muslim due to fear!

Anti-Semitic and homophobic principles

It is quite common for Muslims to be taught anti-Semitic and homophobic principles. Even today, Muslim schoolchildren are taught anti-Semitic and homophobic principles. Gay sex is punishable by execution, and nonbelievers in Islam will end up in hellfire. Cutting off hands of thieves as punishment for their first offence and cutting off their foot for a subsequent offence is a common practise in teaching at least. Death penalty for apostasy [Ertedad or Morted[31]: (ارتداد، مرتد)]—renouncing one's religious faith—is another disgraceful law for the modern day and civilized people, which must not be allowed by world communities. Muslims today must update themselves for a better future for the sake of their own people and communities. All good Muslims—and humanity in general—must stand up and say that a person cannot be put to death or tortured or disfigured for any reason whatsoever. We are supposed to be civilized people; we can't be murdering the murderers. Systematic torturing or disfiguring of people for any crime is totally shameful especially for Muslims who have hurdles to go over in order to catch up with the world.

Muslim mistreatment of their own thinkers and philosophers

In the past, the majority of the scientists who are listed by Muslims as 'Islamic scientists' were either murdered, mistreated, or threatened with death. They were labelled infidels, unbelievers, or interferers in the business of God. They have lived and are living, even today, a life of fear. The, so-called Muslim scientists only become famous after their death when our Muslim brothers can't deny their popularity any longer among ordinary people.

In religion-dominated society, our children are not being led to choose their future beliefs or thoughts; they are rather taught in an authoritarianism

---

[31] *Ertedad or Morted (Persian word): Aapostasy, or changing religion from Islam to any other faith.*

way. This greatly undermines and limits children's future horizons as they grow up in this challenging world of today.

The interruption of science and philosophy in Persia

Real Persian pride, self-confidence, identity and culture come from before and during the Hakhamaneshian dynasty and during Ashkanian dynasty when science and philosophy flourished. Humanity and philosophy plus scientific progress were interrupted gradually by Zoroastrian domination over Persia at the time of the Sassanian dynasty and by an even more intense interruption by the Arab invasion (630 CE). Many teaching places and libraries were burned and destroyed, books were burnt, and thinkers were murdered. I do not want to expand on this and explain how many libraries with many books that were burned to the ground by Muslim invasion of Persian. However, I would like to use a reference regarding burning books by Muslims from a very recent book 'Islam and the Psychology of Muslim' by Professor Bill Warner (2012). He writes with reference to documented history that— the largest and great library of Buddhist, Nalanda, was burned to ground together with thousands of monks were also burned alive by Muslims invasion of India

In the era of Islamic teaching in Bagdad (Iraq)—where the foundation of Islamic culture was being established ruled by Khalifah (Islamic Leader)—the two basic and fundamental law of science were rejected— the laws of nature and the law of cause and effect were rejected.

The new philosophy that was established in Islam claiming that there is no cause and there is no effect has paralyzed the science in Muslim countries—Muhammad Ghazali [(also a Persian) (1058-1111)] was the founder of this philosophy—turning science into faith! The paralysation of the science in Muslim countries carried on ever since—and this is being continued even today. I am an environment scientist and a civil engineer. We work of two laws:

- The law of contradiction—does the data contrast each other?
- The law of cause and effect—the relationship between the first event which is the cause and a second event which is the effect: where the second event is the consequence of the first

Why we don't have Muslim scientist? You can not be a scientist and not believe in the cause and effect—you just can't—it won't work.

The many books in Iran, many of the largest libraries in Iran, India, Egypt… were burnt to the ground by Muslims. The order by the General to burn the books was this: if the books contain any information that is in Quran, we already have it: burn it—if the books contain any information that is not in Quran then it is false: burn it. These are well documented in the old history books: reference 'Islam and the Psychology of Muslim' by Professor Bill Warner (2012).

Nevertheless, the Persian philosophical works, although against Islam, has resurfaced in the form of poems and scientific work during the Islamic period again when Persians managed to dominate over her own affairs and get her confidence back. To save the remaining Persian books, many Pahlavi scripts, owned by farmers, were translated into Arabic and modern Persian scripts. Persians have managed to produce physicians, philosophers, and scientists such as Ebn-e-Sina, Muhammad Zakariya Razi, and mathematicians such as Khwarizmi and Omar Khayyam. They have collected and systematically expanded the

Persian, Greek, and Indian ancient heritage and made further discoveries.

However, the whole works of Persian philosophers and scientist were tarnished again by Mongolian invasion and again by the takeover of Muslim fanatics over Persians affair due to weakness of Persian—which followed on many internal bloody conflicts between Shias and Sunnis (the two main different sects in Islam). Since then, Persia has never managed to get her full confidence back. Many of Persians are fully aware of this phenomenon and the struggle continues.

Muhammad Zakariya Razi

One prominent scientist of the early Islamic period was Muhammad Zakariya Razi (841-926). As a physician and philosopher, he was threatened with death, and his famous book *Mahariq al anbiya* (now a lost treasure) was burned.

One of the main roles played by Persian thinkers in the scientific field was the conservation, consolidation, coordination, and development of ideas and knowledge of ancient civilizations. Razi and other Persian *hakim* (practitioners) such as Fakhr-Din-Razi, and Ebn-Sina, were not only responsible for accumulating all the existing information on medicine of the time, but adding to this knowledge by their own smart observations, experimentation and skills. They were among the central texts in Western medical education from the thirteenth to the eighteenth centuries.

Later on, in the fourteenth century, *Tashrih-al-badan* (Anatomy of the body) was published by Mansur Ebn Ilyas (1390). This contains comprehensive diagrams of the body's structural, nervous and circulatory systems.

Although Persia managed to get her confidence back a few hundred years after the Arab invasion, the general mental trauma and religious dogma left by the Arab invasion didn't go away. Many bloody struggles against the Arab invasion and many religious conflicts between Shia and Sunni carried on before and after the Mongolian invasion in 1219 and brought more state-dominated religious conflicts. As mentioned earlier; after the invasion of Mongolia, Persia has never managed to get her full confidence back and religious supremacy has continued directly over the population or indirectly though influences over the authorities such as the kings of the time. Persians do always see their identity and culture as primary objective and religion is second issue to them—they are fully aware of being hijacked by something like religious phenomenon which made them lag behind other nations and the struggle continues to get the confidence back.

Mansur Hallaj

An exceptional prominent philosopher, poet, and revolutionary writer, Mansur Hallaj (c. 858-922) was publically executed by Muslim rulers. He was truly nothing less than the great man Socrates. The reason for his execution was simply that was true real human with extreme confidence, who dared to say, *'I am the truth'*.

The execution of "Mansur Hallaj" or "Mansur Al-Hallaj" (Arabic way of naming) is depicted in Wikipedia. Mansur Hallaj said, 'I am The Truth: There is nothing wrapped in my turban but divine, the truth.' He was executed for these verses and being open to public about the facts of life. He was one of the most well-known thinkers, philosopher of his time, and was imprisoned for eleven years and finally publicly executed on 26 March 922. This is a shame to the Islamic world; where is an apology?

Years of dogmatic religious domination has caused the murder of many free thinkers; we only know of Mansur Hallaj and few others today. This is still happening even today in the Islamic world where free thinkers are called *kaffir*, infidels, god warriors, and many other accusatory names. A free environment is essential for the advancement of philosophers and intellectuals. In an environment dominated by religious dogma, there will be no hope for social progress, philosophy, scientific exploration, or discoveries. Do any Islam-dominated countries have the right environment for social development, science, and exploration? The answer, simply, firmly, and sadly is no. The shining beams in the Islamic world came by way of invasions of Islam on many countries—and inheritance as the result of the invasion; they are definitely not the product of Muslim rule. Muslims, in fact, murdered many philosophers and scientists when they invaded Persia and other countries, and they burned many books under the name of Islam on the emphasis that they were non-Islamic and on the basis that 'there is one God and there is one book—the Quran'. The Muslim attitude towards philosophers has been hostile all the way through history; however, only their posture for science has been positive. How can you have science without scientists? How can you have a real true scientist without freedom in philosophy?

Who is a scientist?

A scientist is an inventor. Who is an inventor? An inventor is a total devotee to his or her work. Can a Muslim be totally devoted to their work? A Muslim must be a total devotee to God, rather than to work—this is what is required by Islam. This is the problem facing the Muslim world. Who provides the right environment in which a scientist can invent? The answer must be a philosopher—preparing the right mentality. Islam advocates fear and has been made solid and static, and so naive that their ideology is totally against a free philosophy, and yet still they claim that Islam is pro scientist! Such a thought is a farce, ridiculous, and cannot work. And, as mentioned earlier, the base of the Islamic education rejects the two basic and fundamental law of science—the laws of nature—which is the law of contradiction and the law of cause and effect. Why we don't have Muslim scientist? *You can not be a real scientist and not believing in the cause and effect—you just cannot—it will not work, it will not be possible.*

No wonder the shining beams of Muslim society have diminished in intensity, and many Muslims today have found themselves asking why this should have happened. Muslims are anxious to reinstate the Islamic scientists. There are no such things as Islamic scientists or Christian scientists or Jewish scientists. Scientists are simply devotees to their own work. They are free-thinking humans who thrive in a fair and free society. This element of freedom has been taken out of Muslim environments to a large extent as religious thinkers and rulers have established their roots with growing power over the population. People are subjected to religious teaching during all hours of the day; there is not time for them to be able to think. This continuous brainwashing and hypnotism is draining the Islamic world to such a degree that the lives of many people have become a hell here on this Earth.

As I have mentioned earlier, the Islamic world inherited the intellectual of Persian Empire and many other nations whose culture go back three to four millennia before Islam. Therefore, the continuity of human thoughts and intelligence in science and philosophy is beyond the Islamic context. Philosophy and science trace their origins back to the ancient Persian, Greece, India, China, and Egypt…

Members of the Muslim world must build structures in their minds that can create an environment that can absorb scientists, philosophers, and inventors. Without this environment there will be no going forward for our Muslim nations.

Some circumstances in the life of Hallaj were similar to circumstances in Socrates' life. Hallaj was a Sufi, a Muslim, a believer, and also a nonbeliever, and also he advocated the divine power within humans and humanity. Hallaj was everything—a real man of dignity and honour … the pure essence of human dignity. He was simply a great human who could see the divine in himself and in every being. He had respect for himself as well as for every being on this planet. This is why he said, 'I am the truth.' What does this mean? This means each of us and all of us are the truth. We object to being static and we object to being in a static environment that religions want to create for us—to take away our creativity. We want a dynamic environment that we can change and manoeuvre so we can grow continuously, as individuals, from the soul. This means renaissance. Hallaj was a true renaissance man. He believed that we are the key to all of our problems. We want an environment in which scientists, thinkers, and philosophers can thrive to their full potential. This is the fact: *Nothing can grow in a dry land.*

It was and it is the general view of Muslim scholars that it is inappropriate to share matters of real consciousness with the masses, yet Hallaj openly did so in his writings and teachings. He thus began to make enemies for being open to the masses. Hallaj was so conscious that he could see the presence of love and divine in himself and in everybody. Isn't this a wonderful feeling? I am the divine; you are the divine; we are all the divine, the real divine. I am the love; you are the love; we are all the love—the real love. We are the key to the solution to all of our problems. If we don't have this confidence within us, then how can we discover the unknowns, how can we have scientists? As Rumi said:

توخویش درد، گمان برده ای و، درمانی
تو خویش قفل گمان برده ای، کلیدستی

You thought you were the pain, you are the therapy
You thought you are the lock, you are the key

Description of this poem: Rumi told readers that they were the therapy … the treatment—not the pain. They were the key not the lock. We are not the locks; we are the keys to our problems.

In Muslim society, people are not allowed to be the keys to locked matters. Muslims believe that only God can be the key; humans can't be keys! No society can ever truly grow and go forward unless they accept that all people are the keys to all the locked problems.

Hallaj also claimed that humanity is the key to all the locked matters. Due to this extraordinary confidence, Hallaj strongly believe in himself, saying; 'I am The Truth,' or 'There is nothing wrapped in my turban but divine.' Because of this incredibly humanistic and very deep philosophical pronouncement, he was killed. Can anybody imagine this? Such a confidant, brave, and wise man was imprisoned for eleven years and then hanged. Muslims of today should condemn such shameless murder in their history if they are pro science. I am afraid, however, that even today such a true and confident human could be hanged in the Muslim world, and the executioners would bring no shame to the rulers—such a shameless behaviour is the roots of the problems. Where is the shame for the Muslim world? Is it any wonder that we don't have Muslim scientists in Muslim countries today? Virtually all Muslim true scientists, and especially philosophers, have to either live their lives in fear inside their own country, or run away to live without fear in another country.

Muslims speak of 'Islamic philosophy', but to me such claim is absurd. Philosophy must be diverse and dynamic; it can't be confined to a static belief system—taking our creativity away. Islam has nothing to do with a true philosophy; neither does Christianity or any other religion. Such a view of philosophy is hypocrisy to any third-world country that wants to raise its head above water.

Hallaj's claim of being the truth caused the religious dogmatic establishment to utterly hate him. This hate led to a long trial of Hallaj, and his subsequent eleven-year imprisonment in a Baghdad prison. He was then shamelessly, publicly executed in 922. The Muslim leaders should set a public apology for this odious crime.

Hafez, a very famous poet in Persian literature wrote more than one ghazal about Hallaj's execution. Here is an example:

گفت آن یار کز او گشت سر دار بلند
جرمش این بود که اسرار هویدا می‌کرد

Said the friend whose head went to the gallows
Blunder of revealing secrets brought him deathly hallows

Rumi also wrote an interesting ghazal about the execution of Hallaj:

حلاج و شانیم که از دار نترسیم
مجنون صفتانیم که در عشق خداییم
ترسیدن ما چونکه هم از بیم بلا بود
اکنون ز چه ترسیم که در عین بلاییم

We are Hallaj, not scared of executions
We have insane faces, divine, in affections
We were scared of the incoming pain
Why fear now when we are in the pain?

Rumi said that he was living in pain. This is not strange; all the thinkers in Islamic countries who want to make a real difference to their society are living in pain of religious persecution. It is happening now, today. I can daringly say that all true scientists have lived and worked in fear of religious persecution at all times in the Islamic world. Humans need total freedom from religious persecution. Humans need to be free … to be able to explore other religions or beliefs in order to be able to understand from within, from the core of their own essence. Religions should not be an external power; religion must come from within our soul, as Rumi said:

گم شدن در گم شدن، دین منست
نیستی در هست، آیین منست
من چرا گرد جهان گردم چو دوست
در میان جان شیرین منست

Adrift, in adrift, is my religion
To be in a 'not to be' is my ethical passion
Why search the world for a friendly companion?
When it is in my sweet spirit, the best companion

Description of this poem: Rumi wanted to find himself adrift in humanity ... in an environment where humanity was dynamic, not static. It is as if two fluids combine and mix together: this is the true unity of humanity and this was Rumi's religion. As a result of this combination, the original matter disappears, and as result of this unity, Rumi was different person. This is, in fact, what divine power does to humanity in order to make humanity one essence. In this philosophy, *divine is humanity, and humanity is the divine—divine is multiplicity and exuberance*. This is the unity that the early, true Persian culture believed in ... a unity that knows no border or nationality. This unity is Rumi's religion. His religion was him, and what came out of him. It was not an external force that an envoy conveyed to him. In the second part of this poem, Rumi wanted to be in a place where no wise men are supposed to be. He wanted to be with the infidels, unbelievers, kaffirs, and wrongdoers. In fact, there is a story that once Rumi was found among prostitutes listening to them ... listening to their problems and pains.

Furthermore, Rumi pointed out that there is no need to search the world to find friendly compassion, to find a beloved friend, or to find our divine. The beloved friend and the divine (God) is within our sweet spirit.

Religion must not be an enforcement of external power but the power within each of us as individuals. The enforcement of Islam on the minds and souls of children today is a huge problem. The enforcement of Islam on the people in general has been fluctuating and, to a large extent, strengthening through history, so much so that real scientists have been eliminated from Muslim society. It is shocking that it happens today, in our modern world. The total autonomy of Muslim belief on the minds and thoughts of youngsters prevents anybody among young Muslims to jump-in and announce her or his presence and claim to be a free person or a true scientist. The only way to be a true scientist is to be one who is also devoted to Islam, but this is a flawed ambition … in fact, it is not possible. *A real devoted scientist must be a devoted, self-aware scientist, not a devoted, religious scientist.* A society must have the freedom of questioning anybody even—even God. If this is not allowed, then forget about Muslim scientists; Western countries will produce for us! As long as Muslim leaders are geared to disturb and interfere with the minds and thoughts of freedom thinkers, there will be no hope in creating the right environment for scientists.

I have provided good examples in chapters 6 and 7 about Omar Khayyam and his view of religions and the image of an almighty god. Omar Khayyam was an incredibly great person. A great person is simply a human who has dedicated himself totally to thinking and given his entire life for humanity. Putting a religious label on these great people—Muslim, Christian, or Jewish—is an insult to the essence of humanity. For the same reason, we shouldn't call Omar Khayyam a Muslim scientist.

To review the meaning of religion further, let's look at an interesting story from the *Shahnameh* of Ferdowsi.

Sharia law in the eye of Attar of Nishapur

Farid ud-din Attar or Attar of Nishapur (1145-1221) was a Persian poet and theoretician of humanity from Nishapur who had an enduring influence on Persian literature, philosophy, and poetry.

Attar wrote an interesting story—*The Conference of the Birds*. In this epic story; Attar describes a group of birds, which represent individual human souls, under the leadership of a hoopoe, a beautiful bird, who determines to search for the legendary Simorgh (shah or divine). The birds confront their own individual limitations and fears while journeying through seven valleys before they ultimately find Simorgh— find their divine and complete their quest or mission. The thirty birds that ultimately complete the quest discover that they themselves are their own Simorgh, their own Shah or their own divine. This means that, when they are together, they have divine power, they are the divine. This story exactly mirrors the statement of Hallaj: 'I am the truth.'

Revulsion of Attar at the Sharia law on thieving

Attar told a very interesting story that criticizes Sharia law regarding thieving. The story begins when people catch a thief in a marketplace and take him to a square for punishment. The thief's hand is publicly chopped off. Bizarrely, the thief did not scream or show any sign of pain during the removal of the hand. After the punishment, the thief ran away from the square to a wine shop (in Persian میخانه).

It needs to be noted that people in wine shops didn't pay much attention to Islam or religion in general, and they were the people of this world who love this life.

Any way; at the arrival of the thief at the wine shop with severed hand, the thief started shouting and screaming over the trauma and the pain of the severed hand. People in the wine shop asked him to identify the strong motivation that kept him from screaming when his hand was chopped off in the market place.

The thief answered that the people in the marketplace had gathered to see his hand being severed because they found pleasure and delight in the implementation of Sharia law; they were not there to hear his pain and anguish. This is the reason he went to the wine shop where people valued this life and could understand and feel his pain.

This is a very lucid and exceptional story that gives us a strong message: a nation has to be built culturally from the roots in order for people to be able to value this life and protect this life. All the problems start when violence and cruelty are turned into happiness. Gathering people to witness and enjoy the process of cutting off hands, stoning, and execution encourages the celebration of brutality. Gathering people to see the slaughtering of animals for festivals can lead anybody to another level of bloodshed.

The above story shows, how important it is to promote happiness from the roots. The culture of happiness isn't only to make society happier; it is to make a healthy society possible. Happiness also encourages people's brains to function free, to learn more and think better. Happiness makes people to be free of fear—it encourages people to feel for each other and understand each other's pains. Happiness softens people—it will form a tender loving and caring environment. This maybe a utopia world to so many; however, this is the world we have to aim for—nothing less—if we are honest enough and conscious enough.

Attar's indirect sharp criticism of the torture chamber of god (hell)

Attar wrote a very interesting story about those who create torture chambers. The story begins when a king visited a city to see the glories of the city and its infrastructures such as roads and buildings. The citizens prepared everything for the king's visit. After the visit, the king didn't seem very content, and he asked to view the prison. The guide asked, 'Why do you want to visit the prison, your majesty?' The king answered, 'I want to see those who are being tortured in my torture chambers. I want to see the suffering of those who didn't listen to me and didn't obey me. This is how I can see my power.'

This is an almost direct criticism of a god who makes such a sophisticated torture chamber as hell. The criticism of religions is not happening just in our modern times; great people in the past have done plenty of work to show us the problems, and in a much more restricted environment. We need to have vision in seeing those problems that are keeping us sluggish and preventing us from going forward.

Emphasis by Attar that execution is murder

The following is an interesting poem by Attar in which he emphasises that execution is murder. The Muslims call Attar an Islamic scientist.

Attar was simply a human and a true philosopher. Attar was actually against Islamic Sharia law.

In a very interesting story about Anoushiravan-adel, a Persian pre-Islamic king who was famous for being fair and impartial; Attar emphasized that any killing of any captured person is a murder. He actually emphasized that Sharia law opposed the philosophy of humanity (a philosophy without border).

The hidden principles and the hopes in the minds of a society may look childish; however, they are the powers within the heart of the society that establish the roots of the future—the future legal systems and political paths. The great poems in any culture portray such principles and hopes. This makes the poets very popular and so much admired. Therefore, in the minds and souls of these poets, reflected in their poems, is the future character of humanity. Basically, the hope in these poems can shape the future.

Here are messages from Attar that emphasize that execution is murder:

حکیمی بود کامل، مرزبان نام
که نوشروان از او، بودیش آرام

There was an ultimate sage, Marzban by name
Anoushiravan-adel, the king, owed him calm

پسر بودش یکی، چون آفتابی
به هر علمی، دلش را فتح بابی

He had a son like sunlight
Educated to all the insight

سفیهی، کُشت ناگه، آن پسر را
به خَست از درد، جان آن پدر را

A foolish man killed the son of a sudden
Causing pain to the father, a huge burden

مگر آن مرزبان را گفت، خاصی
که باید کرد آن سگ را **قصاصی**

A man told the father, Marzban, 'Hang him
This dog, by Ghasas, you should kill him

جوابی داد او را، مرزبان زود
که الحق نیست، خونریزی چنان سود

Marzban answered back, very quickly,
Shedding more blood, what is the objectivity?

که من شرکت کنم با او، در آن کار
بریزم زنده ای را خون، چنان زار

Should I share in the same blame?
Shed more blood, for what gain?

نه آن بد فعل، کاری بس نکو کرد
که می باید مرا هم کار او کرد؟

'That bad character didn't do well
Same action by me makes life hell

بد و گفتند، پس بستان **دیت** را
نگیرم گفت هرگز آن دیت را

Said to him, 'Okay take diya.'[32]
No, I will never take diya

نمی یارم پسر را با بها کرد
که خون خوردن بود، از خون، بها خورد

No price to my son's head, I can choose
Blood money is blood sucking. I refuse

This is a very strong message from Attar, a so-called Islamic scientist, who said *blood money is blood sucking*. If one does something good, it should be a model for others; however, if one does something bad, then it should not be seen as a model. A model for life shouldn't come from a wrongdoer; it should come from those who make this life beautiful. The death penalty, although an eye-for-an-eye punishment, is still bloodshed and murder. We must not allow ourselves to take the same path as the murderer.

Attar emphasised that Sharia law opposes the philosophy of humanity, which is a philosophy that is derived from many cultures, so is a philosophy without borders. With ghasas (eye for eye, blood for blood), the punishers do the same crime the criminals did. Therefore, ghasas encourages further escalation of the very crime that we want to prevent. This repulsive action of doing bad for bad and shedding blood for blood never brings justice to a society; in fact, it encourages fear, and fear is the worst enemy of intellectuality. Therefore, eye for eye and blood for

---

[32] *diya:* Blood money in Sharia Law

blood reduces the intellectuality of a society, and the society becomes vulnerable to more crime. True justice occurs when there is a degree of love and concern and care for both the criminals and the victims.

This poem of Attar provides humanitarian thoughts. He plants the seeds of a humanistic character and love that comes from the heart of a true human. Attar rejects the action of ghasas, which serves only to raise fear among the population. His rejection reflects the humanity and love in the early, true Persian culture that influenced the Persian Empire and lasted for so many thousands of years.

There is nothing without love. Love is a precondition for the formation of our lives and the Universe. Love is a precondition for the philosophy and intellectuality that shape humanity; otherwise, any thought could claim to be a philosophy. If an idea isn't humane, it shouldn't really be called philosophy. Our real success in life is also derived from our love—passion is the precondition of every real success. No real successful society can be created without passion and love. Love is the bond that makes people stick together and work together.

It is important to know that love is not faith. Love and faith are entirely separate. Love and faith are antithetical because a person who has faith in a belief, such as faith in a religion, will be resistant to any other belief and resistant to any change to her or his ideology. Love goes beyond infidelity and religion, but faith must be in line with religion. Love is to adore and embrace all thoughts and ideas and cherish advancement. Love is colours and variety. Love feeds and thrives on colours and variety while faith sees them as bothers if not the enemy.

Hafez wrote a beautiful ghazal in this respect:

هر کـه شد محرم دل در حرم یار بـماند
وان کـه این کار ندانست در انکار بـماند
از صدای سخن عشق ندیدم خوشتر
یادگاری که در این گنبد دوار بماند

Intimacy with the heart keeps us beloved
Denial of this keeps us apart
The sound of love talk is the sweetest, nothing alike
This is the token, on the revolving dome inscribed

Description of this poem: It is intimacy with our hearts that keeps us beloved. Denial of this closeness to the heart keeps us apart from others. The sounds of love are the sweetest sounds; there is nothing like love. This is the remembrance that is inscribed on our revolving dome (revolving Earth).

Attar's story of the potter and the prophet Noah

In this story, we see Attar's humanity and his skill in making sharp criticism of the prophet Noah in the killing of all the people and creatures of the world except for those in his ark in the name of getting rid of infidels. It can be seen how beautifully Attar rejects the Abrahamic religious vision of the prophet Noah and highlights his Persian vision of god—the god of humanity. Here is the beginning of Attar's story:

نوح پیغمبر، چو از کفّار رَست
با چهل تن کرد برکوهی نشست

When the prophet Noah got rid of the infidels
He sat with forty of his comrades on a mountain

The prophet Noah, after freeing himself from all the infidels and also animals by killing them, sat with forty of his comrades on a hilltop and started a new and fresh life.

بود یک تن از آن چهل، کوزه گر
برگشاد او یک دکان، پرکوزه در

One of those forty was a potter
established a shop of pottery

One of those forty people who survived in Noah's ark was a potter, who subsequently opened a pottery shop. As it is known, Attar was from Nishapur, which is a city of pottery. Omar Khayyam was also from the same city; his poems also reflect a love for pottery—a merger of water and clay was regarded as action of love.

جبرییل آمد که میگوید خدای
بشکنش این کوزه ها، ای رهنمای

Gabriel took a message from god:
Break the pots in the pottery shop

Gabriel took a message from God to Noah: God has ordered Noah to break all the pots in the pottery shop.

نوح گفتش:آن همه نتوان شکست
کین به صد خون دلش آمد بدست

Noah said, 'All the pots? Can't be broken, it's hard
The pots have been made with effort from the heart

گرچه کوزه بشکنی، گِل بشکند
در حقیقت مرد را دل بشکند

It's true that breaking the pot is breaking the mud
However, it would be breaking the potter's heart.

Noah admitted that it was true that if he broke the pots he would, in fact, break mud. However, he then said he would be breaking the potter's heart and the love he had put into his art. Noah said he couldn't do this.

باز جبریل آمد و دادش پیام
گفت میگوید خداوندت سلام

Gabriel came back to Noah again with a message.
Told Noah God has given greetings with this message …

پس چنین میگوید او، کای نیکبخت
گر، شکست کوزه ای چندست سخت

God says, 'Oh, Noah, the good fortune
Oh, breaking the pots is such a misfortune?

ای بسی ز ان سخت تر در کل باب
کز، دعایی خلق را دادی به آب

Oh the much more colossal and difficult affairs

My job, I have drowned all with your prayers

Gabriel came back with a message to Noah again. He said God says hello, but there is still an order from God to break the pots in the pottery shop. God's message said, 'Oh, Noah, the good-hearted prophet! Oh, breaking the pots is so difficult and unfortunate for you. Oh, don't you remember the much more colossal difficulty you had with me over your prayers? I had to drown all the people and the creatures of the world because of your prayers because you named them infidels? Don't you know they were all my creatures that I created with my love and affection?'

Of course, Attar didn't say, here, what sort of god it was who listened to his prophet and followed his prophet's desires. Attar, through this dilemma, showed the nature of God in the Abrahamic religions.

Attar carried on quoting the message from god:

یک دکان کوزه بشکستن خطاست
یک جهان آدمی کشتن رواست؟

Breaking the pottery in a shop is incorrect?
Killing the people of the world is correct?

God complained to Noah and said: 'Oh, Noah, if you refrain breaking the pottery of a shop believing that it is incorrect, then how could the killing of all the people of the world be correct, especially when I loved them after I created them through my love and passion?'

Furthermore, Attar carried on quoting the god's message:

خود دلت میداد ای شیخ کبار
زان همه مردم برآوردن دمار

How can your heart accept, Noah?
To kill all those people of the world, Noah?

How could Noah endure and accept the killing of the entire world population and all the 'beings' under the name of infidel?

In addition, Attar carried on quoting God's message:

کز پی آن بندگان بی قرار
لطف ما چندان همی بگریست زار

For those unfortunate beings of the world
My passionate heart is crying so hard in bewilderment

God's passionate heart was crying so hard for those unfortunate beings of the world who were drowned because of Noah's persistent quest. God continued to cry in bewilderment over such a crime.

Attar sharply criticizes the Abrahamic religious version of the story of the prophet Noah and God. However, Attar has his own god that shows her passions and makes the following criticisms of Noah and the god of Abrahamic religion: It was you who asked me to destroy the infidels— all the beings on Earth except those in your ark.

God tells Noah that God's submission to Noah's request has made his passionate heart cry so hard for all the killing he did at Noah's order. God can't understand how Noah could ask such a thing when Noah can't even break the pots in a pottery shop! God wonders how Noah, who now seems to not have vicious heart, could have asked God to commit the worst possible crime of the world—murder—murder of the whole population of the world!

Of course, this picture of the passionate god of Attar is entirely different from the god of Abrahamic religion. This picture of a passionate god is the Persian divine that is the essence of humanity, harmony and love, which is in the mind and the soul of Attar. As well as Attar, Rumi also criticizes the Abrahamic almighty god in the story of Moses in his book *Masnavi Manavi*. Persians literature is all about humanity, and therefore there are many criticisms of religious zealousness, either directly or indirectly, in much of the poetry. A very direct form of criticism of religious scripture has never been possible in the Muslim nations, and is not allowed even in today's modern world.

The above story from Attar is a very deep tell tale story that defines the whole of Abrahamian Religions—this is the foundation on which all of these religions is based on. What is this foundation?—*murdering the whole population of earth for being infidels*.

People tell me: Each religion is different—why are you painting all the Abrahamian religions with the same brush? Of course, they are different but, at the end of the day, they are the product of each other—Islam is the product of Christianity. Abrahamian religions are based on the storey of Noah—the order to murder the whole population of Earth for being infidels ... is this not terrorism? The reason that Christianity is much softer than Islam is due to the true nature of Jesus Christ who was an ultimate peaceful loving man—however; the roots of these religions are the same ... you only need few extremists to pick up the idea and make this life a hell for all of us.

CHAPTER NINE

WHY THE LONDON BOMBING?

Abstract

This chapter will show that extremism and terrorism, both of which endanger our modern world, have roots in the loss of identity and lack of rooted cultural values. Conversely, our consciousness of cultural awakening and identity is the way to tackle extremism and terrorism at their roots.

There is a definite lack of new ideas and new vision in defining a life that is very well connected and rooted to our past real cultural values, identity, and literature. This lack of change has made it possible for extremists to hijack the belief system and advocate their image of the world.

We, as a modern society, have to be able to define our lives through our literature, true culture, and philosophy that have roots in our history and in our ancestors. *This definition of life is spirituality, which is missing in our modern life.* Denying the value we received from our ancestors because they lived in the Dark Ages is an insult to our roots, to our integrity, and to our identity. We would not even be human without the hard work of our ancestors. Any new vision of today must have a connection to our past heritage; otherwise, there is no continuity. And, when there is no continuity, there is a break, which causes suffering. If there is no continuity in a vision, then that vision isn't really a true vision that can connect us to each other and create the unity that we need as humans.

The lack of our vision into our past humanity is giving signals to our future generations that we have just fallen out of the sky and become human by some order, such as the order of an almighty power. There is no such thing as free lunch; nothing comes so easily. Our ancestors worked hard and sacrificed themselves to make us what we are today—human. A precarious belief that 'things just happened and came easily to us' is making our generation and future generations forget that everything needs to go through a process, to go through hard work and progression. Our ancestors worked extremely hard and generated ideas, thoughts, and philosophies to form those values and principles that make us human today. The great work of our ancestors has to be admired for the sake of our unified future.

It is amazing to see so many young people showing their anxiety and revulsion in hatred, killing, and other distractions, but at the same time advocating even a more repugnant way of response such as supporting bombers who indiscriminately kill. The principles of humanity must not be forgotten even in an environment of war. I must not fight my enemies with the full intension of eliminating them. My war with my enemy must be limited, with the full intension of avoiding the war as far as possible. Creating hate out of any type of war is against the principles of humanity.

A brief review of 2005 London bombing

On Thursday, 7 July 2005, a series of four bomb attacks struck London's public transport system during the morning rush hour. At 8.50 in the morning, three bombs exploded within fifty seconds of each other on three London Underground trains. A fourth bomb exploded on a bus shortly afterwards at 9.47 in Tavistock Square in London. The bombings led to a severe, day-long disruption of the city's transportation and mobile telecommunications infrastructure.

Fifty-six people were killed in the attacks, including the four suspected bombers, and 700 were injured. The incident was the deadliest bombing in London since the Second World War. Do we have an answer for these types of problems? Freedom is like a bird. Can this bird—the phoenix—fly away from us in a country such as United Kingdom? Well, it can, if we try to limit its territory. Freedom is the most precious experience of humanity. It requires a new understanding at every stage of our life on this planet. Freedom—the phoenix—has no border; this is the basic meaning of freedom. Freedom that has border—or a cage—is free within the cage but has no real freedom. The true meaning of freedom applies only when there is freedom everywhere in the world; otherwise, our freedom will be in danger. And, for its protection, more and more war would be required, which goes against the principles of humanity and against the very nature of the freedom that we are supposed to be advocating.

The roots of human rights and democracy

Democracy, human rights, freedom, and humanity are all elements of civilization, the values of which the West holds dear, and hopes to cling on to. Many don't realize that these values originally came from the East. But are we in the West taking these precious values for granted?

These precious values are the result of thousands of years of human effort and sacrifice, not only from the Greek and Persian cultures, but also from many other cultures—Egyptian, Indian, and Chinese, for example. Consider the words *human* and *humanity*. They date back six to nine thousand years in the root of the Persian culture. Additionally, *wise*, *vision*, *artery*, *ark*, and *sun* and many more words also date back to the same period in the root of the Persian culture. To highlight the importance of antiquity even more, just take a look at the amazing picture of Venus at the beginning of this book, and look at the goddess culture images in museums or webs. These date back to the same period and even farther back. This is where Rumi, 700 years ago, got his ideas from—his ideas of love within, self-confidence, values, humanity, and the interconnectedness of the world. Rumi's ideas come from deep Persian culture; it is important to remember that his ideas didn't just drop from sky. Shakespeare's thoughts and ideas didn't just drop from sky either; they came from somewhere and, then, he managed to expand them. Look at the similarities between these two authors in this poem by Rumi:

تو مجنون و لیلی به بیرون مباش
که رامین تونی ، ویس رعنا تونی
تو درمان غم ها ، زبیرون مجو
که پا زهرو درمان غم ها تونی

اگر عالمی منکر ما شود
غمی نیست ما را که ما را توئی
اگر تا قیامت بگویم ز تو
به پایان نیاید ، سروپا توئی

Don't search outside you for Lily and Majnoon[33] (Romeo and Juliet)
You are both, Ramin and the beautiful Vis[34]
Do not search outside you for treatments of grief
You are the anti-venom and the treatment to all grief
If the whole world denies us
No pains to us, as you are us
If I carry on saying about you to eternity
Still no end, as you are my soul and my identity

Description of this poem: Rumi said that Romeo and Juliet are within each of us. We are both, Romeo and Juliet. Therefore, the love and lover are both inside each of us. Furthermore, we are the treatment for our own grief. We are the anti-venom and the treatment to all the grief of the world. He admires this path with confidence even if the whole world denies us. If we choose the right path with our consciousness, we will succeed. This is the uppermost appreciation and admiration of us and our individual worlds. Each of us is a world unto ourselves, and each of us is divine. But we are definitely not almighty gods as many people with static ideology may claim. We are the divine; we have Romeo and Juliet inside of us. This is Rumi's real, true message of humanity.

---

[33]. *Lily and Majnoon: love story in Persian literature*
[34]. *Ramin and Vis: love story in Persian literature, similar to Romeo and Juliet of Shakespeare.*

The values of humanity are not confined to Persian culture; in fact, all cultures have some combination of these golden values that can be excavated and explored. To some extent, these values were formulated and reshaped with new ideas, and applied to Western society at the time of the Renaissance and thereafter by great western philosophers; it was this that resulted in Western civilization as we know it today. In fact, Simorgh—the Phoenix—rose from the ashes at the time of the Renaissance. In reality, Western civilization, as we know today, is the result of thousands of years of human effort rooted in many cultures. It is important to be aware of this in order to convey the message that humanity and morality don't just appear spontaneously for us without hard work.

Moreover, it is very important to know the difference between culture and history. History is the struggle of powers that results in wars, bloodshed, and conflicts, while culture is the frustration of war. *Culture is a learning process based in the values and the experiences that come out of the history and help people learn how to live together in peace. Therefore, culture opposes nationalism and xenophobia. The experience of living together and loving each other and knowing how to live together without any prejudice, without any conflict or quarrel, is culture. We evolve today to move into tomorrow's world. Humanity isn't like a bullet coming out of the barrel of a gun aimed at the future.* Neither is it perfectionist religious ideology! We live in this modern world of information technology, and we should never give in to perfectionist religious ideology. *Humanity must evolve from its old form to a new form; otherwise, it will remain static, old, and doomed without a path to creativity. History dies, but culture, humanity, and values are reborn and evolve.*

Cultures are rooted in thousands of years of human exploration and effort in learning different ways of living together. This is why culture is an invaluable humanity asset. Culture doesn't embody the historical figureheads of a society. For example, Hitler isn't the culture of Germany; instead, he is part of her history. However, Werner Heisenberg, Immanuel Kant, Friedrich Nietzsche, and Friedrich Hegel are part of German culture, as Sigmund Freud is part of Austrian culture and Shakespeare is part of English culture. It was these philosophers and theorists who made the move towards Western civilization.

In the same principle; Persian historical figureheads such as Khomeini or Reza-Shah aren't part of the culture of Persia. The figureheads of Persian culture are Hafez, Rumi, Ferdowsi, Attar, Khayyam, and Obeid Zakani. It is the work of these thinkers, philosophers, and theorists who will influence the Persian—or Iranian—renaissance.

Freedom and democracy in the West, although only a partial success, but are huge achievement that must be valued, admired, and cared for by all of mankind. This great human achievement must be encouraged to take the next step forward. Humanity must be awake to these great values that were left for us by our ancestors, and we must not take them for granted, claim ownership, or become prejudiced. Snobbery and selfishness in a positive way, without prejudice, can be good. This is due to the fact that we do need self-confidence, which comes from selfishness, in order to be able to believe in ourselves and to be able to think. *In fact, it is not selfishness that we don't adore; it is the arrogance that we hate. We do and we must adore selfishness for the sake of self-confidence.* These are delicate human matters that must be discussed openly in our classrooms and media. Discussion can strengthen humanity, which will grow stronger with reasoning and strong self-confidence.

Our educational system is failing, to a large degree, in training the youngsters of today to understand these precious and golden values of life. This is why religions attain ground and gain strength and are able to fill in the vacuum that education has left behind. All of our social problems are rooted in misunderstanding the roots of humanity, values, and the true meaning of culture. This is why we are failing in winning the hearts and minds of people in the world, especially the youngsters. We separate one nation from another in human achievement, and this separation is what causes problems. Individuals must be able to find their roots in the values and the glories of human achievements. If they don't have the chance to do this, then they will find their roots in something that no one likes.

Our educational system is failing in defining the meaning of life and the values of life. This life is our god and our destiny; this life is our spirituality. We must infiltrate the message into the hearts and minds of people of all nations, especially children in our classrooms. We must make sure our philosophy of life, our spirituality, grows so much that it dwarfs religions in comparison.

When most people hear the word *spirituality*, they immediately think of religious spirituality, but that is only a very small part of the meaning of the word. True spirituality is a principle of humanity that we can tap into in order to value this life. Ethics and spirituality are very important subjects in any society. They can be used to guide youngsters in their understanding of what is important in this life. The young people who go on rampages and participate in the indiscriminate shooting of people are a clear indication of how neglectful our system of education has become regarding life and the principles of humanity. The importance of this life and the values of humanity, which are in fact spirituality, must never be out of our minds and souls.

All people in a society try to find their identity within that society. If this is not achievable, then they might be able to find their way into extremist groups. Some of these are religious extremists and some are nationalistic extremists. The London bombing was the product of an identity crisis. People who couldn't find their identity within a productive society slipped into a vacuum and joined an extremist group where they found an identity and a cause that encouraged them to harm society.

Philosophy, the solution

Because we are human, the principle upon which we connect to each other has to be humanity. Both science and philosophy must come to our aid as we surge forward on the path towards this humanity. Science isn't the only solution to our problems. *Philosophy must work towards putting the discoveries of science to peaceful productive use that will benefit all mankind in all nations—that stops warfare activities.*

The world needs new creative ideas and new philosophy to find a way of emphasising morality and the values of humanity. It is very obvious that there must be something wrong with our system of education, and the way we think of our world. To tackle the roots of the problem, we must broaden our vision even more and look at the many rooted cultural values with which at least some people around the world can associate and identify. We must bring to the surface those identities and values of humanity that remain in cultures. These values can lead us to a new thinking, a new vision. They can open up societies for more diversity and more sharing. This can reshape the minds and thoughts of our youngsters to a much broader spectrum, encouraging them not to be so naive and so indifferent. Such great work has already commenced in earnest by a Persian professor Manuchehr Jamali, who has written over 150 books in the Persian language. At my earliest opportunity, I shall write more books in English expanding on the true and real meaning of humanity in Persian literature.

Conclusion

Due to the lack of new vision and philosophy, we keep finding simple solutions to our world problems. For example, we export democracy or 'freedom' to nations by invasion or change a regime or just through ballet boxes. Democracy, freedom, and secularity come from the richness of philosophy and thought. Democracy is the belief that an individual person is responsible for all the bad and good irrespective of any supernatural ideology. We need the confidence that people are capable of building their heaven here on this Earth. Democracy advocates that we are the key to unlock all the problems in our path. Therefore, democracy and a supernatural power such as an almighty god do not go together hand in hand and in harmony. Democracy has to come from the root of a society with social infrastructure. Democracy must grow within the cultural background of a community that has roots within that community, which give them the pride, dignity and self-confidence. Democracy must be respected by all the people in a community in order to be able to function. Therefore, democracy isn't a commodity that can be imported; it must be built from within.

The lack of new vision and philosophy has made us naïve in thinking that democracy can happen overnight. Such naïveté and the idea that there is a simple solution to our world problems are causing many more problems and also blocking the real path to democracy. Albert Einstein said, 'everything should be made as simple as possible, but not simpler.'

The problem is that people keep applying simple solutions that keep failing, and there seems to be no shame in the failures. Simple solutions can result in naïveté … a vacuum or void that can easily and quickly become filled with something undesirable that creates more division and more problems. Thus, as the division escalates, we are giving more and more opportunities to extremists. The starvation, disease, and war in one part of the world can undermine the democracy, human rights, and freedom in another part of the world. Humanity must dearly adore and desire a freedom that has no borders, on which the future of our children can depend. We have to be the masters of our own destiny, morality, and ethics by continuously developing and sharing new ideas. We need new visions that can fill in the vacuum that is left in the morality of our society, before the vacuum is hijacked by extremists.

CHAPTER TEN

THE DEAN OF HUMANITY

Introduction

It is known that Greece gave the Western civilization the word *democracy* as well as the principles of civil society. In practise, the Greek city-state of Athens and the surrounding territory of Attica experienced twenty years of democracy around 508 BCE. Although Athens is one of the first known democracies, parallel to Greek democracy there was Persian democracy for many hundred years in a different form and shape which was more humanitarian in the name of *shar-e-khoram*[35] (written in Farsi شهر خرم) in which people and ruler had to sit around a tablecloth (*sofreh*[36]) and celebrate many events or festivals such as Norooz (New Year). The Persian experience of democracy must not be put aside just because it was not called democracy. Democracy in Persia existed under a different culture with a different name and philosophy; is this not quite reasonable? It is obvious that democracy in Persia with a different culture must have had a completely different name. What is that name? That name was shar-e khoram.

---

[35] *Shar-e Khoram was the city of happiness. It was the Persian principle of civil society and democracy. Its purpose was to make people happy.*
[36] *Sofreh: A cloth on which food is served. People sit around the sofreh and eat together—a show of unity and togetherness.*

Humanism was the cause of humanely culture and the origin of human right in the west. However, in Persian culture a similar corresponding humanism culture gradually took shape around and after 1000 BCE and up to around 200 ACE in the name of *hu-man* or *vahu-man* or *ha-kha-man*. The philosophy behind this was good thinking and good wisdom in an atmosphere of friendship, and this was called dean[37]—dean of humanity or *dean-e-mardomi*[38] in Persian language (written in Farsi دین مردمی). The dynasty names Hakhamaneshian and Ashkanian have this exact meaning. Dean was a vision of humanity in exploration and finding the way forward. Dean wasn't a static idea; it was rather a fluid and dynamic ideology. The word *dean* took the meaning of religion and became a static idea when Zoroastrianism took over Persia around 200 CE. This word was then picked up by the Muslims. The word *dean* in the entire Muslim nation has lost its original meaning to religion among general public. However, the word *dean* hasn't lost its original meaning in literature. As Ferdowsi in the storey of Iraj said:

جز از کهتری نیست، آئین من
نباشد بجز مردمی، دین من

Being younger than you, is my only ethic
Nothing, but the dean of humanity is my epic

---

[37] Dean: This is a Persian word that comes from the Persian word for seeing (dean or bean) and vision (again from the Persian word beanesh). Dean is a vision of humanity in exploration and finding the way forward. Dean wasn't a static idea; it was rather a fluid and dynamic idea.
[38] . Dean-e-mardomi: This is Persian word, meaning; the religion of humanity

The Divine and Wisdom

In the West, a *dean* is the head of a college or university—in UK it is used as a head of a research department. The original Persian word dean (دین) had almost the same meaning—vision, wisdom exploration and research. I like to use this word to describe 'cooperative human progresses'. There does not seem to be a word in English that describes this sort or achievement. So, in this book, *dean* is exploration and visions that emerge out of humanity wisdom when people think together and work together as a cluster and exchange thoughts and knowledge. In this chapter I will briefly explain the meaning of this vision of humanity I call dean.

Dean is a vision of humanity. But, what is humanity? The word *humanity* obviously comes from the word *human*. Human is from two words, *hu* and *man*. *Hu-man was the divine of wisdom in Persia. This is the connection and the link between people that encourage them to stay together to be productive to progress and to remain afresh throughout.* The word *divine* that comes from Latin *divinus*, from *divus* 'godlike' (related to *deus* 'god') must have had the origins through what I call *dean*. The divine was known to be the cluster of humans who were linked together to be productive. Without this cluster there is no existence of the divine. *It is very important to understand the point here—hu-man (the divine) is not the cause of the link but* is *the link.* To make this point clearer, I give you an example: Imagine of a glue that sticks two objects together and makes them one—the two objects are one but there is no sign of the glue. The glue is the divine—it can't be seen but it is there and is the link and the cause of the cluster. This idea of a cluster is an impressive and very cohesive thought that has no boundaries in thinking and does not separate between believers and nonbelievers. It is simply the link of people connecting with one another so that they create a cluster; this cluster is the divine or Simorgh (Phoenix). So long as people are not together, there is no cluster, and therefore, there is no divine and no God; it is as simple as that—no god. Therefore, *in the dean of humanity, the existence of the divine depends on us ... if people can get together and be productive, then, there is divine—is this a crazy idea—I think it is a very interesting unifying idea that I haven't seen anywhere else.*

A gathering together to create the divine was the link between adoration and discipline. Therefore, humans have the essence of divinity, the essence of being together, the essence of existing in a cluster, and therefore being divine, Simorgh, because the divine was the seed in the human soul, which must be grown and cultivated.

To be productive was to be enlightened. Therefore, the enlightenment that comes out of the core essence of human vision was the divinity or dean. Additionally, *dean* in early, true Persian culture, means vision from within ... vision that is born within and grows from the roots, nature, and the seeds of humanity.

The divine or Arta (god) was the first gem or the first essence of humanity. This is a direct connection between humanity and the divine. The divine is within humanity and *is* the humanity—there is a direct connection. Therefore, the requirement that a middleman (mullah, priest, rabbi) must assist in creating the connection between humanity and the divine in this philosophy is meaningless. In this culture, divine and humanity have the same essence of foliage or plant. For these reasons, the divine and goddesses in Persian native culture were related to plants, flowers, and trees. For example, the cedar tree was the symbol of humanity—as it stands tall and high. Additionally, cedar tree was the representative of the seeds of divine due to being evergreen. This symbolizes that humanity and divine are evergreen (productive). In the same way *Myrtus communis*, a plant commonly known as myrtle (*mored* in Persian) is also evergreen. It is very aromatic and is representative of first day of month. The first day of every month in Persia used to be called *Hu-Ram*[39]; [it is called Khoram (happiness) today in Persia]. Ram or Raam is the name of Persian goddess Venus who is the cluster of the soul of humanity. Persians used to use this plant, myrtle, over the crowns and wear it to celebrations.

The general view of Persians about the divine was the cluster of humanity, and this cluster was Simorgh. Simorgh scattered herself as one would sow seeds over the ground to grow and nurture the world and liven the world. This means every being has the same essence as the divine. In this philosophy, the divine turns into soul and matter. *Divinity was the essence of humanity in Persia.*

Hu-man[40] or the divine brings chivalry into the world, a manner that comes from her own essence; basically Arta is chivalric. Chivalry is a moral system that advocates caring for others and protecting others even if the protector's life is endangered in doing so. Originally, the divine didn't mean god or creator; it had nothing to do with the sudden creation of the world. The divine was rather a sacrificial abstract that sacrificed her to be the world and to be the being. Arta, or the divine, was the first essence in every human. Therefore, the term *humanity*, in itself, has the meaning of chivalry. Humanity is chivalric. This was the core of culture in Persia, which used to embrace many populations such

---

[39] *Hu-Ram: The present Persian word of 'Khoram': meaning hhappiness. Ram is the name of Persian goddess*

[40] *Hu-man: a Persian word: antonym of dosh-man (the Persian word for enemy).*

as Dailamites, Arabs, Indians, Tajiks, Afghans, Persians, Kurds, Jews, and many more.

Hu-man has the meaning of egg or seeds of Arta, Erez, or Iraj. These are all references to divinity and the divine. Iraj was the first mythological Persian king—appointed as Persian king by his father, Fereydoun, as he was younger (being younger had the advantage in goddess culture). Iraj, unarmed, approached his two older brothers and begged them to put aside hatred and settle their differences in a peaceful manner—he has offered leave the power for peace. However, the two older brothers killed him because they were jealous of his charisma and character.

This is what Iraj, in the *Shahnameh* of Ferdowsi, said to his older brothers, Salm and Tur, before they murder him:

جز از کهتری نیست، آئین من
نباشد بجر مردمی، دین من

Being younger than you, is my only ethic
Nothing, but the dean of humanity is my epic

Description of this poem: Iraj says the only difference between him and his brothers is that he is younger. Being young gave him a divine power, all Persian divine were young—fifteen to eighteen years old. *Iraj says that his ethic is the dean of humanity, the same dean or vision that his brothers have.* If there is no difference between their goals, his brothers should not kill him. Despite the pleading and heroic strength and astonishing manners of Iraj, his older brothers murdered him. This epic story and astonishing tragedy from the *Shahnameh* teaches the consequence of a society with and without army.

In the epic story of Iraj, he says of his vision as: *dean of humanity, is the vision that emerges from the essence and cluster of humanity—the vision that materialises the cluster of humanity—togetherness and unity is the dean of humanity.* Iraj expresses the gem of the state in Persia. He says that his vision is the dean of humanity. In other words, he expresses that his natural instinct (like any people)—the gem hidden within him—has evolved into a vision that humans are brothers and sisters and one family from one cluster. A vision that rises directly from the essence and the nature of every human is the appearance of the divine or the power of love. This is the real vision and the real dean of humanity.

It is important to note the different meanings of age in the cultures of male god and the female god. *In the culture of male god, the elders were the source of initiatives, while in the culture of female god, the young were the source of initiative.* It is the young who are the source of initiatives and who are the founders of change. Again, *young* does not directly relate to age; rather it relates to minds and thoughts that are not old fashioned … that are eager for change. In Ferdowsi's *Shahnameh*, Zahhak eats the brain of youngsters; this means absorbing the initiatives of the founders of change.

The Persian divine Hu-Ram was always young and always fifteen to eighteen years old. Rostam in Ferdowsi's *Shahnameh* was also young when he went for Seven Khan (Juan), an expedition to rescue the Persian king, Keykavous. Basically, all the divine characters in Persian mythology are young. In the dean of humanity, the power of youth is the power of initiative, the power of spirit, the power of exploration, and the cause of new vision. Therefore, Iraj, who is the hope and desire of a Persian state and power, is also the initiative for the dean of humanity. With Iraj, the dean of humanity becomes the foundation of a Persian state.

This context highlights Persian vision as the vision of humanity. Basically, Iraj is the first mythological divine character—or humanity—in Persian culture. Adam and Eve are the first symbolic characters in the Muslim and Christian traditions.

In *The Selections of Zadspram* (published in the ninth century) Iraj is known as *wan-i-jud-besh*. This is a tree that has all the seeds of all the souls. Above the tree is Simorgh (the Phoenix) who is the cluster of the souls of all humanity. This cluster is the cluster of the entire human race on this Earth—not only Persian, Turkish, Arab, Western, American, Indian ... but the cluster of all humans together. The word for *human* in Persian Language is *mardom*[41], which means the seeds of cluster, meaning Simorgh.

Dean is a vision that gives birth and nurtures from the gem and the essence of each individual person. What grows from this essence? Humanity grows from the human essence, which is Iraj or Arta. The exclusivity of this essence or seed opposes fury, anger, and hurt, aggressiveness and threat. This means that, in the essence of humans, there is no anger, hurt, aggressiveness, or *jihad* (religious duty of Muslims) or threat. Humanity is a soul and spirit that has grown from the cluster of all humanity that is called Simorgh, and therefore in its essence, it opposes jihad, which is aggressiveness and threat. It is for

---

[41] *Mardom: The Persian word for people. This is from two words, mar and tom, or dom. Mar is another name for goddess and tom or dom are the seeds or egg. Therefore humans are the seeds of the divine, a similar idea to egoism.*

this reason that any vision that comes from the essence of humanity opposes anger and threat.

The dean of humanity protects the soul and the wisdom of every individual against any harm. When Iraj's brothers wanted to kill him, in Persian mythology, he gave testimony to his brothers based on this dean of humanity that is the essence of the Persian culture. This is the testimony. As Iraj says to his brothers in the *Shahnameh* of Ferdowsi:

پسندی و همداستانی کنی
که جان داری و، جانستانی کنی
میآزار موری که دانه کش است
که جان دارد و، جان شیرین خوش است

Taking part in a story of hatred, is no life
You have a life; you must take no one's life
An ant bearing a grain, bring no strife
Due to ant's joyful soul and a sweet life

Description of this poem: The one who has soul (life) must not take someone else's soul, as Iraj or Arta is the collective of the whole life, and individual life is from the cluster of the whole life. Therefore, taking someone's life is, in fact, taking your own life. Happiness and pain are flavours that exist in all of our lives and souls. Every individual is from the seed of the cluster, the cluster of humanity. The essence of humanity is to reject any harm to life or wisdom of anyone, as the bad taste of harm will make his own sweet life bitter.

Apart from that, wisdom is the eye and the guardian of the soul. This means that wisdom is responsible for the decoration and discipline of this life. *Therefore, wisdom is the mate of the soul and the principle of government in every person. Consequently, wisdom has role in politics as well as the social aspects of life and manners.* Harming wisdom is also harming the soul; the two can't be separated. In order to harm the soul, the wisdom—the guardian of soul—must be stopped from functioning. In another words, the wisdom must be neglected and put aside such as in the story of Zahhak in the *Shahnameh* when the wisdom (brain) is swallowed or eaten away to gain the ability to harm the soul. The natural essence of each individual human is the avoidance of harming any soul or wisdom.

The fabric of the dean of humanity is based on the soul and the life, which has priority over belief, race, tribe, or nationality. Belief, race, tribe, or nationalities are side issues in relationship to the soul and life. There can never be an excuse in taking part in a story that accepts the taking of someone's life, or even leads to a punishment of death. Only life is sanctity, not a personality or a belief or a leader or a god or a prophet.

Dean of humanity of Iraj opposes anger, threat, and malice, which take away chivalry and love in humanity. Life and the guardian of life—wisdom—are sacred, and therefore no one is allowed to harm them. This is the meaning of the sacred—stopping bodily harm irrevocably once and for all. The sanctity (sacredness) of life embraces everyone and does not know Turkish, Persians, Japanese, English, Arab, Chinese, American. Neither does it know Jews, Muslims, or Christians. Due to the fact that everyone has life and this life is sweet, no one is allowed to harm this life. *There should be no death punishment for one who takes a life; rather, a murderer should be put in prison with the full intension of rehabilitation.* Anyone can have any belief or religion from any background, whatever race or sex. None of these are important; it is the life that is the seeds of the cluster (Simorgh) or Arta—this is the culture of the dean of humanity.

Harming the soul of humanity and harming wisdom are the biggest sins; these are the dean of humanity. This is a testimony from the Persian poet Hafez:

مباش در پی آزار و هرچه خواهی کن
که درشریعت ما، غیر از این گناهی نیست

> *Don't seek to hurt anyone, do whatever else*
> *In our Sharia, harming is sin, nothing else*

This Sharia that Hafez is talking about is not Islamic Sharia that distinguishes between the life of a believer and a nonbeliever. The core of the Abrahamic religions is their faith and their distinction between believer and nonbeliever. They discriminate against nonbelievers. If these religions do not manage to hurt a nonbeliever here on this Earth, then they have plenty of complicated torture equipment waiting for the nonbelievers in their afterlife. They are purposely creating an atmosphere of fear. Sin in these religions is well connected to their god; sin is an insult to their god … it is blasphemous. If God orders to kill, then the killing is holy. In Islam, the belief is more important than the life of a person. However, in the dean of humanity or Arta, it is the body and soul of human that is holy, and *if any god orders a killing, then that god is no longer a god but a demon. Dean of humanity allows people to change their god at any time, as 'god' is from the wisdom.* It is not a static and unchanging god. God, in the dean of humanity, is a dynamic god and constantly changing. Moreover, the change in this god is the cause of the existence of this dynamic god—no change, no god. Furthermore, *if there is no change in this god, then the god is dead*. It is as simple as that. *God is dead in those nations that remain static and can't change.*

Dean of humanity—Iraj's dean in *Shahnameh*

Dean of humanity declares that, hurting or harming anyone's soul (body) or wisdom is an offence. According to the dean of humanity, making people afraid of anything, such as a god or a hell, is also an offence—because it hurts their wisdom. Fear is the worst enemy of the path to wisdom and intellectuality. A productive social infrastructure or democracy can never be created in a fearful society. People must be made mentally free of any fear to choose their own individual destiny. No religions should advocate fear; how can anyone establish a democracy in a society that allows fear? This is common sense and the principle of humanity. Acceptance of the principles of humanity provides dignity to the society where mind and wisdom can grow. This is why Ferdowsi said:

مگر هرچه در مردمی درخورد
مر آن را پذیرنده باشد، خرد

Anything that is connected to humanity
Wisdom accepts that as dignity

Wisdom accepts only those who are humane. The nature of human beings is humanity. *Religion doesn't come from a natural wisdom of humanity; rather, it is an artificial product to benefit a certain ideology, race, or tribe that usually has hidden agendas.* This is why there are so many religions in this world; otherwise, we would have had one religion as we have one 'humanity'. The reason that humanity is one is that it derives from human wisdom and morality that evolved throughout thousands of years of human experience on this Earth. Wisdom in Persian language is *kharad*[42]. *It is what binds forever humanity and truth.* In the description and characteristic of Siavash[43] in the *Shahnameh* Ferdowsi said:

همه مردمی، جُستی و راستی
جهان را به دانش بیاراستی

You've explored all the truth and humanity
Attire the world with knowledge and morality

The world needs to be decorated with the truth and humanity. Why do truth and humanity come together in Persian poems? Because truth is the first essence of humanity. *Truth and humanity shape our day-to-day conversations, form our character, and deepen our wisdom.* Truth is the expansion of the first essence of humanity who is Iraj or Arta in the *Shahnameh*. This is the phenomenon that we call freedom today. Freedom is a relaxed environment where minds can grow and take the next step of life through wisdom and awareness without any fear—advocating the fear of hell-fire goes against freedom.

Being right in Persian culture has the meaning of truth, as truth is the essence of Iraj and the word *right* is the process of evolvement. If

---

[42] *Kharad is human intelligence and awareness, or wisdom. It is a decision not made just by the brain but by the whole of the body and soul, taking every possible thing into account.*

[43] *Siavash is the Persian Heroin Shahnameh who sacrificed his life for the principles of humanity, not only protecting Persia, but also protecting the enemy of Persia too (principles of humanity).*

anyone for any reason or for any order or for any law harms or hurts the soul or the wisdom of humanity, he or she is considered a lie. Hurting people and harming wisdom propagates fear in the heart of the society. *Fear of God makes us lie to each other. Hypocrisy develops when religious fear of a god encourages people to live lies.* A society or a population that does not lie does not propagate fear, oppression, or assault. This does not come under the category of moral advice; rather, this is the natural instinct of humanity, and it must be invoked. *It is, in fact, the natural instinct of humanity that is shaped and classified as the dean of humanity.* This is the vision that appears from deep inside the dean of humanity.

Creating fear or harming anyone's body or wisdom in the name of Allah or Yahweh or Ahora-Mazda, whether here on this Earth or in the afterlife, is against the dean of humanity. *Dean of humanity does not build a wall separating two different souls or wisdoms or separating the believers from nonbelievers. Dean of humanity brings all the people together irrespective of their beliefs or backgrounds.*

Lie or false isn't just in our conversation. *Lie is hurting spirits—lie is hurting wisdoms—lie is hurting thoughts—lie is hurting souls—lie is hurting the consciences.* These hurts and harms terminate the trusts and is the cause of all false and lies within the heart of humanity.

The thoughts and visions of the dean of humanity are portrayed very nicely in a story in the *Shahnameh* by Ferdowsi that clearly shows the meaning of the dean of humanity and the difference among the four popular religions (Zoroastrian, Judaism, Christianity, and Islam) and the dean of humanity. This is explained in the following section.

Religion in the eyes of Ferdowsi as a thinker

Ferdowsi described truth in a concept of *allegory of elegant sackcloth* as it is made of sinews working in unity and harmony, a representation of ultimate truth. In Persia, fabric was sinew[44](the Persian word for this is تاروپود), ligament, and a representation of harmony, unity and God.

In Ferdowsi's allegory of elegant sackcloth, the elegant sackcloth is the truth (dean of humanity) and it is being pulled apart by religions of different faiths to tear the truth (dean of humanity) apart in order to protect their own truths. Therefore, they are tearing apart the real truth for their own gain and for their own faith. The sackcloth has four corners; these four corners are being pulled by the four religions of the world. They are as follows:

- Religion of farmers, Zoroastrian
- Religion of Moses, Judaism
- Greek religion, Christianity
- Tazi[45] Religion, Islam

Zoroaster, Moses, Jesus, and Muhammad are pulling and tearing apart the sackcloth or the truth for the defence of their own truth. In despite of all the efforts, the sackcloth is not torn apart and no one takes possession of it. Therefore, none of these wise men owns the truth. Worse than this, they are tearing apart the truth, and the unity of all of these religions is also undermined by this action. Well, what is this real truth that is being pulled? This truth is life and humanity. This very lucid and telling allegory of the sackcloth shows that the truth can't be

---

[44] *Sinew: Uunity as a fabric*

[45] *Tazi: A common term used for Arabs by Persians.*

owned by any one of the four religions. Ferdowsi is saying that none of these wise men has the truth or can own the truth. This story was carefully crafted and hidden within the story of Alexander in the *Shahnameh* so it couldn't be quite visible to prying eyes and it would be protected against religious persecution. Here is the story as told by Ferdowsi:

دگر آنک دیدی ز کرباس نغز
گرفته ورا چار پاکیزه مغز

Therefore, you've seen the elegant sackcloth
Four wise men holding and pulling the sackcloth

چنان چارسو از پی پاس را
کشیدند زانگونه کرباس را

In four directions, for defence of their own faiths
They've pulled in such a way the sackcloth, the real faith

نه کرباس نغز از کشیدن درید
نه آمد ستوه آنک او را کشید

Didn't tear apart the elegant sackcloth
Also those who pulled were not worn out

تو کرباس را دین یزدان شناس
کشنده چهار آیدت از بهر پاس

You should know that the sackcloth is the truth
The four are pullers defending their own truths

یکی دین دهقان آتش‌پرست
که بر واژ برسم بگیرد بدست

One is farmer religion, Zoroastrian, the fire faith
Comes for collection of tax to keep the faith

دگر دین موسی که خوانی جهود
که گوید جز آن را نشاید ستود

The next is Moses' religion, called Judaism
Who says, pray to nothing but this truism

دگر دین یونانی آن پارسا
که داد آورد در دل پادشا

The third, the Greek—Christianity—the truthfulness
Take the justice to the heart of kingdom

چهارم ز تازی یکی دین پاک
سر هوشمندان برآرد ز خاک

The fourth, the Arab, the pure Muslims
Put down to the dust, the heads of intellectuals

همی برکشند دین از آن، آن از این
شوند آن زمان دشمن از بهر دین

They keep puling from each other, the truth
Become enemies in the name of the truth

No one, at least up to Ferdowsi's period (940-1020), had ever put forward such understandable dialogue between historic religions and the truth that can't be owned by anyone. This message is a very strong message, which can be summarised as: *No one has the truth. No one can own the truth. The only way to the truth is in unity as the fabric of all thoughts, beliefs, and faiths.*

This very understandable dialogue is the real secularism; it is the heart of secularism. Therefore, there is no need of the East to try to borrow secularism from the West because a borrowed ideology would never be as lucid as this. Eastern countries keep translating many books from Western countries on secularism in the hope of establishing a secular society without paying enough attention to their own literature, cultural wisdom, awareness, and background. Secularism must come from within the heart of a community; it cannot come merely by severing religion from a state. That is a negative approach. Severing religion from a state won't be successful if an alternative social structure isn't there to replace it. If it is successful, it won't last long. Secularism is the philosophy of learning the importance of living and loving this life, and loving each other irrespective of faith, nationality, or religion. It is this philosophy that can make it possible to sever religion from state. Any direct method of severing religion from state would lead to only a temporary solution. Any temporary solution in a society can lead to repeated revolutions and unlimited bloodshed with dangerous and grave outcomes.

We should never forget that the West has built an alternative social structure and then taken a step in severing religion from state. The West, to a large extent, has managed to build a philosophy of learning the importance of living this life, irrespective of faith, nationality, or religion. It was these principles that initiated the Western civilization.

It is 'the path of thoughts and thinking of humanity' which has to be guided in a right direction—in an evolving and progressive direction. Until this is not solved ... the division among humanity will continue and miseries of humanity won't stop. It's the clear thoughts of humanity that can combine and work together—not the conflicting artificial thoughts or supernatural thoughts that humanity has no connection with. The supernatural ideas or beliefs can only tear the truth and human dignity apart for the benefit, selfishness and arrogance of individuals.

Artificial thought are manmade without real cultural background and *supernatural thoughts are those that have connection with an almighty god that owns the ultimate truth.* Supernatural and artificial thoughts can only pretend unification of humanity but it can never make it happen in real, true or factual scene.

CHAPTER ELEVEN

HUMANITY IN THE EYES OF PERSIANS

The root of humanity

The root of humanity in the eyes of Persians is based on the principle that all people from any tribe, nation, religion, ideology, or any level must be able to live together under their own wisdom and thoughts, and they have to be able to think together for a better life on this Earth. *Ghadasat-e-jan*[46] is the highest principle in the root of Persian culture. Naturally, the first principle of the state would have to be the freedom of thought in order to create the right environment in which people are allowed to explore and learn the way of living together.

Persian culture is neither looking to find an absolute truth in the form of a religion; neither does it attempt to publicise and implement the ideology as the basis of a society or a state. Such conduct is against the perception of Persian culture, or the divine, that has the same essence as beings and same essence as mankind. Philosophy, humanity, and values used to be summarised into a phenomenon of the essence of humanity called the divine or god. The divine wasn't an external power, but rather

---

[46.] *Ghadasat-e-jan: Pprevention of any sort of harm to human body or wisdom (non-harm or non-violence).*

the power within the core and soul of humanity in unity and working together.

The Persian divine or philosophy is the basis of all findings, innovations, and experiences. This is why the essence and the characteristics of humans are based on new findings, experiences, and innovation. Divinity in Persian literature opposes the acknowledgement of a 'true religion' or a 'true ideology'. Persian culture believed that there is no single true religion or ideology because a person's or a society's philosophy of tomorrow could easily be different from the philosophy of today. As people and societies move forward, they are alive; they are not dead. Living together in a society is based on the kharad of people, for protection and looking after each other's souls and wisdom and nursing each other. The root of Persian culture believes that ghadasat-e-jan is the basis of a state. This means that protecting each individual's soul and wisdom is the responsibility of the state irrespective of any belief or ideology that individual may have. As Ferdowsi said:

به نام خداوند جان و خرد
کزین برتر اندیشه برنگذرد

In the name of the divine of soul and wisdom
No thought can be greater than this perception

Description of this poem: Ferdowsi tells us that nothing can be greater than the perception of the divine of soul (body) and in the name of the divine of wisdom. This is the god of wisdom and the god of soul. This is different than the gods of established religions. The god of wisdom and the god of soul are the protectors of wisdom and soul irrespective of any religion, beliefs, race, or nationality. Everyone has wisdom and soul, and therefore no one is allowed to harm the wisdom or soul of another. This is a true meaning of secularity in which people can live without fear of religious persecution and without the fear of a painful afterlife.

Wisdom (kharad) is born from the soul of humanity

Persian culture believes that kharad (wisdom) is the eyes and guardian of the human soul, life, and spirit. Furthermore, kharad is born from the soul of humanity. And, naturally, the self-consciousness of the kharad is to protect and nurture all life in this world without any prejudice. As Ferdowsi said:

خرد، چشم جان است چون بنگری
تو بی چشم، شادان جهان نسپری
نخست آفرینش، خرد را شناس
نگهبان جانست وآن را سه پاس
سه پاس تو: گوش است و چشم و زبان
کزینت رسد، نیک وبد بیگمان

> *Kharad is the eye of our soul, if you're a visionary*
> *Without eye you won't live in the world joyfully*
> *The first in the formation of the world is visionary*
> *The guardian of soul three times appreciatively*
> *Thanks to ears, eyes and tongue, collectively*
> *Good and bad are from these three, certainly*

Description of this poem: In Persian literature, kharad is a sieve. Kharad sieves to find things that aren't known. It is at this point that kharad has the job to explore from the soul, taking all the possible side effects into account. Wisdom (kharad), that stem from life, is the main *samandeh*[47], true destiny. It is the kharad of humanity that establishes a state, law, and order.

The objective is kharad of humanity, which has the power and the ability to establish law and order, a stable society, and government without any external divine force but only an internal divine power. We, as humanity, have the internal divine force within us when we are united. The argument is that the divine force is within the humanity's soul. Bahman[48], who is Kharad-e-Samandeh or ark[49], means the actual discipline, within each individual human—this change to Arta, which is justice, truth, and law.

Justice, truth, and law come from wisdom

It is Bahman that appears in the picture of Arta. In the other words, justice and truth and law come from the kharad of humanity. This

---

[47] *Samandeh*: True destiny. It also means state.

[48] *Bahman*: The God of thinking and wisdom that is hidden in every human; it appears in an enlightenment but remains hidden. This means that the truth is not obvious in enlightenment but rather is hidden. It must be explored for and found in the shadow and darkness of the same enlightenment.

[49] *Ark*: Persian word, the word of monarchy, anarchy comes from this word ark. Anarchy has bad meaning today but in the old days, it had a good meaning. Anarchists were those who could protect people without waiting for an order from the top.

Bahman changes amongst people to the actual dialogue (hamporsi[50] in the Persian language) and rhythm and unity.

Humans, in fact, with their own essence, are in direct dialogue with the divine. All human thought comes, basically, from this dialogue; each individual is a building block of humanity or the divine. Based on this principle, the dialogue between people can be understood as dialogue with the divine.

Persian culture is based on the equality of everyone, as everyone is from one soul, which is the soul of the divine. All people are the seeds of the tree of the life, which means divine, which is life. Kharad is the direct reflection of the soul. Therefore, soul and kharad are sacred and no law, power, or any god has the right to harm them. Taking away the freedom of kharad in thinking is hurtful to the soul as kharad is the guardian of soul. Hence, the freedom of kharad in thinking is considered sacred in the Persian culture. Furthermore, the practicality of this philosophy is defined in a Persian word of Shahrivar[51], which is the present name of a month in the Iranian calendar.

Shahrivar, which for thousands of years had been the desire for a state among Persians, means an establishment of a state from the kharad of the people. The state and the ruler must be chosen afresh each time, based on the kharad of the people—not based on their beliefs, religion, or ideology. Electing a ruler based on her/his religious beliefs would only result in the enforcement of her/his beliefs on the people, and this

---

[50] *Hamporsi: Free dialogue among people as they learn from each other.*
[51] *Shahrivar: The month sixth in Persian calendar. The bases of running an estate from human wisdom: secondly, the society that gives saint respect to human wisdom.*

is clearly against the explorative and creative nature of the human being.

In Persian culture, humans are like seeds of one 'interconnected bunch' (like a bunch of grapes)—a bunch that can be likened to the divine. By being united and staying in dialogue with each other, people in a society can create a harmonious union. In other words, humanity or the divine power of people becomes the state.

The unity of a society is the outcome of their dialogue to find the way of living together. The unity isn't in believing in same leader, the same religion or faith, or the same holy book.

Bahman and Arta, which are the foundation of each individual, are the basis for discovery and innovation. Therefore, Persian culture, which has established roots within the soul and spirit of all Persians for thousands of years, promises the formation of a resourceful state and an inventive society.

The principle of all grand ideas such as civil society, human rights, social rights, people power, and modernism that the East have taken from the West have no roots in Islam and also no roots in Christianity or Judaism. All these principles were picked up by the Westerners who were thrilled largely by the Greek's creative culture and to some extent by other Eastern creative cultures. Based on these creative ideas, the Western world was able to initiate the foundation of its present civilization.

We as Persians or Iranians are now looking into a similar process of 'fermenting of the grand principles of Persian culture', in order to facilitate the establishment of a new state and a creative society in Iran.

CHAPTER TWELVE

SECULARISM AND THE SANCTITY OF LIFE

Secularism and the root of Persian culture

Secularism is defined as the principle of separation between government institutions and the persons mandated to represent the state on one hand from religious institutions and on the other from religious dignitaries. This largely means severing religion from state. However, secularism must come from within the heart of a community, not just by severing religion from state, which is a negative approach. If the attention and priority is given to values and cherishing this life, then automatically religion will be set aside. This is exactly the message in Persian literature—the emphasis and admiration in valuing this life is plentiful in Persian literature. It is the respect for this life that makes us respect everyone, to respect all of being, and to respect the very environment that we live in. Hafez wrote a very interesting poem about humanity, which is the heart of secularism. He said that, through the doorway of humanity, there is no vanity or objection ... there is no master or porter.

As Hafez said:

هر که خواهد گو بیا و هر چه خواهد گو بگو
کبر و ناز و صاحب و دربان بدین درگاه نیست

Whoever; tell them come. Whatever; let them say
Vanity, objection, master, porter isn't in this doorway

Description of this poem: *This is a direct reference to the goddess cultures: Whoever wants to come, tell them come. Whatever they want to say let them say.* You can't find vanity, objection, masters, and porters in this doorway. This is the true meaning of secularism. A true secular society respects everyone and allows them freedom.

The true meaning of secularism is admiring and cherishing this life on this Earth to its full glory. Secularism is to be highlighted as giving value and dignity to the life on this Earth. A state has to worry about people's lives on this Earth not the life after death. Based on these principles, life would be much more prioritised than it would be if driven by a religious belief. It is the priority that we should be after; the priority of this life to any afterlife must be shown in our classrooms, media, and the nations in general. Therefore, there will be no need for a negative approach in severing church from state. Apart from this, the negative approach of severing church from state may have worked in the West to some extent. However, it will definitely be more difficult to make the same method work in Muslim nations. Severing the mosque from the state would be a completely different phenomenon than severing the church from state. Severing the mosque from the state is not practical in a nation in which religion is superior to the life on this Earth. Every nation and every culture has a path to the future. It is important to find the correct path that has roots in the identity of that nation.

Introduction of goddess and spiritual values

The root of Persian culture is purely based upon giving value and dignity to life on this Earth. Early Persians respected life and nature through goddess worship. The goddess has been called by many names by different cultures in different periods in Persia: Yazdan, Parvardegar, Khoda, Khodavand, Afaridagar, Afarinandeh, Artaparvar, Raam, Simorgh, Khoram, Shad, Farhang, Daadaar, and many more. The word *parastesh* (pray) comes from *parastari*[52] (nursing). It was Persians who introduced a divine or a god to the Arabs in the first place. The word *namaz* (pray) and the word *Islam* originated from Persian words used in the stories in the *Shahnameh*. The words *salam*, *shalom*, and *Islam* come from the name of Salm in the story of Iraj. The story of Salm, Tur, and Fereydoun in the *Shahnameh* goes back to earlier than 3,000 BCE.

To the Persians, caring for and nurturing people and nature was the actual prayer to the divine in the root of the culture. The same applies to many native cultures of the area. This culture of caring for the life on this Earth is the heart of secularism. Therefore, there is no need to import secularism to the area in order to establish the roots of democracy. Persian culture is many times more secular than the imported Western secularism. *There is no need to borrow unnecessary words.* Borrowing words that relate to morality and values can ruin the Middle East's Golden Culture because it will cause the native culture to be put aside. Borrowing unnecessary words can ruin the internal culture and take the confidence away, as confidence comes from the richness within. Moreover, copying values from the West gives an admission of

---

[52] *Parastesh, parvaresh, and parastari: Persian words; they are from one source. They mean pray and looking after someone and nurturing or nursing. Looking after someone was an actual prayer to the divine.*

emptiness, emphasizing that the East has nothing to offer. This causes a loss of confidence; once confidence is lost, all hope will go with it. Furthermore, the borrowed words always have many times less meaning to the people; they are less understandable than native words.

Persian culture is Simorgh—love, beauty, dance, and music

Love, beauty, and music are flow, being, and life. This can be seen in the portrayal of Simorgh and Raam (Persian goddesses) in this book. There is a plate kept in Saint Petersburg Museum in Russia. In this picture, Simorgh is giving birth to Raam. Raam is the first birth 'being' of Simorgh. Raam is happy and joyful as she is being protected by the bird; while dancing she is offering grape to Simorgh. This is showing the culture of give and take. This is to show that all being is in 'give and take', love, beauty, and happiness.

Being is love, beauty, music, dance, flow, and happiness. From these, humanity takes shape; this is evolution, which is called Simorgh. The portrayal of Simorgh is the symbol of evolution or formation in Persian culture. Persian culture believes in formation or evolution, not in the creation as it is known in Islam, Christianity, or Judaism. Persian culture believes that there is no separation between love, beauty, and music. Every being came from love, from beauty, and from happiness through evolution.

Persian culture believes that humanity is born from a divine source. Therefore, every human has the power of the divine within her or him. The ultimate power of the divine is at the place where humanity gets together in celebration, love, and happiness—this is harmony. The divine is within humanity: *Divine is not an ultimate power or ultimate thoughts but the ultimate harmony*. The divine that is within us evolves as we evolve ... as we learn through the span of time. The divine is us when we are together and work together and think together in harmony. The divine is unity; the divine is the bond between us that creates that vital harmony—making us productive. If there is no unity, then, simply, there is no divine and there is no god. In the early native Persian culture, the divine is not always present. However, the divine is imminent; it can be present at any time if we can become united. One person has no divine power, two persons have divine power as they can create bond and harmony, and this bond and harmony is divine. The bond—the actual unity and connection between two people—is divine (Bahman). The divine is not the cause of the bond, but is the actual bond. To make this clear ... I set an example here: Imagine of a glue that sticks two objects together and makes them one—the two objects are one but there is no sign of the glue. The glue is the divine (Bahman)—it can't be seen but it is there and is the link and the cause of the link, the actual link and the actual part of the whole being. This is why divine is a social bond and has thoughts like a human mind and explores like a human and gives birth every day to a new era, a new communal-bond, unity, and a new harmony. This is what the Persian divine is—the connection, the bond, the harmony and the unity: not unlimited power that can't harmonize with anything. The divine is *yough*[53] in the Persian language and *yoke* in English. The bond and unity of humanity has always been the target of those who wanted to control the people. Any power that wants unity *under his or her name* does not respect the fact that the people 'believe in themselves'.

---

[53] *Yough: Yoke is from this word: A wooden frame normally used to connect a pair of horses or oxen who must work together.*

When the Abrahamic religion came into being, they targeted the bond and the unity and proclaimed that unity is not the connection among humans; instead, they insisted it was the connection and bond between people and God. The Abrahamic religions argued that unity is from an almighty god not from humanity. Therefore, in this way, the source and the originality of the great value of humanity has been undermined and taken away from humanity and given to an almighty god. Now we have a problem taking this source and originality back and returning it to its original source or to its original owner. Making heaven was in our hands, and it was the duty of humans to build a heaven here on this Earth. This power of building heaven has also been taken away from humanity and given to the almighty god who is so big that we have no access to him and there is no harmony between him and us. Furthermore, *the almighty god sends us a message that he will not allow making heaven here on this Earth, but he will rather make it for us only in our afterlife. This is the biggest cheat that humanity has ever experienced!* I want heaven when I am alive not when I am dead! We have to get together and make this life a heaven for us, for our future, for our children, and for our grandchildren.

Life is sanctity

The aim of this book is to reveal the early, true Persian culture and the values of humanity in this culture. This culture has, in its roots, a prime value for humanity and life, irrespective of any belief or nationality. The root of Persian culture gives the value of a saint to every individual life on this Earth. Even the lives of criminals are protected by this culture. This culture has a lot to offer to the modern world.

Persian culture is derived from justice and love. One of the portrayals of this culture is in the story of Fereydoun, Iraj, Salm, and Tur in Ferdowsi's *Shahnameh* that promotes the dean of humanity as discussed in chapter 10 (dean of humanity).

The goal is to promote and apply the root of Persian culture to the future of Persian society—to, in fact, rewrite the Persian constitution. This applies to all the countries in the Middle East too, in order to promote and engage their rich literature in evoking humanity from its core value. We want religions—including Islam—to live in an environment where humans are protected from any bodily harm and from any harm to their minds or wisdom. This is only possible under the framework of the root of native culture where the values of humanity of that nation are shaped. This is the same for people living in United Kingdom where all the sects and religions, including Islam, live side by side happily and without any conflicts under the framework of British culture.

With this strategy, a coherent plan for the peace in the Middle East and the world in general can be introduced. Democracy and peace can be introduced only through values that come out of culture and the right education through evolution rather than by religious ideology or by force. The troubles in the Middle East are caused by loss of identity, loss of core values, loss of dignity, and loss of ethics. Identity, values, dignity, and ethics come from the root identity and root culture and are kept sacred in literature. They do not come from an ideology or religious doctrine. Human minds can be stopped from stimulation under one ideology or religious doctrine. Middle Eastern culture goes back nearly 10,000 years. There are gold mines in these cultures, and the ore must be extracted and reintroduced and tuned up for today's world. The way to do this is to reshape and stimulate the minds for innovative ideas and recreate that self-confidence that has been lost in the region for over two millennia.

Persian culture has a huge influence in the Middle East as it has always been an iconic culture for almost all. Therefore, the success of Persian culture can strengthen the belief of others in the area to fulfil their desire in finding the path for democracy. This is why Persian culture can play a great part in democracy, peace, and stability of not only the Middle East but also the world as a whole.

Definition of culture

As defined in chapter 2, culture is from Latin word *cultura*. *Culture* is related to *cultivation*; culture is growing from the roots; culture is the process of growing, and part of the evolution route of humanity. And as explained, the behaviour of people—their mental content or norms—should not be referred to as culture. Furthermore, any system or religious law such as Sharia law has nothing to do with culture; they are rather against culture. Whereas culture is cultivation and wants to grow and change, Sharia law or any established system wants no change in order to keep its own rule and guidelines. A deeper understating of Persian literature can lead us to the following definitions.

The meaning of culture is always 'making bouquet of flowers' of thoughts collected from different nations that have grown far away from each other. Every struggle gives a gift to a culture. The only reason for a struggle having a historical value in a culture is due to one great thought. This great thought gives birth to a great new experience; only that one thought from the whole struggle is collected into a 'bouquet of flowers' of culture, although the final result of the struggle may produce a negative effect.

In light of this definition, we seriously need to avoid using phrases such as 'bad culture'. Bad things can't be called culture. A culture is the art of living together in peace and harmony gained and experienced through thousands of years of experience of living this life, irrespective of any religions factions or sects.

Pre-Islamic Persian culture, which dates back to almost 7,000 BCE, was not Zoroastrian as many may think. Persians used to believe in the power of mind and nature. They used to summarize their beliefs and ideas into philosophy gathered in the portrayal of a free bird called Simorgh (Phoenix). The words *Jam-e-Jam*, *Peri*, *Shah-e-pariyan*, *Zohreh*, *Raam*, *Shahr-e-khorram*, and *Jahan-araei* are from the root of this culture of Simorgh, the Persian Phoenix or the culture of the goddess.

Persian culture demonstrates and stresses the values of humanity, respect, and ethics in keeping people united and helping them to work together. This emphasis that all the living deserves a better life tomorrow is what we have to work for. In the root of Persian culture is the essence of humanity (the divine), which is love, and this love sacrifices for a new beginning. In fact, the divine sacrifices herself, scatters, as you scatter seeds, to form this life and this world. *Divine spreads the seeds of life to create life.* Therefore, the divine is within you, within me, within our souls, and within every being and life on this Earth in order to harmonize the life. *This is why doing good or loving people or nature was the actual prayer to god or the divine.* The word *parastesh* (praying) in the Persian language comes from *parastari*, which means caring for or nurturing those who need us. In the root of

Persian culture, caring for those who need us was the actual prayer to divinity; there wasn't such a thing as praying to an almighty god with super power and super strength. Persians didn't used to believe in the promises of punishment and reward and hell and heaven. The belief was that heaven and hell are both here on this Earth. We will get our rewards here on this Earth within this life span.

What makes Persian culture so unique?

The soul and wisdom (*jaan* and *kharad*) in Persian culture were holy, regardless of any belief. All people were equal and deserved equal respect, just by virtue of their existence. Sin, in Persian culture was something that harmed the life of anybody, whether a believer or a nonbeliever. In Persian culture, believing a god, not believing in a god, or obeying a god was meaningless, since 'god' or the divine is harmony within humanity. God or the divine wasn't an external force to believe in or to have faith in. Having faith in an ideology was laughable because ideology is in constant change. My beliefs tomorrow are going to be different from my beliefs today, so how can I have faith in an ideology that is in constant change? We are here to live this life and care for each other; a divine source is to strengthen the philosophy of this life. The centre of respect in Persian culture was to live this life and respect this life; while in Islam, Christianity, and Judaism, the centre of respect is the belief (faith). This is the reason for disrespect of the people who want to be free and to be free of the doctrines of these religions. The only people who changed our world to a modern life are those who were free-minded people and dedicated to exploration. The work of these people had nothing to do with an external force such as a god.

Therefore, the respect in Persia's culture is for humanity and this life—not for a supernatural god or prophet. It was for this exact reason that Persian culture managed to spread into many parts of the world during its time. Today, we can still see the traces of this culture in many parts of the world in our everyday vocabulary. For example:

- The word *sun* originates from *sanam*.
- The words *anarchy*, *artery*, and *monarchy* originate from the words Aark, Arta, or Artaparvar (names of Persian gods)
- The word *star* originates from the Persian word *setareh*, which means star.

It is important for the international world to know the early, true Persian culture and to be aware of the root of humanity and its origin and path and the core values of humankind. It is the core identities that can give confidence and belief and therefore stimulate minds. We strongly believe that this is the only way for, not only Persians, but also all other nations to start rethinking from their roots again, which is the only way to recover our long-lost dignity.

Persian culture sends us the message that we are responsible for all the good and the bad in this world; we are responsible for all our sadness and happiness; we are the sponsors of justice and repressions. Testimony of this message is plentiful in Persian literature. A good example is a rubai of Omar Khayyam:

ماییم که اصل شادی و کان غمیم
سرمایه‌ی دادیم و نهاد ستمیم
پستیم و بلندیم و کمالیم و کمیم
آئینه‌ی زنگ خورده و جام جمیم

We're the joy and the core of the sadness
We're the sponsor of justice and repression
We're wicked, the great, the perfect, and the flawed
We're the crystal ball and oxidized mirrors

Description of this poem: We are the main cause of our own sadness and happiness; we are the sponsors of justice and all the unfairness and repressions; we are wicked and great; we are perfect and flawed; we are the magic crystal ball and rusted mirrors. Magic crystal ball refers to our vision that we are the key to all of our problems; we can see and plan the future. The oxidized mirror is the sign of a dark mirror and blocked vision. The message in this poem is clearly that we are responsible for our destiny; we cannot leave our destiny to a super god or to an almighty god; neither can we blame such a god for our fate. The message of Khayyam, here, is exactly the opposite of the message that comes from Islam.

Finally, it is only within the culture of humanity, which comes from the deep identity and literature of nations, that we can bypass the lies of religions and give respect, dignity, and consequently confidence to people who are the true owner of values of humanity. Without such respect, dignity, and confidence, there will be no love. If we don't work together with our hearts and love, neither freedom nor democracy is possible. Any shortcut solution will always be short term and will eventually result in more bloodshed.

CHAPTER THIRTEEN

GODDESS CULTURE

Introduction

At a time when the survival of humans was a constant struggle, life was much more admired; indeed, it was perceived as a miracle, and rightly so. I have seen the birth of my child in hospital; I have never ever seen anything as miraculous as the birth of a child. The earlier beliefs and thoughts of humanity began with this wonder of the miracle of a woman's body bringing forth a child—a new life. This was the beginning of belief in the goddess.

Many recent archaeological discoveries of the goddess cultures provide validation to the theories of the former religions and their respect for women. This principle of respect for women created a religion with an incredible social equality that is almost unbelievable to us today.

This created a peace-loving, egalitarian society spread across the whole of Europe as well as Persia, Egypt, and India wherein the mother goddess was worshipped as the centre of belief or religion. The mother goddess wasn't a super goddess asking for obedience. The goddess was a way of thinking. It was principles and a philosophy in which every woman was respected as goddess. This is not a strange issue; even today this is more or less practised to some extent in very cultural-based nations. The respect for women, to some extent, that we see in Western civilization must be rooted in such a culture; more research is required to reveal this. The idea isn't to go back to goddess culture; the idea is to be able to think about where we were and where we are heading.

The pursuit of the science of archaeology has unearthed thousands of artefacts from Neolithic Europe, mostly in the form of female figurines. These discoveries have contributed to opening the eyes and minds of many researchers as they made discoveries about earlier civilizations that the world doesn't know a great deal about. These new phenomena of ancient civilizations are now emerging—further studies of goddess culture is finally getting a voice in field of archaeology. The concept of the goddess is becoming more understandable as the origin of the core value of humanity.

Marija Gimbutas's goddess discoveries in Europe

The leading pioneer in goddess culture research is the archaeologist Marija Gimbutas, who comes from a very well-educated family. Gimbutas earned a status as a world-class expert on the Indo-European Bronze Age, During the 1950s and early 1960s. In her work *she studied European prehistory religions, and challenged many traditional assumptions* about the early period of European civilization.

Marija Gimbutas studyied the patterns and symbols of cult objects for thirty years. She developed the field in archeomythology (the fields of archaeology, comparative mythology). She believed the key in discovering the meaning of prehistory is through interdisciplinary research. Gimbutas's concluded that Neolithic (Stone Age, Stone era) sites or site in Lithuania and across Europe pointed to long-term stable egalitarian (democratic) societies *with women at the centre, materially and spiritually*. This became her basis of the *matriarchal (women domination) studies movement and the Goddess movement.*

Gimbutas discovered water to be representative of the mother goddess as the life giver. This is a very lucid finding, which matches well with goddesses in Persian mythology and literature. Water is an archetype from where all life flows; this was understood and recognized by our ancestors. The amniotic fluid produced inside the woman's womb during pregnancy used to be called *water* in Persia. The connection of water to the goddess or the divine is plentiful in Persian literature. It used to be viewed as water and seeds being like magnets, pulling each other to form life ... the being. In Persian literature, juice, wine, and essence of being are well connected as water and divine power (goddess).

In her discoveries, Gimbutas showed the differences between the Old European (Stone Age) system being a civilization of the goddess culture and the Bronze Age Indo-European patriarchal or male dominated culture. She concluded that this change happened due to invasion of male-dominated, Kurgan people. The most interesting part of her finding which relate to the study of this book is her finding of old European goddess culture in which societies was peaceful—they honoured homosexuals, and they supported economic equality. This is an amazing discovery regarding humanity ... further research on these areas and its connection with Middle Eastern goddess culture can reveal additional interesting bumpy path that humanity has travelled.

A similar event also happened in Persian when Zoroastrian, a male-dominated religion, took over Persia around 200 CE and imposed its hierarchical rule of male warriors. *The goal of the Zoroastrian takeover—a religious takeover—was to make a nation equal in strength with European male-dominated nations. This is an amazing parallel event that happened both in Europe and Persia that no researcher has ever investigated.*

Gimbutas found one of the earliest symbols in human history—the zigzag, which was used by Neanderthals around 40,000 BCE. The letter *M* or *W* in the zigzag shape was found to represent water. Another category of symbols she managed to attribute to the goddess were the chevron and *V* symbols. It is very interesting that she related the *V* to the bird goddess and also to understand the bird goddess as a protector; this is an amazing similarity with Persian true culture. *The Persian Simorgh is also a bird goddess and also a protector—as seen on the image at the beginning of this book.*

It is very important to note that in her discoveries, *Gimbutas did not discover a single universal great goddess; rather, she discovered a range of female deities.* This finding is very significant and matches with the findings of Manuchehr Jamali in Persian culture.

In a tape entitled 'The Age of the Great Goddess,' Gimbutas discusses the various manifestations of the Goddess that occur, and stresses the ultimate unity behind them all—from all over the Earth—as feminine.

Gimbutas's findings regarding the humane goddess culture gives us hope that we do not have to go far in finding solution to our problems; we need only to explore our roots, which we have tragically forgotten. The East has a much greater challenge in researching and advocating their own literature or the goddess culture, which is much more advanced than that of European culture. The challenge of Eastern nations is Islam, an ideology or religion that strictly sees itself as superior and therefore prevents or suppresses any research into a much more humane and unifying culture ... especially a goddess culture.

There have been few criticisms of Gimbutas' findings which is appreciable and normal—we do need critical studies to open-up the subject. Anthropologist Bernard Wailes blames her for not doing critical analysis—I just can't imagine how this could be possible with thousands of artefacts she has managed to find and study: hard evidence. David Anthony has disputed Gimbutas's assertion that there was a widespread matriarchal (mother having central roles) society prior to the Kurgan incursion, noting that Europe had hill-forts and weapons, and most probably warfare, long before the Kurgan Invasion.

There are easy answers to these criticisms. A goddess culture doesn't mean that there is no warfare at all and no need for protection; it is quite the opposite. The Phoenix, which is the core of goddess culture, has claws that are for protection. Tragedies are the core of the goddess culture in which a hero has to go to war to defend the weak and at the same time to refrain from war. There are plenty of tragedies in the *Shahnameh* of Ferdowsi that are meant to show this exact message—how should I go to war to defend the weak and at the same time refrain from the war? Persian literature, amazingly, opens up the doors to solving many of humanity's complex problems.

Persian literature is the key to elaborating much of our ancestors' culture and beliefs. It is the very rich Persian literature that can reveal plenty of hidden matters and illustrate the evidence in favour of Gimbutas' finding. The reason for this is the continuation of goddess culture in

Persian. The goddess culture continued in Persia up to 200 CE, long after Europe had put aside the goddess culture.

Cultures all throughout Europe participated in the goddess culture, with the women as spiritual leaders, not necessarily political or social leaders.

Gimbutas goes on emphasizing that, due to respect for life and birth, the egg was the most obvious symbol in goddess culture, which is still present today. Most cultures use eggs in some form or another to celebrate renewal and the coming of spring. This is, in fact, a common practise in Persia today (Iran) for celebrating Norooz, the coming of spring; eggs are painted several colours. Of course, the same sort celebration is also popular in Europe and is practised in spring; the Easter holiday is celebrated with colourful Easter eggs.

Gimbutas most important relating studies were on artefacts such as vases, water containers, figurines with image of eggs. Furthermore, she discovered and studied a dish from Malta contains Goddess symbols, dating back to 3,000 BCE. Her finding of artefacts of snakes and relating it to goddess culture due to shedding skin as regeneration has amazed me. There are plenty of hard evidences in Persian culture regarding snake and goddess culture—any animals such as snake that shed skin were representative of renewal, change, beauty and freshness—goddess.

Culture of the goddess

The known culture of goddess around the world goes back 40,000 BCE and eventually evolves to a very interesting human culture. The culture of the goddess in Persia lasted longer than it did in other nations and eventually turned into a culture of love, music, dance, freedom, and happiness before being subdued by Zoroastrian and eventually Islam.

As we know from researches and textbooks; human lineage diverted from last common ancestor with its closest living relative, the chimpanzee five million years ago. Modern humans originated in Africa about 200,000 to 250,000 years ago and began to reveal full behavioural modernity around 50,000 years ago. It is a general understanding that our ancestors have been organizing themselves as hunter-gatherer societies till about 8,000 years ago and naturally went through difficult times in this period—realizing their life was finite and they would all die if they did not value this life. This must have led to them to praise women and even pray to them as the origin of birth as the only way to survive. This resulted in the development of the primitive religious beliefs that were nothing but their own depictions and imagination of this world and the survival in this world which must have lead them to female fertility and birth. This is the best religion in the world—a religion that comes out of human instinct for survival rather than supremacy over others. Societies in this way naturally developed a common ground to believe-in and worship in the being, in the birth as the origin of life, which led them into the goddess phenomenon.

Eventually the culture of goddess played a major part in shaping values and respect for humanity and nature. This is the process of evolution of mind and thought that made us to be human today. These goddess cultures are our heritage, our identity through which humanity has been shaped. Persians took the culture of the goddess to a much higher level of spirituality and values, and this has shaped and enriched Persian literature (poetry), which is admired greatly even today—the only true identity known to all Iranian is their literature.

Many people assume that the 'peaceful' goddess cultures knew no weapons or other tools of war, but this theory is preposterous. We cannot look at goddess cultures as utopian societies. It is obvious that any system must have weapons for defence against intruders, even to protect against wild animals. There has always been the moral struggle: How does one go to war and at the same time refrain from war. As mentioned earlier, the tragedies of the stories in the *Shahnameh* of Ferdowsi refer to this principle.

The culture of the goddess was stopped by the introduction of Zoroastrian and Abrahamic religions across the world. We should not forget that many principles of the Zoroastrian and Abrahamic religions were actually taken from the culture of the goddess and then manipulated to suit their agenda to control their followers and take over others. For example, places of worship were often built on goddess sacred sites, and Abrahamic holy days were superimposed over goddess cult sacred days. Symbols such as eggs and various evergreen plants, which had traditionally been used in specific celebrations, were given different meanings. The culture of goddess was very open and diversified to suit different needs; in fact, it was very philosophical and civilized.

The following few lists are made to guides the readers in searching for images of goddesses in internets. The images show that the goddess changed through the span of 35,000 years. They also show how ideas and thoughts were shared between nations and between continents over the years.

- The Venus of Willendorf, estimated to have been made 24,000 BCE.
- The Venus of Dolní Věstonice dated to 29,000-25,000 BCE.
- Persian Venus, Simorgh (Persian Phoenix)—1500-year-old. Phoenix and Venus are hacked on silver plate kept in Saint Petersburg Museum, Russia.
- Alexandre Cabanel, paintings of the birth of the mythological goddess Venus
- Sandro Botticelli, painting of Venus, having emerged from the sea as a fully-grown woman.
- Greek Goddess Aphrodite, the goat-footed Pan, and Eros, 100 BCE
- Anahita, Ancient Persian Goddess, was the goddess of life-giving fluids. Rivers and lakes were sacred to her.
- Persian Golden cup decorated with an image of the Persian goddess Zohreh or Raam. It is known to be from the Ashkanian Dynasty and is over 1,800-year-old. This cup is owned privately by an American.
- Ancient Arabic, triple goddesses: Al-Uzza, Al-lat, and Manat. These goddesses were once worshipped across the Arab world, especially at Mecca. The black stone in the yoni, beneath the Ka'bah is believed to be the symbol of Al-lat, the Great Mother Goddess.
- Indian goddess and child statue, Norton Simon Museum's Asian Art Collection.
- Hindu Goddess Parvati Statue in Brass
- Venus of Arles

- Anahita Temple: Ancient temple of goddess Anahita in Kangawar

Venus, as we know today, evolved throughout the history of humanity. The many goddess images found in Europe and other places must be very useful in finding the process and the evolution that Venus went through. It is most perfidious to refer to the images of Venus as erotic or pornographic. To a large extent, the same will apply to many artistic representations of goddesses that has been found in Europe and analysed by Marija Gimbutas and others. On the other hand, there is no doubt that our ancestors also produced some erotic and pornographic images, as we have today. Nevertheless, don't we have enough skills to distinguish between these simple issues? Do we know of the sexual freedom in the goddess culture? We should not look our past with today's vision of the world. We have to understand our past environment to some extent in order to be able to look at our past with some acceptable vision.

Marija Gimbutas' findings indicate that the 'old European' goddess culture lasted for tens of thousands of years. Europe generally lived in unity and peace; there are notable defensive fortifications around these hamlets. Funeral customs indicate that males and females seem to have shared equal status. This does not disprove the goddess culture, but rather is the proof of equality. Many historians and archaeologists believe the following points in discoveries of goddess culture in Europe:

- Their society was matrilineal; children took their mothers' names.
- Life was based on lunar (not solar) calendar. The lunar-based calendar in Islam comes from goddess culture. To the Persians, the moon was divine; it is seen often in Persian literature. Rumi,

in one of his very famous poems, said he is devoted to the moon.

- Time was experienced as a repetitive cycle in the European goddess culture rather than linearly as we think of it today. However, in the era of the Persian goddess, time was neither linear nor repetitive but metamorphic; time was an accumulation of knowledge and understanding like a tree trunk and the branches. The branches of a tree depend on the trunk and the roots, which represent past time; past time wasn't a time that had gone forever. The past remained as our identity and cumulative values and dignity.

The suppression of goddess worship in Western Europe occurred a few thousand years BCE, when the Indo-Europeans invaded Europe from the East. But in Persia, it carried on with strength until 200ACE when Zoroastrianism took over Persia. However, *Zoroastrian takeover of Persia has never been accepted by Majority of Persians*. Persians continued the struggle for social equality against the rule of Zoroastrian fanaticisms; the struggles such as Kerm-e Haftvad, Bahram-e Choobineh, Sofra, Mazdak, Mani, Salman (Mahyar) and Rostam-Farokhzad ... These are only the recorded struggles. Only in one of this recorded struggle—Mazdak—over 12,000 supporters were massacred in one day, including Mazdak himself. This is only one of the many struggles of our ancestors for our social right.

The continuous, rigorous and tight rule of Zoroastrian has forced Persians for continues struggle for social equality. Adding border conflicts between Persia and Roman Empire—continues struggle has weakened Persia such that they have lost the war against 'Arab religious ideology' invasion causing a huge setback of humanity.

The prolonged life of the goddess culture in Persia left a trail of deep philosophical human mythology. As time went on, and invasions and wars occurred, this mythology was preserved in poetic literature in a coded message. This is how the rich literature of Persia took shape and why Persia remains one of the world's unique and rich cultures.

Moreover, the Persian goddess culture didn't disappear suddenly; the goddess culture was carried on among the people of Persian, unofficially, but publicly and privately, for many years. However, the goddess culture became more and more scarce at the height of Zoroastrian power and after the invasion Islam in 644 CE.

Apart from all that, amazingly and astonishingly, the culture of the goddess in Persia, as it vanished; it found its way into the rich literature of Persia, which is admired greatly even today even though its message is difficult to understand. The reason for the difficulty in understanding Persian literature is the lack of knowledge of the goddess culture among today's readers. The foundation of Persian literature is based on the goddess culture, but the Islamic way of life in Iran has tried many ways to hide this very important image. As an example, Rumi admired greatly the Persian Venus and described her as the sum of the two worlds. He said the celestial stars are checkmated by her beauty and the Messiah will bow to her. This is an amazing and astonishing depiction of the goddess by Rumi. The importance of Rumi in keeping alive the culture of goddess—the true Persian culture—is enormous. Rumi hardly ever mentioned the name of Mohammad or god of Mohammad in his poems, as it would have been too dangerous for him to do so. This is the actual poem from Rumi.

خلاصه دو جهان است آن پری چهره
چو او نقاب گشاید فنا شود زُهره

ستارگان سماوات جمله مات شوند
به طاس چرخ چو آن شه درافکند مهره
چو روح قدس ببیند ورا سجود کند
فرشتگان مقرب برند از او بهره

The summary of the two worlds is the Peri way
Peri is the daughter of Venus
Inexistence becomes Venus, by taking the mask away
Daughter of Venus is so beautiful that Venus comes in existence
Checkmated, the celestial stars entirely, in this way
Like putting lock stopping a wheel in such a way
Would bow to her the Messiah without delay
Gracious angels fulfil their desire, with hooray

Description of this poem: Peri in this poem is goddess (daughter of Venus) who is called the summary of the two worlds; this world and the world of after death. This Peri is so beautiful that once she takes her veil away, Venus (who is also beautiful) becomes in existence. Rumi carried on using the same language of religions in adoring Peri; that the celestial stars are checkmated and the angles fulfil their desire and the whole world, basically, become happier. Rumi did explain who this Peri is in this poem:

برچشمه ضمیرت، کرد آن پری، وثاقی
هرصورت خیالت، ازوی شدست پیدا
هرجا که چشمه باشد، باشد مقام پریان
با احتیاط باید، بودن ترا در آنجا
این پنج چشمه حس، تا برتنت روانست
ز اشراق آن پری دان، گه بسته، گاه مجری

Tied to the fountain of your soul, the Peri

> *Came alive from her, your dream, to the entity*
> *Wherever is fountain, there is dignity of Peri*
> *With caution, you must be there with empathy*
> *Till five fountains of your senses are lively*
> *Know they're from the glow of this Peri*

Description of this poem: Who is this Peri? This Peri has a nest in the fountain of your soul. The entire organ of recognition of humanity, whether sense or spirit such as thoughts, illusion, image, and dreams, are this Peri. This Peri has a nest in every individual person's soul. This is why we have thoughts, illusions, images, and dreams within our souls. This is why, wherever there is a fountain of water, there is also a Peri. Why? Because, wherever is fountain of water, there is life and there is being.

From these poems of Rumi it is clear how spiritual the life was and how much respect was given to life. Peri (goddess) was the expression of the gentility, originality, or purity of humanity to its real value and meaning. This purity of humanity means that the god or goddess is within us not beyond us. This originality of humanity automatically rejects the requirement for any middleman in our communication with god such as preachers or prophets. This is a dangerous theory to those who want to rule over people! Therefore, they had to fight against this theory, and they have done so. As a result of this, they have left trails of bloodshed and vicious wars and killings throughout history. The story does not finish with religion-related wars. Even others who are not religious take their philosophy from these religions in order to control people; one example was *Hitler, whose political rituals closely resembled religious rituals.* The idea of suppression, wars, and supremacy has to come from somewhere—either directly or indirectly—most come from religion.

In a separate poem Rumi explain of the difficulties he has in opening his mouth and telling the truth—the narratives. This is the poem from Rumi.

دریغ شرح نگشت و ز شرح میترسم
که تیغ شرع برهنه است در شریعت او

Ah, couldn't say enough: scared of telling the narratives
Due to Sharia bared swords and its imperatives

Description of this poem: In this poem Rumi suddenly confesses that he is not free in expanding his thoughts due to the bared sward of Sharia-law in Islam. Freedom of speech and freedom of thoughts are not allowed in Islamic world—everyone is scared in revealing their purity and essence. This is the exact reason of hidden messages in the literature of the area and Persian literature. Freedom of thoughts in our literature had to come in poetic form to disguise the prosecutors … Sharia-law in Islam. The messages in poems comes in a short and cut messages—half finished, inchoate messages, in sort of allusions hints and clues—and yet had to claim of telling the messages in a sort of madness and drunken way … to avoid giving chance to murderers in prosecuting them.

In another very famous poem, Rumi explains that he had to break Sanams (another name for goddess) in front of Mohammad in order to find the desired sweetheart Sanam. There are a few places where Rumi dared to bring in Mohammad's name.

As Rumi said:

ما چند صنم پیش محمد بشکستیم

تا در صنم دلبر دلخواه رسیدیم

For Mohammad, we have broken a few Sanam
To reach to the sweetheart, the desired Sanam

Description of this poem: Why did Rumi have to break Sanams? He had to break Sanams in front of Muhammad in order to gain the trust so he could go after his desired Sanam. This is the case and was the case for all intellectuals in the Islamic world. You have to fight with your soul and spirit and kill or break your ability, which is the Sanam inside you, to gain the trust of the religious hierarchies before you can freely find your own desired Sanam. This is exactly what all Persian thinkers had to do—Ferdowsi, Khayyam, Attar, Hafez, and the rest.

The Indo-Europeans invasion of Europe

When the Indo-Europeans invaded Europe, they brought with them some of the 'refinements' of so-called modern civilization—the horse, war, belief in male gods, exploitation of nature, and knowledge of the male role in procreation among others. Goddess worship was gradually combined with worship of male gods to produce a variety of pagan polytheistic religions, among the Greeks, Romans, Celts, and other European cultures. Author Leonard Shlain, in his book *The Alphabet Versus the Goddess*, offers a fascinating alternative explanation. The following text from his website (www.alphabetvsgoddess.com) gives us an idea of the premise of this book:

> … rewired the human brain, with profound consequences for culture. Making remarkable connections across a wide range of

subjects including brain function, anthropology, history, and religion, Shlain argues that literacy reinforced the brain's linear, abstract, predominantly masculine left hemisphere at the expense of the holistic, iconic feminine right one. This shift upset the balance between men and women initiating the disappearance of goddesses, the abhorrence of images, and, in literacy's early stages, the decline of women's political status. Patriarchy and misogyny followed (L. Shlain 1937, 09).

Professor Manuchehr Jamali, Persian writer, writes another fascinating alternative explanation regarding our past heritage in Persian Language—this is my translation:

> Culture goes back thousands of years in the history of humanity, but it is still our present invaluable roots and identity that can be triggered at any time. One example in the European civilization was the Renaissance. This was a cultural movement that took advantage of Greek and European culture; humanity went through its roots for a rebirth (M. Jamali 1928,12).

> Bad events in our history such as war and bloodshed can also be triggered at any time. One real or mythological event in our past, whether good or bad, has remarkable connections to almost all of our behaviours today. Our present happiness and sadness has roots in our past too. Our past bloodshed can appear in front of our eyes as if it has happened yesterday, such as the Second World War which happed at the height of Europe's civilization with the rise of Hitler in Germany causing massive amounts of bloodshed in a blink of eye (M. Jamali 1928,12).

A testimony of Jamali's theory is Rumi. Rumi showed the importance of our past and regarded our past as being our roots:

حقایقهای نیک وبد به شیر خفته میماند
که عالم را زند برهم چودستی برنهی بر او

As with a sleeping lion; there are good and bad facts
Brandishing a hand over them can cause havoc

Description of this poem: Havoc in the above poem has two meanings—havoc to change everything in a good way and in a bad way. Rumi highlights the reality that our past good and bad facts can be triggered at any time by just taping, shaking or brandishing our hand over facts, even by giving it a tender loving care—it can resurface—as a sleeping lion would. This shows the importance of our past facts. Society must always be aware of these facts and try to resurface the value of humanity and prevent the repeat of violence and aggression.

The domination of Zoroastrianism over Persia in 224 CE destroyed the early, true Persian identity and culture, resulting in a gradual diminution of goddess worship and the place of women in society. This was a direct result of the gradual shift of respect from women to men. The worship of the goddess had traditionally enhanced the integrity of women and placed them in a position of respect. This shift upset the balance between men and women as it initiated the gradual disappearance of goddesses in Persia and pushed them into their hiding place—Persian literature.

Initially, Zoroastrianism and later Islam in Persia never acknowledged the existence of the Persian goddess culture; rather, these systems denied reference to this culture, even going so far as imposing the death sentence for anyone who created any artwork that referred to the Persian goddess culture. Unfortunately, all the Muslim nations refer to the art of the goddess as abhorrent images! However, Europe managed to explore the art of goddess during Renaissance, and a great deal of evidence of this can be seen in European museums today. The plentiful artwork in Europe has closed the hands of religion over society to a large extent.

Treatment of Women by Abrahamic Religion

There are many known evidence in our text books showing Pagan religion (before Abrahamic religion) wasn't all mindless and senseless beliefs after all—they were rather well established cultural ideas well connected to goddess culture in this period. This period of our history has been 'cursed' by our, so called, modern religion as believing into multiple deities (polytheism)! Why polytheism is cursed? Why our passed history has been neglected and has been cut off from us as bad, evil and dark? We need to explore these, so called, dark areas of our history, rather than putting it aside and judging by the same old yardstick. It is important to find out why something that is labelled 'evil' has been so labelled—maybe it isn't bad after all—perhaps it has been given the bad-label for the benefit of beliefs (religions) to gain supremacy. The past pagan religions are known to be well connected to root of humanity and goddess religion. It was the rise of Abrahamic religions that has suppressed the goddess culture rather than making the use of the gained experience and advancing it to the next stage of humanity—they have instead ruined a culture and started a new artificially made discipline to fulfil their own desire. This has taken humanity to a wrong unnatural path resulting in human moral stagnation and wisdom collapse—resulting into many other religions for supremacy and consequently unlimited wars and bloodsheds.

As Abrahamic religions evolved, the Pagan religions were suppressed and the female principle was gradually driven out of religion. Women were considered lower to men—the role of women as major figure became limited—as an example: a woman's testimony and inheritance in Islam halved over man.

In fact, all public activity for women has been taken away in Islam. Women's witness was not measured significant in Jewish courts; women were not allowed to speak in Christian churches; positions of supremacy in the church were restricted to men. Young women are often portrayed in the Bible as possessions of their fathers. After marriage, their ownership was transferred to their husbands.

Due to superiority of female over male prior to Abrahamic religions, public activity for women couldn't have been curtailed over night—it went through process over a time span: the religions would of course deny this. For example; Women played a major role in the early Islam and Christianity. However, the process of suppressing women started as religion consolidated and gained power. The process of suppression of women can clearly be seen from letters remaining from early Christianity called epistles—the letters in the New Testament from the apostles (those who were sent away) to Christians. These are formal didactic letters, which were common in early Christianity and in ancient Egypt.

The importance of women in Islamic world has fluctuated throughout history; they were socially admired when they were needed at the time of troubles—wars—and socially subdued when Islam was at peace and had power over the society. Moreover, the stoning practise of women is usually more common when religion is at its most powerful state. This cowardice behaviour happens in Islamic world even today—without any shame.

The importance of women in Christianity also has fluctuated throughout history. The lowest point in the fate of women was reached during the very late Middle Ages, when many tens of thousands of alleged female witches (and a smaller proportion of males) were massacred by burning and hanging over three centuries.

Limitless crime, war, and killing followed the introduction of the so-called modern religions—the Abrahamic religions. The early Abrahamic religion gave birth to other religions such as Islam again for supremacy and rivalry. The idea of using religious phenomenon for supremacy over others has carried on ever since. Even others who were not religious took their philosophy from these religions in order to control people; one example is *Hitler, whose political rituals closely resembled religious rituals*. The idea of suppression, wars, and supremacy has to come from somewhere; either directly or indirectly, most come from religion.

CHAPTER FOURTEEN

DEMOCRACY

Introduction

As we all know, democracy is a political system based upon the concept of 'rule by the people'. But people can't directly rule, so people have to elect a government that can rule. Therefore democracy is a form of government in which the foundation of supreme power is based in the people and exercised directly by people or by their elected agents under a free and fair electoral system. The most common type of democracy is majority rule democracy based on one member, one vote with each vote being of equal value. There are also two major types of democracy 'direct democracy' and 'representative democracy', which is not the point of concern here.

In general, there is no universally accepted definition of 'democracy' or 'liberal democracy'. However, equal opportunity and liberty have both been recognized as significant characteristics of a democracy since prehistoric times. These principles are reflected in all citizens being the same before the law and having equal access to legislative processes. For instance, in a representative democracy, every vote has equal weight; no irrational (unreasonable) limits can apply to anyone seeking to become a representative. Moreover, in a representative democracy, freedom of people is secured by legitimized rights and liberties which are generally protected by a constitution. Basically, democracy that is known to us has its origin from Athenian democracy, which was a direct democracy of its citizens. Athenian citizenship excluded women, immigrants, and slaves; essentially only upper-class to upper-middle-class, native-born Greek male adults were able to take part. How about democracy in Persian civilization that was running in parallel with Greek civilization? Can we really say there was no sign of democracy in Persian civilization but only in Greek civilization?

We all know there was a Persian civilization running in parallel with the Greek civilization, and it is well known that the Persian civilization was far more humane and advanced than the Greek civilization. Therefore, the concept that the early democracy happened only in Greece but not Persia has to be quite misleading. We can't discard democracy in Persia for the reason that democracy in Persia wasn't simply called democracy.

Khoram-Rooz[54] was a celebration of democracy in Persia for over a thousand years. Manuchehr Jamali wrote about this in his book, *Humanism and Humanity in Persian Culture before Zoroastrianism*. From the first to the eighth of December there used to be the celebration of Khoram-Rooz in Persia, which was the celebration of democracy. However, this celebration of democracy was banished by Zoroastrianism and then gradually forgotten. *Any nation that loses its festivals loses its identity too.* Once the identity is lost, confusion kicks in putting people in disarray with no clear path for going forward. Such a confused nation, one day, is Westernised and the next day is Easternised or Islamicized without any confidence or any clear path.

---

[54] *Khoram-Rooz: a Persian word for day of happiness.*

This is exactly what is happening to Iran today. And, of course, it is also happening to Arab nations that are embracing more of a mixture of Islam and Western ideology.

All Muslim nations are confused nations that can't figure out the future path for democracy, whether Islamic democracy, Western democracy, or Eastern democracy. Their only achievement is the number of labels they give to their democracy!

Western democracy or Islamic theocracy

There has been great achievement in self-awakening in the Middle East due to recent Arab revolutions but are they ready for real change for a path to a democratic system? It is feared that the answer would be no. Arab revolutions have to pass through many hurdles in order to experience a type of democratic maturity and open the path to democracy. There are two main hurdles that must be conquered before democracy can prevail in Muslim nations:

- Islam is preventing any easy progress to political maturity because the main focus is on belief and religious duties rather than the root culture, root values, and literature of that nation that is not religious orientated.
- Western democracy can prevent a home-grown democracy, which comes from a nation's own heritage.

Home-grown democracy is the same democracy that we know today, but it is based on the values and principles that are rooted within literature and culture. Culture and religion are two different matters, which can briefly be explained as follows:

- Culture is the values that have been evolved and reshaped themselves throughout the whole span of the history of that nation. Culture continuously evolves to reshape itself. Culture is the phoenix.
- Religion is god-given rules to live by—rules that have been established many years ago in god-given scripts that cannot be amended or reshaped by humanity.

Every principle and value within a religion comes from humanity, but it is captivated within that religion like an imprisoned phoenix. Plenty of our humanity principles that have been lost due to religious theocracy—in fact stolen by religious tactics—can be found within religion. Some of these principles can be found intact in the religion, and some have been twisted 180 degrees to fulfil the authoritarian rule of religious leaders.

The path to a real democracy within any nation begins with the exploration of the root culture by allowing philosophy to gain ground and start forming a strong base, giving room to thinkers and philosophers in order to explore their identity and values within their own culture and literature that glorifies that nation and gives them dignity. This process can increase the power of reasoning and intellectuality within that nation, which is a crucial step to self-belief and consciousness. This is achievable; the reality of the past shows that freedom and dignity weren't as scarce as we know today. Our ancestors have left for us a great wealth of humanity that has been demonized by religious theocracy. *Our ancestors have been given a bad image by this religious madness, which has discredited everything in our past so that the religion itself could claim to be the moral base and foundation for humanity.* This is a harrowing process that came about through hypocrisy and religious zealousness that went on for thousands of years causing wars, starvation, and horrendous killing of millions of innocent people. This is why the names of religion are always paired with the world *hypocrisy* in any nation's literature. As Hafez said:

دور شو از برم ای واعظ و بیهوده مگوی
من نه آنم که دگر گوش به تزویر کنم

Oh, preacher, go away. No more nonsense theocracy
No longer that person I am, listening to your hypocrisy

There are many such examples in Persian literature that show a very strong tie between religion and hypocrisy. In fact, without hypocrisy no religion would have ever existed. *Hypocrisy is the root and foundation of these religions.*

Every Islamic country is trying to instate a vision of Islamic democracy, and there is no common ground between them. In fact, there can never be coordination under the name of theocracy and dictatorship. There is no common ground between the theocracy and democracy. In reality, these two ideologies are as far apart as an Islamist is from an Infidel. In fact, *Islamic democracy is Islamic hypocrisy.* If an Islamist is honest, he or she must denounce democracy, as there is no common ground between Islam and democracy. This is the beginning of the entire problem in Islamic countries. The unity under religion can happen only under fear and dictatorship, and fear is the worst enemy of intellectuals. No wonder there are not enough intellectuals in the Islamic world. In the Islamic world, there has been no experience of home-grown democracy, but there has been rather the experience of home-grown dictatorship. When democracy is proposed for the Islamic world, the moderate thinkers consider the democracies in the West and they quickly conclude that a democratic system can be established overnight by copying a Western constitution. However, we must not forget that it took hundreds of years for the West to establish the democracy that we know today.

Democracy was achieved in the Western world when people fought against stubborn religious zealousness and took the values out of the responsibility of religions and gave them back to people. The value and dignity has been given to the people for just being people, irrespective of their beliefs or religious backgrounds. In fact, Western democracy has taken the power out of the hands of God and given it to the people. Democracy is the product of infidelity to the religious views—setting the prime objective as the people not god. Therefore, there can never be a common ground between democracy and religious theocracy.

On the other hand, a real peaceful Islamic life is possible only under an infidel rule, not under Islamic rule; a clear example of this is the life of practicing Muslims in the United Kingdom. Muslims in United Kingdom practise their religion in total comfort and harmony and at the same time they live happily with all other sects, believers, and even nonbelievers. Everyone has total respect for everyone else. Such a system is almost impossible in any of the Muslim countries unless they reach back and take the path of their roots, establishing those values and respect that were left from their past heritage … values that cherish this life. Religious belief can flourish among family and friends, but cannot be imposed on a whole society of people who belong to many sects and are believers and nonbelievers.

Current advances towards democracy in Arab countries today are taking the wrong path. Because Islam focuses on the afterlife, they do not see this life as a main agenda. Democracy doesn't come only out of ballot boxes; democracy comes out of the stimulation of minds and thoughts. *Democracy means valuing this very world we live in to its full glory.* My belief, my God, my goal must be here in this world, for which I have to work. Democracy is to cherish *this* life, not the afterlife.

I want a minister or a member of parliament to look after my street, my school, my community, and my environment for a better life irrespective of any belief I may have. This maturity hasn't been achieved in our Islamic nations to give at least a glimmer of hope for the future. This is why, in our Islamic countries, there will be neither Islamic democracy nor Western democracy. This may be a disappointing overview, but it is very important to understand the problem; *understanding a problem is a major milestone in solving a problem.*

Is Western democracy possible for the East?

Democracy is power of the people, not power of a god. Democracy believes in the mental power of the people. It believes in community, society, and nation. Because a god doesn't have a part in democracy, democracy doesn't recognize the religious concept of 'infidel'. Democracy embraces all the people from all sects or religions. Democracy can never be based on a religion; democracy has to be put somehow at higher position than a religious belief, as democracy must supersede religion, not the other way round. Religion cannot supersede a democracy as it is biased from its roots against unbelievers and other religious practises. Democracy is respect and self-belief that 'I' as an individual person am responsible for all the bad and good. 'I' as an individual person am capable of building a community and working in the community, and there is no limit to what I can do or what we can do together for a better life on this Earth. 'I' as an individual person am capable of building my heaven here on this Earth. We are the key to unlocking all the problems in our path; this is why we are here on this Earth. Democracy does not require belief in a supernatural entity such as a god. The leadership and each individual in a democracy must be fully responsible for her or his action without relating the problems to a supernatural source such as god.

With such a description of democracy, it is obvious that democracy can't be imported. Democracy must grow within the cultural background of a community. The cultural background is the identity and literature of that nation; the cultural background gives self-respect and pride to that nation, which cannot be achieved by an imported democracy. Democracy must be respected by all the people in that community in order for it to function. Democracy comes out of the values within the cultural background of the nation. This is what I call home-grown democracy. It is only this kind of democracy that has the chance to gain the highest possible respect within that nation. It is natural that a nation would look after and cherish a democracy that has roots in its own identity and cultural background. An imported democracy that has roots in some foreign culture would not be respected, and this could result in no democracy at all, but instead another dictatorship.

The only reason people are asking for a democracy under the Islamic system is that they lack a real political institution. There is no real political institution other than Islam or dictatorship in these countries.

Those moderates who are after real democracy pick up and copy Western democracy. Almost all the people in the Islamic world are pro-democracy, but hardly anyone knows the real path their nation must take to achieve democracy. The only path to democracy is the path that leads to home-grown democracy, not an imported democracy or Western democracy. The institution has to be laid from the root culture in these nations, exploring rather than exploiting the values and dignity in these cultures. This is the only way to achieve a real democratic system in the Islamic world.

Democracy is one, but there are many ways to it

It is very important to find the pathway to democracy, a pathway that will lead through the values and dignity of the cultural background of the people it will serve. Democracy has to be rooted in the society; the rooted connection must be searched for and found. *There is one democracy, but there are thousands of ways to it ... each way has its own philosophy.*

Our heritage is much more than our collective memory; it is our collective literature—a treasure for our future and for our destiny. Literature provides lively and lasting values, community, shows our dignity, identity, and shows who we are and where we are heading. Without these paths, confusion can easily kick-in and the trust of the people can be swiftly lost on those who lay the principles or the constitutions. This scenario perpetually happens in all the modern political movements in our third-world countries.

A Pakistani commentator has exposed the harrowing lives of Pakistanis in Pakistan. He says the people in Pakistan can't have a life. If they want to live, they have to go to India or to the West. If they want to die, they should stay in Pakistan. In fact, this is more or less the scenario in many Muslim nations where, unfortunately, there is no hope and no future for young people. The worst-case scenario for any nation is the total loss of hope by the young generation, especially in developing countries. When hope is lost, the trust will be lost too and therefore there will be no future.

The naïveté of thought in the Islamic world

The naïveté of thought in the Islamic world has created an atmosphere of fear and tension for those who want to be different, who want to think differently, who want to explore, who want to cross the barriers and frontiers of thought. The biggest enemy of intellectuals is the atmosphere of fear—any fear. Even the fear of God should not be encouraged. In fact, fear of God is the worst fear for a path to intellectuality. Intellectuality is dying in the Islamic nations, and this must be taken very seriously. Why is it happening? We cannot just bury our heads in the sand and pretend we see no problem. The Islamic books that are published freely as messages of current thought and knowledge are totally farcical in comparison to our modern world's literature. Why have Muslim nations lost their position in the frontier of knowledge and civilization? It is because of the loss of freedom to travel on the intellectual path. Everybody must be free to question without any fear of persecution, without even the fear of God. Muslims are preventing their own people from asking the most basic questions. How can there be hope in such an atmosphere?

Due to lack of identity, culture, and understanding, many young Muslims think the world is based on conspiracy and fabrication. This is an easy and irresponsible conclusion. Let's not forget, there is no such thing as a perfect country, a perfect democracy, or a perfect world; let's not look for a utopian land. The utopian ideal is fine, but a perfect society is not possible. In any system there are always flaws. A system must be judged in a wider spectrum of thought rather than on a few single events.

A perfect society is simply a society that is perfect; everything in that society is perfect. Having such perfect society is impossible, but working towards it is the ultimate desire of humanity. There are critics who search for a perfect utopian society in their own communities, and when they can't find it, obviously, they become suspicious and pick up conspiracy theories. There is nothing perfect in this world, and we don't want a perfect or pure world. Perfection and purity are in our minds, and rightly so; when these perfect ideas come to practise, those who get closer to perfection need to be admired.

We hear many critics who regularly comment that there is no freedom or democracy in the West. This may be correct in the pure sense of the meaning of democracy. However, there is actually no freedom or democracy in its pure sense. But, do we really want democracy in its pure sense? The answer, in fact, should be no. We want democracy and freedom that is practical, possible, and within the social capacity of our environment. We do not have sanctity except the mythological characters. Mythological characters are ideal characters that are shaped and polished from collective ideas of purity over a span of thousands of years. The Islamic world needs freedom to be able to expose the mythological characters from their own literatures and bring out those purities that have made their literature so rich and so famous for so long.

The most precious experience is freedom

The most precious experience is freedom from fears and freedom of speech. No people should live a life in fear—fear of a system, fear of a society, fear of a god, fear of persecution, or fear of each other.

> *Freedom, freedom, freedom*
> *Free of any fear, the most precious item.*

To be free of any fear must be the prime objective of anyone who wants to build a genuine and healthy society. Even prevention of crimes should not be achieved through fear; it should ultimately be through principles and a constructive path. Through a constructive path, a free society can be formed in which people can exchange ideas with freedom of speech. What is freedom of speech? It is to hear from those from whom we don't want to hear!

Definition of freedom is given in chapter 5 (Atheism) with reference to Persian mythology and the two steps of freedoms are discussed in detail. Nevertheless, with reference to oxford dictionary there are two similar steps for freedom which are as follows:

- Absence of subjection to foreign domination or despotic government (oxford dictionary)
- The power or the right to act, speak, or think as one wants without hindrance or restraint (oxford dictionary)

There is hardly any difference between my definition (taken from Persian mythology) and oxford dictionary definition regarding the first step of freedom given in chapter 5. However, the second step of freedom discussed in chapter 5 is the core discussion which talks about creating an environment that initiate personal talent, purity, essence, consciousness, and the roots of their nature—persuade self-confidence and a person must not be encouraged to follow a pre-defined goal and ideology such as religion.

Every social system and ideology wants to be supported by the people, and therefore they have to claim to be in favour of freedom and even lie about it, as freedom is what humanity wants most. In its simplest form, freedom is being able to do what you want to do. In general, political and financial freedoms enable us to act quicker and to earn more without so many bureaucracy and obstacles. We all like easy life and engage in our hobbies rather than working for money. Freedom gives us more manoeuvrability in exploring life. However, freedom doesn't mean no principles or rule of jungle, at some point, more freedom for me means less freedom for you. Freedom can't be established by a weak government, freedom comes out of confidence and strength which is very important and a vital factor. This is where the complexity of freedom starts. This is where expert philosophers are required who would access and find freedom within the true cultural background of a nation and explore those respected values further. An imported freedom will not be respected in its adoptive nation and will finally break up; in fact, we have seen this happen in many nations. This breakup doesn't mean that the nation does not deserve freedom; it just means the approach was wrong. As I have said, freedom must come from the rooted values of a nation, which can be found in plenty by exploring the literature and true cultural background.

Systematic teaching to make people socially dumb

The most important part of our lives is our childhood. In almost all nondemocratic countries such as our Muslim nations, young people are systematically taught to be socially dumb and unconscious. This is done through so-called brainwashing. Yes, this is a very serious matter. This brainwashing is the cause of racism, xenophobia, and snobbery against each other and against their neighbours. This is a disaster and a very serious problem; in fact, it is the root cause of all the troubles and bloodshed in Muslim nations.

A person who finishes a system of education must have social and moral consciousness that helps him or her have respect for others who may have different beliefs. These educated people should have been taught how to advocate progressive principles for society that is based on a strong bond among all people. However, the reality in Muslim countries is quite the reverse: *our academically illiterate villagers are socially more conscious than our educated city people*. This is a sad misfortune, and is the cause of all the instability and conflicts and miseries. Our educated people are systematically put on a path on which they are unable to take the initiative to create a real social bond with others who have a different belief or religious background.

Here is how this happens: There is a real systematic process that is happening even today in our Islamic world. In virtually all the Muslim nations, young people are brainwashed to be socially oblivious. This begins when they begin school and continues all the way through university. They are taught—brainwashed—to be and to remain unaware of the social aspects of life. The system may teach our young people to be scientists or doctors, but they, at the same time, brainwash them to believe in one thought, one direction, one idea, and one religion—and that is Islamic way of life. Basically, students aren't allowed to learn about diversity and the values of diversity in the social aspect of life. They are given one 'truth', and that truth is their religion ... their god-given religion.

For people in Muslim nations, the only hope to be a real intellectual and thinker—if there is even any chance or opportunity for real intellectuality—is not through the educational system but *strangely* after the educational system when that they can clearly open up their eyes to the outside world. Therefore, it takes young Muslims ten to twenty years to open up their eyes after their systematic education. Then, to explore and to become conscious, it takes another ten or twenty years. By this time, consequently, the person as a thinker must be around fifty or sixty years old ... imagine the dilemma. At this age, the thinker has to face being classified as an infidel, kaffir, unbeliever, and god warrior. This is a disaster. How can a person be a god warrior? This is the dilemma facing the thinkers in the Muslim nations. It is an almost impossible task for our true thinkers and philosophers to work sincerely in the Muslim world. However, there has to be hope—only harder and serious work is needed: human awareness and consciousness will rise again from its ashes and will—one day—fly again.

We, as humans in this complex world, need to be systematically trained in the social diversity of life. Instead, too many in both the East and West are being sent along a defined path by a faith. We ought to be socially wise so we can understand our past heritage and our ancestors who have worked so hard for us and even sacrificed their lives for us. We ought to be able to understand others and to be able to communicate with and understand those who are different from us because they follow a different faith and religion—or even because they are nonbelievers.

The process of communicating and understanding others makes us wise. Wise people do not fight because they are able to find common ground on which they can work together. If wisdom is not encouraged to take its course to full strength, stupidity, foolishness, naïveté will continue resulting into wars and bloodshed.

Nonetheless, we are not purely wise; we are also artists, and our god or divine is from nothing but our own artistic impression of our minds in trying to harmonize with our surrounding. Therefore, a true god—or the divine—is ultimately the art of humanity in harmonizing, rather than knowledge that drops from sky. Consequently, there cannot be only one god because of the diversity of minds and the way we think and the way we see the world. One god means one thought, one impression, or one idea, which is practically impossible. Therefore, believing in one god is to believe in one thought and one idea, which can easily undermine the strength and diversity of our thoughts and philosophy.

Even Muslims can believe in pluralism and diversity of gods if they get their philosophy right as we all are different and we have different views of god. My vision of an almighty god is different from my brother's vision, as we are different people. Pluralism and multiple gods are a sign of sharing … a sign of understanding and working together as gods do. Pluralism, sharing, and understanding are the hallmarks of democracy, and this is lacking among Muslim nations.

Morality

The general understood description of *morality* as seen in many text books is manner, character, and proper behaviour. It is known that, the word morality comes from the Latin word *moralitas*. Furthermore, it is defined that moral can be anyone's practice or teaching within a moral code! A branch of philosophy, called Ethics, studies morality in the sense of defining right and wrong. In its common sense that, 'morality' refers to whatever is right or wrong. But, who defines right or wrong? The answer to this must be 'nobody but human': there must be no god given definition for morality as it can be socially divisive. This doesn't mean morality can't be absolute—there are principals in morality which can't be relative such as harming wisdom and soul of humanity, a universal morality. It is very much bothering to me to hear that morality is relative—defining morality as relative can give an excuse to anyone to undermine our dignity.

Lack of ethics and morality can result in rivalry for political and economic supremacy. Modern technology, unfortunately, is trying to conquer nature rather than respecting the beautiful and wonderful nature that our very existence is based on. Morality is the hard work of humanity and evolved throughout the span of human life on this earth. It is important to be aware of this in order to convey the message to our children that morality doesn't just appear spontaneously for us without any hard work. The world needs new creative ideas and new philosophy to cherish humanity and find a way of emphasising morality and the values of humanity to a level that there can be trust. As defined throughout this book, we have to have confidence; we have to be the masters of our own destiny, morality, and ethics—exploring and continuously developing and sharing new ideas. We need new visions that can fill in the vacuum that is left in the morality of our society, before the vacuum is hijacked by opportunists

Another of our problems is the connection of the word of 'morality' to religion; basically the belief of the general public is that, if there is no religion, there is no morality! This is the basic problem facing humanity today—if we as a thinkers and intellectuals had the initiative and supremacy, this wouldn't have been general public view. Morality was invented and shaped by humanity and then stolen by religions. We owe our morality to our ancestors who shaped the ethics and humanity and passed it to us. Morality can't be owned by any religion or any nation—claim of ownership would be an insult to humanity. Morality is a process; morality is an evolvement, not a god-given product.

Perhaps the only reason that morality is tied into religion today is that it is has been enforced by religious decree. In fact, morality is the principle of being a human. Morality has been stolen from humanity by religions and given to god. Morality and values are the core of humanity; they are what makes us human. Morality and the values of humanity have been shaped and have evolved for over thousands of years by our ancestors with many sacrifices as they passed them to us. Therefore, it is an insult to our ancestors if we dismiss our past by labelling our ancestors as unintelligent and not progressive. Our past is our roots, and we are connected to our roots; it is where we developed our signature of being human. Our past is our identity. As Rumi said:

هر کسی کو دور ماند از اصل خویش
باز جوید روزگار وصل خویش

Anyone who has distanced from the roots
One day again, seeks connecting to the roots

Description of this poem: Once again Rumi admired the roots in this poem. Rumi said that, no matter how much one denies the past—the roots—eventually he or she will come back to the roots.

The responsibilities of the ethnic minorities

Ethnic minorities in the West who have backgrounds from third-world countries or Muslim nations have enormous responsibilities for their own people back home. Ethnic minorities have left their homeland so they can make a difference in the lives of their own people back home as well as integrating into the Western society. *Integrating into Western society does not mean losing one's own identity; it means learning a way to live together*. People from all cultural backgrounds must never ever forget their identities and roots. We can leave our roots, but our roots will never ever leave us, as our roots are from our consciousness, and our consciousness will never die but stays with us and haunts us till the last breath of our lives. We have a huge sense of responsibility—responsibility towards our own nation, towards our own people. Our people are our identity, and we will never have true happiness unless we contribute to those people who need us. A believer who refrains from highlighting his nationality and culture and tries to be identified just by religious identity will not have a restful mind.

Muslims living in the West have a huge responsibility to learn from the West to find a way to contribute to their native homeland in whatever way possible, whether mentally or economically, in order to improve the life standard of their native land.

The responsibility of Muslim women in the West is also enormous. Women are much more caring people than men, and they must act as the goddesses of their homeland. The children of the Islamic world are our own children; we must never forget this. Who is going to build their future? Taking care of impoverished people is an actual prayer to the divine, or God. This is not like praying to God, but it is the actual and the true prayer to God. The impoverished people need to be guided and helped over the hurdles and the difficulties which they are feeling with their own flesh, bone and blood—the problems which are preventing them to show their ability in this dynamic world. People from third-world countries who live in the West must never allow themselves to play politics. We must open up to the world and show our faces. The Eastern people living in the West are the face of their own people. We want to show our faces to the world and tell them about ourselves, show them our culture, our identities, and the contribution that we can make to the world.

By covering our women's faces behind a *hijab* we are hiding away from the problems, and this is being irresponsible. Anyway, who is going to look at your face when there are so many women in the street? Apart from this, there isn't much problem with wearing a scarf for religious or whatever reasons, but wearing a veil or *niqab* is hiding away from those vital responsibilities. We are here to open up our eyes and to show our faces and the faces of our people who we have left behind. We have to show our faces to the world and tell them who we are and what we really want. We have to be icons for the changes in our own-third world countries. We have to take responsibilities; not doing so is disgraceful, shameless, and inhumane. We must not hide our faces against those vital responsibilities that are facing us all. We have to show that we have not just run away from those problems from our own countries; rather, we have come over to find solutions to those problems that seem to be unsolvable. If we do not take on these responsibilities, then that is a clear indication that we have just run away from the problems that we have left behind and we can't be bothered about the miseries, misfortunes and agonies of our own people. How can we behave so irresponsibly and yet open up our mouths and judge the West?

There is plenty of work that must be done; there are huge challenges facing the third-world countries, and we must take responsibility for making things better. Blaming our problems only on the actions of the West is irresponsible and does not enable us to accept our own responsibilities. Blaming the neighbours for our failings is the easiest strategy, and proof of being totally irresponsible.

We are immortal

My Muslim brothers keep on asking me about life after death. Aren't we all brothers and sisters? Aren't we one entity? We should be together, work together, care for each other as one body and *stick together as if we have been attached together with Super Glue; this makes us immortal.* If we really could achieve this unity only under the name of humanity without any religious sects, then there would be no separation between us, and therefore we would become immortal.

The separation between us also separates us from our goals, and therefore each individual of us as a single being is mortal.

The separation between us is the separation between us and our divine or god. In this separation, there is no god, no belief, no values, no dignity, and no humanity.

The separation between us is the separation between us and our goals, hopes, and wishes; without you, each of us is like dead man walking.

These separations are the main cause of the degradation in our mortality and the cause of all our problems. We need to explore thoughts and philosophy in order to turn separation into unity. As Rumi said:

بشنو این نی چون شکایت می‌کند
از جدایی‌ها حکایت می‌کند

Listen to the tale of this reed
The separation pain, it reads

Description of this poem: Reed in this poem is a special Persian or Arabic flute called *ney*, one of the oldest musical instruments still in use. The ney produces a sussing sound of pain, and this pain is referred to as separation pain—separation of humanity from the soul, from within, and from the divine that is within us that shapes our being, our characters, and our spirits.

We make our death (mortality) here in this life, and also our everlasting life (immortality) here on this Earth. If we can't explore from within, we are not alive. If we are suppressed and subdued thoughtfully, we are mortal. As Rumi said:

آزمودم! مرگ من در زندگی است
چون رهی زین زندگی، پاینده‌گیست

Experienced, this life is my death and destiny
A path through this life is to the eternity

Description of this poem: Rumi had so much respect for this life, and he admired those who lived the life. A person who lives only for the life after death doesn't live *this* life. That's why Rumi expressed that our death and destiny are here in this life, when we are physically and consciously alive, and our path to eternity is here too. Therefore, losing a person would be a sorrow just like losing a part of our body, but life carries on. Within the philosophy of friendship, we are part of the whole community, and therefore we are immortal as a community. The fact is, we as individuals are very vulnerable and mortal, but as a unified people we are divine and immortal. We are part of one body; if a part of a body becomes injured, the rest of body will follow in accordance.

As Saadi, the Persian poet, said:

بنی آدم اعضای یک پیکرند
که در آفرینش ز یک گوهرند
چو عضوی به درد آورد روزگار
دگر عضوها را نماند قرار
تو کز محنت دیگران بیغمی
نشاید که نامت نهند آدمی

> *Humanity is of one body, likeness*
> *The root of its formation is of one essence*
> *If a part of a body receives soreness*
> *The rest of the body will follow in accordance*
> *If you are indifferent to people's soreness*
> *You can't be described as a human likeness*

Description of this poem: This lucid poem articulates humanity to its full glory. Saadi defined humanity as one body because humanity is formed from one essence. So if a part of the body receives agony and pain, the rest of the body will feel the pain and agony too. If we are indifferent to people's pain and agony, then Saadi suggests, this is immoral and asks this question: How we can be addressed as a human? Feeling people's pain is the principle of the culture of humanity—*feeling people's pain is the principle of being human*. It is important also to note that Saadi referenced the *formation* of life not the *creation*.

It is very imperative to be, to exist, to be alive, to stay alive, and to have confidence that we have a healthy life ahead of us. *It is very crucial to be alive and stay alive.* We have to believe in ourselves and believe that we can change the world. We *are* the world. We urgently and desperately need such confidence if we are serious about making a difference to the miserable lives of the many people who are left behind in this world for any excuse. We can think, we can explore, and we are capable. We need this confidence.

Descartes, French philologer said, 'I think, therefore I am'. However, there is a very much stronger message that comes from the root of Persian culture. As Rumi said, *'I explore, therefore I am'*. This is the exact wording from Rumi:

ترا اگر نفسی هست جز که عشق مکار
که چیست قیمت مردم؟ هر آنچه میجوید

Till your last breath, nurture love solitary
Exploration is merely, the price of humanity

Description of this poem: The price of humanity is exploration. The admiration and appreciation of Rumi for nurture of love, kindness, and exploration is unique in this poem—*without exploration love can't be nurtured*. He talks of the connection of nurture of love and exploration. Additionally, he carries on stressing that the price of humanity is exploration, to be an explorer—without exploration nurture of love is impossible.

I doubt, therefore I am

The first principle of thinking is to be able to doubt everything we have been taught as beliefs. If we don't doubt, we can't think. *Any belief system that doesn't allow doubt is like a rope around our necks tied to a peg in a stable in order to limit our movement*—treats us as you treat a donkey—is this not an insult? We are explorers who are not subdued to a predefined destiny of life, death, and after death as defined by religions. We are explorers; we can explore our way through our lives with our artistic talent, with our scientific talent, with our engineering talent, and with our medical talent, and so on. We have wealth of knowledge in bringing the unity and happiness and making a healthy society. We have this power; we can do this. We are alive; we must stay alive and work seriously for those who are alive, for our children and for our grandchildren and for the generations to come.

Our heritage is much more than just being selfish. *Our heritage comes from our collective ethical values that are rooted in our past and that have evolved through the span of thousands of years.* These values are like pebbles that have travelled through mountains and valleys and have been polished to form the literature that we have today. These are pure treasures that can't be just put aside as history. These values were born from the effort and the struggles of our ancestors who worked hard and contributed to humanity. We owe it to our children, our grandchildren, and the future generations we will never meet to keep these values in our literature alive by the joy, delight, happiness, pleasure and enjoyment of hard work, research and exploration.

APPENDIX

List of terms used throughout this book:

- Abrahamic religions: Judaism, Christianity and Islam.
- Anoushiravan-adel: A famous Persian pre-Islamic king who is publicised for being a fair and impartial ruler and used as an iconic character in Persian literature—either as a true or sarcastic figure.
- Ark (ارک = دژ ِ بهمن): Persian prehistoric word for *wall* or a secure place. The word for monarchy, anarchy comes from this word. Anarchy has a negative meaning today, but it used to have a positive meaning. Anarchy used to be referred to government soldiers placed all around the country, defendants against intruders, for protection of people without waiting for orders from the top—otherwise; it would have been too late to act against the intruder.
- Arta: divine or soul or humanity, which is also Simorgh (Persian Phoenix). The English word artery is believed to have come from Arta.
- Baba Tahir, (بابا طاهر): An eleventh-century poet; Persian literature/Kurdish literature.
- Bahman (بهمن): the month of February in the Persian calendar. Bahman: the god of thinking and wisdom who is hidden in every human—it appears during enlightenment, but otherwise remains hidden. This means, the truth is not obvious in enlightenment but rather hidden in the enlightenment and must

be explored in the dark areas or in the shadows areas of that enlightened environment. Any enlightenment forms a shadow or dark area that we can't see unless we explore.

- Bahman: The bond—the actual unity and connection between two people is bahman (divine). Bahman is not the cause of the bond, but is the actual bond. For example: a glue that sticks two objects together and makes them one—the two objects are one but there is no sign of the glue. The glue is bahman—it can't be seen but it is there and is the link and the cause of the link. Bahman the god of social bond harmony.
- Charshanbe-Soori: A *firework-like* festival held on the last Tuesday evening of the year (The evening is called the Wednesday evening in Persia).
- Culture: Culture, in this book, refers to cultivation, the process of growing, and part of evolution, the route of humanity.
- Day (دی): The month of December in the Persian calendar, named after the god of love and happiness, Khoram.
- Dean (دین): This is a Persian word that comes from the Persian word for seeing (dean or bean) and vision (again from Persian word beanesh). Dean is a vision of humanity in exploration and finding the way forward. Dean wasn't a static idea; it was rather a fluid and dynamic idea.
- Dean-e-Mardomi (دین مردمی): The religion of humanity—I call this "dean of humanity" in this book.
- Diya: Blood money in Sharia law.
- Eizad-Banoo (ایزد بانو): A Persian word that means the god women—goddess or Venus or Zohreh or Raam seen in the image given at the start of this book.

- Ertedad or Morted (ارتداد، مرتد): Apostasy, changing religion from Islam to any other faith—the consequence being the death penalty.
- Farhang (فرهنگ): A Persian word for civilization and culture; it is also the name for the Persian Phoenix (Simorgh).
- Farvardin (فروردین): The month of March in the Persian calendar or Arta-Farvard; the god of celebration and festivals.
- Ghadasat-e-Jan: (قداست جان) Prevention of any sort of harm to soul (human body) or wisdom (the ideology of no-harm and no-violence).
- Ghasas (Sharia law): Eye for eye, blood for blood—revenge.
- Ghazal: A poetic form consisting of many lines of verses in which the poet puts herself or himself to be an ideal person or an iconic person for the past, present, and future, representing the path of a person to an ideal world on this earth. *Ghazaliyat* is the plural of Ghazal.
- Halal: Permissible by Islamic law.
- Hamporsi: Free dialogue among people in order to learn from each other.
- Haram: Not permissible by Islamic law. See the word Hu-Ram and similarity with this word. In fact anything from the land of Hu-Ram was disallowed by Islam.
- Hu-Man: This is the Persian word for (هومن). This is antonym of doshman (Persian word for enemy). This is where the word of 'human' comes from.
- Hu-Ram: Persian word for (خرّم) khoram (Persian word for happiness). Ram is the name of Persian goddess. See the word Haram and similarity with this word. In fact anything from the land of Hu-Ram (happiness) was disallowed by Islam.

- Jamshid: The first iconic man and god in Persian mythology. He was named after the god of thinking and reasoning, and he ruled Persia for over 300 years. It is very important to know that he was not a king but a god.
- Kharad: Human intelligence and awareness (wisdom). It is a decision not made just by the brain but by the whole of the body and soul, taking every possible thing into account before making the final decision.
- Khoday-nameh: The articles that were left over from Persian ancestors in farmers' hand (Libraries were burned by Arab invasion of Persia) from which the Shahnameh is written.
- Khoram: (خرّم) A Persian word for happiness.
- Khoram-Rooz: A Persian word for day of happiness.
- Lily and Majnoon: Persian love storey in many Persian text books—similar to Romeo and Juliet.
- Man: (من) has the meaning of 'me' in the Persian language and it also means thinking in Persian literature.
- Mardom: Persian word for people. This is from two words mar + tom or dom. Mar is another name for goddess and tom or dom is the seeds or egg. Therefore, Human or Mardom are the seeds of the divine. This means human has the egg or essence of divine—similar idea of egoism.
- Norooz: Persian New Year.
- Parastesh, parvaresh, and parastari: These Persian words are from one source. They mean pray, looking after someone, and nurturing. Looking after someone was the actual prayer to divine.
- Pierre: Reference to an old wise man or a sarcastic reference to a man with religious authority.
- Ramin and Vis: Persian love story such as Romeo and Juliet.

- Religion: Religion in this book refers to Zoroastrian, Judaism, Christianity, and Islam.
- Religions of light: A reference to Zoroastrian, Judaism, Christianity, and Islam.
- Rend: A humanity character who appears as a mystery character that can't openly show her/his true face or character; therefore the character sends indirect messages and hides behind a mask. It is much easier to criticize the unjust by being a Rend rather than a philosopher—a philosopher would reveal too much and get caught.
- Rubai (plural: rubaiyat): A complete poem, consisting of four lines of verses in which the poet puts himself to be an ideal person or an iconic person for the past, present and future; representing the path of a person to an ideal world on this earth.
- Samandeh: True destiny; it also means state.
- Sassanid Empire: Persian Empire from 224 to 651 AD.
- Seventy-two: The number seventy-two, or 70+, in Persian culture, was the symbol of unity—the unity of Arta (goddesses), the principles of human unity and dignity.
- Shahnameh of Ferdowsi: The Persian mythology book: it has national epic of Iran and related societies, consisting of some 60,000 verses.
- Shahrivar: Sixth month of the Persian calendar. The basis of running an estate from human wisdom; secondly, the society that gives saintly respect to human wisdom.
- Shams Tabrizi; The spiritual instructor of Rumi. Rumi is a total devotee to Shams, so much so that Rumi calls him God.
- Shar-e Khoram (شهر خرّم): The Persian word for democracy. It also means city of happiness. It was Persian principle of civil society and democracy to make people happy. Furthermore, there are more words for democracy in person culture that are

Raayenitan, Raadhenitan and Raatenitan. (راینیتن، رادنیتن، راتنیتن جوانمردی، رادی کردن، بخشیدن و آزادمنش)
- Sharia Law: The moral code and religious law of Islam (eye for eye, blood for blood …)
- Simorgh (Persian Phoenix): God of souls or body (Arta) or the cluster of the whole soul. No human, even an agnostic, would fight her/his own soul. Simorgh is the seeds of humanity, where humanity grows. This is why Simorgh is so popular and there is hardly anyone against this philosophy. Persian Simorgh is also a bird goddess and protector of weak people. Simorgh saves a newborn child (Zal, Persian Hero) and looks after the child—up to the age of eighteen and then gives him back to his father SAAM (سام).
- Sinew (تار و پود): Unity as a fabric.
- Siavash: Persian hero in Shahnameh who sacrificed his life for the principles of humanity, not only protecting Persia, but also protecting the enemy of Persia too (principles of humanity).
- Sizdah-Bedar: A picnic-like festival held on the thirteenth day of Persian New Year.
- Sofreh: Similar to tablecloth that is laid on the ground and around which people sit and eat together.
- Spirituality (معنویت): It is to be able to define life and morality.
- Tazi: A common term used for Arabs by Persians.
- Working-wisdom (خرد ِ سامانده): The wisdom that listens and finds the mistakes and corrects itself and therefore moves forward.
- Yalda: The first night of winter, the longest night. This is celebrated in Persia. This shows how importance the darkness was to Persians. Persians use to embrace darkness not to run away from it as Plato did.

- Yough: Yoke is from this word. A wooden frame normally used between a pair of horse or oxen.
- Zahhak: Mythological character, god; symbol of dictatorship and injustice, who ruled Persia for 1,000 years. It is important to know that he was a god—a vicious god—not just a king.
- Zakani (Obeid Zakan): Persian poet and satirist of the 14th century
- Zohreh: Venus, Aphrodite or Raam
- Zoroastrianism: A monotheistic religion and philosophy based on the teachings of Prophet Zoroaster. It was the official religion of Persia from 200 CE to 650 CE—against majority of Persian people's will.
- Zunnar (Zonnar or Zonar): A waist belt made with thirty-three or seventy-two threads in a variety of colours—representing the unity of nations. Seventy-two, *also*, represents Arta or the love of nations. This word's meaning was changed by 180 degree and used to demonize people—see the following:
- Zunnar (Zonnar or Zonar): This beautiful word's meaning was changed and used as a reference to demonize people: A reference to a distinctive cloth forced upon the Dhimmi, Christians and Jews, to signify their inferior and submissive status to Muslims as required by Sharia Law.

BOOKS CITED OR RECOMMENDED

1. Bertrand Russell, *Historey of Western Philosophy*, London: Routledge (an imprint of the Taylor & Francis Group), 2001.
2. Bill Warner, *A Two-Hour Koran*' USA: Canadian Scholars' Press (CSPI), 2010.
3. Bill Warner, *Factual Persuasion*' USA: Canadian Scholars' Press (CSPI), 2011.
4. Bill Warner, *Islam and the Psychology of Muslim*' USA: Canadian Scholars' Press (CSPI), 2012.
5. Ferdowsi, *Shahnameh of Ferdowsi*, Tehran: Amirkabir Press, 1986.
6. Hafez Shirazi, *Divan-e Hafez*, Tehan: Eqbal Press, 1982.
7. Manuchehr Jamali, *After the Div—called Akvan*, London: Kurmali Press, 2001.
8. Manuchehr Jamali, *Devious way of thinking*, London: Kurmali Press, 1987.
9. Manuchehr Jamali, *Happy Wisdom*, London: Kurmali Press, 1998.
10. Manuchehr Jamali, *How can people become phoenix*, London: Kurmali Press, 1999.
11. Manuchehr Jamali, *Human, the yardstick for a state*, London: Kurmali Press, 1991.
12. Manuchehr Jamali, *Humanism and Humanity in Persian culture before Zoroastrians*, London: Kurmali Press, 2006.
13. Manuchehr Jamali, *Minorities and freedom*, London: Kurmali Press, 1985.

14. Manuchehr Jamali, *Must run away from truth*. London: Kurmali Press, 1989.
15. Manuchehr Jamali, *Persian Republic*, London: Kurmali Press 2010.
16. Manuchehr Jamali, *Philosophy, the way of disconnecting with the truth*, London: Kurmali Press, 1996.
17. Manuchehr Jamali, *Rendi, the identity of Hafez Shirazi*, London: Kurmali Press, 2004.
18. Manuchehr Jamali, *Resurrection of Simorgh (Phoenix)*, London: Kurmali Press, 1997.
19. Manuchehr Jamali, Rumi, *the believer of Sanam (Venus)*, London: Kurmali Press, 2005.
20. Manuchehr Jamali, Rumi, *the joy and Resurrection of Ram the child of Simorgh (Phoenix)*, London: Kurmali Press, 2004.
21. Manuchehr Jamali, *Secularism in Early, true Persian culture*, London: Kurmali Press, 2002.
22. Manuchehr Jamali, *Self-renaissance is Strength*, London: Kurmali Press, 1978.
23. Manuchehr Jamali, *Shahnameh and us*. London: Kurmali Press, 1996.
24. Manuchehr Jamali, *The kiss of devil*, London: Kurmali Press, 1984.
25. Manuchehr Jamali, *The rebellion Wisdom*, London: Kurmali Press, 2003.
26. Manuchehr Jamali, *The view from a cliff*, London: Kurmali Press, 1985.
27. Manuchehr Jamali, *Zale-Zar and Zoroaster*, London: Kurmali Press, 2002.
28. Marija Gimbutas and Joseph Campbell, *The Language of the Goddess*, Thames & Hudson publisher, 2001.

29. Marija Gimbutas, *The Civilization of the Goddess: The World of Old Europe*: California: University of California Press: 1982.
30. Marija Gimbutas, *The Goddesses and Gods of Old Europe: Myths and Cult Images*, California: University of California Press: 1982.
31. Maulana Jalaluddin Balkhi (Rumi), *Koliyat-e Shams-e Tabrizi*, Tehran: Talayeh Press, 2008.
32. Maulana Jalaluddin Balkhi (Rumi), *Masnavi Manavi*, Tehran: Majid Press, 2002.
33. Michael Wood, *The story of India*, UK: BBC Books, 2007.
34. Muhammad Ibn Jarir Tabari, *History of Tabari (16 Volumes)*, Asatir Press, 1973.
35. Omar Khayyam, *Omar Khayyam Rubaiyat*, Tehran: Atileh_Honar Press, 2002.
36. Richard Dawkins, *The God Delusion*, Transworld Publishers, 2006.
37. Richard Dawkins, *The Selfish Gene*, Oxford: Oxford University Press, 1976.
38. Saadi Shirazi, *Golestan*, Tehran: Payam Press, 2002.

INDEX

A

Abrahamic 78, 79, 113, 118
Abrahamic religions are the roots and seeds of nihilism 118
According to the dean of humanity, making people afraid of anything, such as a god or a hell, is also an offencebecause it hurts their wisdom 206
Afghans 2, 200
afterlife 23, 28, 42, 81, 86, 115, 118, 119, 139, 140, 152, 205, 217, 222, 261
A gloomy and sad face has to be melted to flow 146
ancestorsXII, XVI, 3, 4, 7, 9, 12, 29, 72, 73, 80, 81, 99, 145, 147, 150, 183, 184, 189, 235, 237, 239, 242, 243, 258, 269, 272, 279, 284
An ideology has to be replaced by a new, rooted philosophy that dwarfs the original ideology 93
anthropology 26, 249
anti-Semitic 155
Any belief system that doesnt allow doubt is like a rope around our necks tied to a peg in a stable in order to limit our movement ... 279
Any brightness creates a shadow and a darkness area that is unavoidable 63
Any god-given script is an insult to humanity, and to god too 76
apology 123, 161, 165

Arabic countries 66
Arabization 76
A real devoted scientist must be a devoted, self-aware scientist,
   not a devoted, religious scientist...168
Artificial thought are manmade without real cultural background 213
As legendary a man as I, hasnt seen the globe......................................124
Atheism... 20, 24, 87, 91
Atheist..4, 24, 25, 95, 111, 112
Attar... 82, 95, 105, 135, 169, 171, 172, 174, 175
Attar emphasised that Sharia law opposes the philosophy
   of humanity..174
Attar in which he emphasises that execution is murder. 171

B

Bad things cant be called culture 229
Bahman changes amongst people to the actual dialogue
   (hamporsi in the Persian language) and rhythm and unity 219
Bahram-e Choobineh 8, 243
ballet boxes 11, 129, 192, 261
Balochistan 2
beauty is divinity 18, 59, 116
Being able to feel other peoples pain is one of the most important
   principles of the culture of humanity 73
Being cheerful is the full meaning of life 110
belief XIV, 5, 12, 22, 23, 24, 25, 27, 32, 35, 38, 39, 43, 59, 77, 81, 92, 96,
   99, 112, 113, 116, 118, 119, 129, 133, 136, 165, 168, 175, 183,
   184, 192, 204, 205, 216, 222, 226, 228, 230, 231, 233, 248, 257,
   258, 260, 261, 268, 271, 275

Belief in the afterlife, such as heaven and hell, was only for the uneducated 59
Be the divine 22
biological evolution 4, 72
blinding people and giving them walking sticks 77
blood money is blood sucking 174
bloodshed 10, 170, 174, 188, 212, 232, 246, 249, 268, 270

C

Christianity 110, 111, 202, 208, 209, 211, 220, 224, 230
civilization1, 5, 7, 15, 73, 79, 81, 82, 90, 122, 186, 188, 195, 248, 249, 264
Civilization is harmony of the flowers of thoughts 80
Civilization is the path of understanding 81
consciousness 3, 4, 19, 38, 68, 76, 78, 96, 97, 136, 143, 144, 148, 164, 183, 187, 217, 258, 267, 268, 269, 273
conspiracy 39, 265
Converted to Islam for a few days sake to pretend being the same ... 46
core   IV, 5, 14, 15, 23, 24, 36, 55, 66, 83, 85, 86, 87, 104, 110, 112, 113, 116, 117, 133, 140, 149, 166, 198, 199, 205, 216, 227, 231, 232, 234, 237, 267, 272, 310, 311
creationism 34, 38, 76
creative mind 139
Culture is a learning process based in the values and the experiences 188
culture of female god, the young were the source of initiative 201
culture of male god, the elders were the source of initiatives 201
culture opposes nationalism and xenophobia 188

D

dance	IV, XII, 31, 104, 120, 224, 239

Darkness and brightness are the two sides of one coin, complementary to one other 63
Darkness gives birth to our findings 61
Darkness is where we all come from 61

dean of humanity	119, 198, 201, 203, 208, 227, 282

Dean of humanity allows people to change their god at any time, as god is from the wisdom 205
Dean of humanity brings all the people together irrespective of their beliefs or backgrounds 208
Dean of humanity declares that, hurting or harming anyones soul (body) or wisdom is an offence 206
Dean of humanity does not build a wall separating two different souls or wisdoms or separating the believers from nonbelievers 208
dean of humanity is based on the soul and the life, which has priority over belief, race, tribe, or nationality 204
dean of humanity, is the vision that emerges from the essence and cluster of humanitythe vision that materialises the cluster of humanity 201
Dean of humanity of Iraj opposes anger, threat, and malice, which take away chivalry and love in humanity 204
dean of humanity protects the soul and the wisdom of every individual against any harm 203
dean of humanity says, the existence of the divine depends on us ... if people can get together and be productive, then, there is divine 198

Defined spirituality 43
definition of life is spirituality, which is missing in our modern life 183
deities 8, 87, 91, 236, 251
democracy10, 11, 55, 66, 97, 118, 186, 189, 192, 193, 195, 206, 223, 227, 228, 257, 258, 259, 260, 261, 262, 263, 265, 270
demonize 14, 132, 287
destiny ...11, 85, 94, 95, 115, 117, 128, 138, 190, 193, 206, 218, 232, 263, 271, 276, 279, 285
dictators.. 68, 104, 125, 127
Different name of goddess in Persia 223
dignity 9, 18, 30, 31, 78, 84, 106, 107, 110, 114, 131, 134, 163, 192, 206, 222, 223, 227, 231, 232, 243, 246, 258, 260, 263, 271, 275, 285, 311
Diminution of my intellectual.. 153
Diminution of my intellectual capacity in obedience to God is exactly the diminution of God in its formation or creation of humanity.... 153
divine VI, XIII, XVII, 16, 17, 18, 19, 20, 21, 22, 24, 29, 32, 34, 35, 36, 40, 47, 56, 58, 59, 60, 62, 75, 78, 79, 88, 89, 90, 94, 95, 98, 99, 102, 115, 116, 117, 124, 128, 140, 150, 151, 161, 163, 164, 166, 167, 169, 181, 187, 197, 198, 199, 200, 201, 202, 215, 216, 218, 219, 220, 223, 224, 229, 230, 235, 242, 270, 275, 276, 277, 281, 284
Divine is all of the beauty and colours.. 59
divine is humanity, and humanity is the divine 167
divine is multiplicity and exuberance.. 59, 167
Divine spreads the seeds of life to create life... 229
Divinity 199, 216
dogma... 67, 84, 160, 161
dogmatic..84, 91, 107, 161, 165

doing good or loving people or nature was the actual prayer to
    god or the divine 229
domination 64, 100, 104, 106, 114, 157, 161, 235, 250, 266
dowry 109, 110
dream 90, 91
dynamic .... II, 14, 25, 28, 36, 39, 46, 77, 79, 99, 163, 165, 167, 196, 205,
    274, 282

E

Eastern goddess 7, 235
Egypt 3, 72, 89, 158, 163, 233, 252
ELAHEH XVI
enlightenment 20, 58, 108, 136, 198, 218
ethical evolution .... **XVI**, 3, 15, 79
Every being is beautiful 116
*Everything should flow through music and harmony rather than be
    forced and threatened by punishment* 117
experiences and the art of living together. 52
explore .... **VI**, VII, 3, 10, 60, 76, 107, 127, 128, 143, 147, 153, 166, 215,
    218, 236, 251, 258, 264, 267, 269, 276, 278, 279

F

Faces are idle and fixed, but meaning must flow 146
Faith is the mother of fanaticism 48
Faith is the stagnation of thoughts 48
Fear is the worst enemy of the path to wisdom and intellectuality .. 206

Fear of a god, which is advocated in religions, is an insult to
humanity 120
Fear of God makes us lie to each other 208
feeling peoples pain is the principle of being human 277
Ferdowsi .... XIV, 34, 40, 56, 64, 65, 66, 68, 69, 70, 83, 89, 90, 96, 101, 105, 123, 125, 127, 131, 150, 151, 168, 200, 201, 206, 207, 208, 209, 210, 216, 217, 227, 288
Ferdowsis allegory of elegant sackcloth 209
Ferdowsi used the word *formation* rather than *creation* 105
five deities 99
Freedom 97, 114, 185, 189

G

Gimbutas .... XII, 7, 8, 10, 234, 235, 236, 237, 238, 242, 289, 290
God   IV, VI, XII, 18, 19, 20, 22, 23, 24, 25, 26, 27, 29, 32, 35, 40, 41, 58, 64, 66, 69, 78, 84, 87, 88, 90, 91, 93, 94, 95, 97, 109, 111, 113, 114, 120, 122, 125, 127, 128, 132, 141, 145, 149, 150, 152, 153, 156, 161, 162, 167, 168, 198, 201, 204, 205, 218, 219, 223, 230, 231, 232, 261, 269, 270
Goddess .... IV, XII, 199, 223, 233, 239, 241, 243, 248, 250
God doesnt need our submissive thoughts and obedience 152

H

Hafez 102, 103, 105, 133, 150, 175, 205, 259, 289
Halal 133, 143
happiness ...... **IV**, XII, XVI, 19, 34, 42, 59, 84, 85, 109, 110, 113, 114, 115, 116, 117, 132, 133, 140, 195, 199, 224, 225, 231, 232, 239, 249, 256, 273

Haram .... XVI, 133, 143, 283
harmony... 5, 20, 29, 59, 81, 82, 94, 98, 117, 120, 140, 146, 181, 192, 209, 225, 226, 229, 230, 260
harrowing process that came about through hypocrisy and religious zealousness 259
History dies, but culture, humanity, and values are reborn and evolve 188
Hitler, whose political rituals closely resembled religious rituals 253
Hu-Man 199, 200
humanity .... XII, XV, 3, 13, 21, 22, 27, 31, 32, 35, 38, 39, 64, 65, 72, 78, 83, 84, 88, 92, 99, 106, 107, 108, 109, 110, 111, 112, 115, 117, 119, 120, 121, 122, 123, 125, 126, 128, 129, 131, 133, 139, 140, 141, 145, 147, 149, 150, 151, 153, 164, 166, 167, 168, 169, 172, 174, 175, 186, 188, 190, 196, 197, 198, 199, 201, 202, 203, 205, 206, 207, 208, 209, 212, 215, 217, 218, 220, 221, 224, 226, 227, 229, 230, 231, 239, 249, 258, 265, 272, 275, 276, 279
Humanity 120, 157, 188, 189, 196, 197, 199, 200, 201, 202, 256, 277, 288
Humanity isnt like a bullet coming out of the barrel of a gun aimed at the future 188
Humanity must evolve from its old form to a new form 188
Humans, in fact, with their own essence, are in direct dialogue with the divine 219
hu-man (the divine) is not the cause of the link but is the link 197
Hu-RAM XVI
Hypocrisy is the root and foundation of these religions 259

I

I AM GOD 94
I am the truth **123**, 127, 160, 163
I doubt, therefore I am 60
I explore, therefore I am 49
I explore, therefore, I am VI
If there is no freedom, there can be no going forward 97
If there is no happiness, then, there is no life 113
immortal 56, 117, 275, 277
Indians 2, 200
Integrating into Western society does not mean losing ones own identity it means learning a way to live together 273
intellectuals job isnt to prove or disprove the existence of such a god 91
Islam **XIV**, XVI, 66, 103, 110, 161, 162, 163, 167, 205, 220, 223, 227, 230, 242, 244, 252, 259
I think, therefore I am 49
It is, in fact, the natural instinct of humanity that is shaped and classified as the dean of humanity 208
it is not selfishness that we dont adore it is the arrogance that we hate 189

J

Jamshid 121, 123, 124, 125, 126, 127, 128, 129, 130
Jamshid made heaven here on this Earth 122
Judaism 27, 28, 39, 110, 208, 209, 211, 220, 224, 230

K

kaffir 161, 269
Kerm-e Haftvad 8, 243
Khayyam is a well-articulated rend who knows no boundaries, knows no submissive character, and is free of any such believes 149

L

Lack of ethics and morality can result in rivalry for political and economic supremacy. 271
lie is hurting souls 208
Lie is hurting spirits 208
lie is hurting the consciences 208
lie is hurting thoughts 208
lie is hurting wisdoms 208
Life is happinesswithout it life is meaningless 84
Life is Sanctity .... VI, 226
Love and faith are antithetical 48
love cant go hand in hand with creationism 33
love is superior to all the beliefs or religions 48

M

makes people to be the enemy of their own freedom 53
Mani 8, 243
Manuchehr Jamali .... IX, 1, 7, 14, 288, 289
Manuchehr Jamalis fascinating alternative explanation regarding our past heritage 249

Mazdak 8, 243
meaning of life 24, 110, 112, 121, 122, 145, 147
Mithraism, a mystery religion that began in Persia and expanded to Rome 57
moral evolution 72, 76
morality 13, 18, 24, 27, 34, 66, 75, 83, 88, 90, 92, 94, 95, 113, 193, 207, 271, 272
murdering the whole population of earth for being infidels—foundation of these religions 181
Muslim ... 152, 155, 156, 160, 161, 162, 163, 164, 165, 168, 202, 208, 209, 224, 260
Muslim nations 75, 77, 118, 134, 251, 264, 268, 269, 270
myth is the product of thousands of years of experience 51

N

names of religion are always paired with the world *hypocrisy* 259
Nihilism 118
None of the leaders is dropped from the sky 111
No one can own the truth 212
No one has the truth 212
Not allowing people to openly explore their ancestral heritage is an insult to the heritage and to the dignity of the people of that nation 77

O

Obedience to God is humiliation to human intellectual capability 153
Omar Khayyam 4, 5, 15, 41,
    42, 85, 106, 108, 109, 112, 113, 115, 117, 119, 120, 131, 133, 134,
    137, 141, 142, 143, 144, 148, 149, 152, 158, 168, 231, 290
Omar Khayyam was on a mission to change the world to his ideal
    world 115
One who thinks is from his own essence 121
our academically illiterate villagers are socially more conscious than
    our educated city people 268
Our ancestors have been given a bad image by this
    religious madness... 258
Our essence, our values, and the true meaning of humanity has been
    stolen from us and given to an almighty God XIV
Our heritage comes from our collective ethical values that are rooted
    in our past and that have evolved through the span of thousands
    of years.. 279
Over 12,000 Mazdak supporters were massacred 9

P

People who pray to an almighty god arent really praying to a
    god they are praying to power 111
Persian Culture 224, 226, 227
Philosophical definition of the divine.. 44
Philosophical definition of this life 44

Philosophy must work towards putting the discoveries of science to peaceful productive use that will benefit all mankind in all nations 191
Phoenix ...... IV, XII, 20, 28, 29, 30, 31, 32, 35, 40, 79, 83, 98, 99, 188, 198, 202, 229, 237, 241, 281, 283, 286, 289
Plato 55, 58, 64
Platos version of enlightenment has made the enlightened individuals superior to others and has created super humans and dictators and almighty gods who have dominated over people for many centuries 57
poem **XIII**, 14, 19, 21, 22, 28, 33, 34, 40, 42, 62, 65, 66, 67, 69, 70, 78, 89, 94, 98, 102, 103, 105, 110, 114, 124, 125, 126, 129, 133, 134, 135, 136, 137, 138, 140, 142, 143, 144, 145, 146, 149, 164, 167, 176, 200, 203, 232, 244, 247, 272, 276
power of me 141
Procreative spirituality 43, 44
psychic 38

Q

Quest for supremacy may destroy our own environment 13
Quick solution of ideologies such as religion add more to the skin and pay less attention to the core 37

R

Raam .... IV, XII, XIV, 145, 147, 199, 224, 229, 241
reasoning 5, 120, 122, 125, 127, 189, 258
religion is a thorn in the flesh of every wise person 74

Religion is nothing but a walking stick 76
religions broke the chain of continuity of the thoughts of humanity 8
Religious believes are static ideas 77
Rostam 8, 55, 56, 57, 64, 201, 243
Rostam goes into the darkness and effortlessly makes his way through—he is able to see through in the darkness with his own eyes 57
Rostam story of Haft Khan-e Rostam shows that darkness and clarity are complementary to each other rather than being against each other 63

S

Saadi 72, 73, 105, 277, 290
Sanam .... XIV, XV, 58, 98, 289
Sassanian .... XIV, 127
Secularism is admiring and cherishing this life on this Earth to its full glory 222
selfishness 34, 129, 189
separation .... XIII, 27, 29, 32, 35, 39, 190, 224, 275, 276
September 11 39
Shahnameh 56, 64, 68, 83, 101, 121, 122, 123, 127, 128, 129, 150, 168, 200, 201, 204, 206, 207, 208, 223, 227, 288, 289
Shahr-e-Khorram 229
Sharia-law 172, 174
Simorgh ..... IV, XII, **XIV**, XV, 20, 29, 30, 31, 35, 74, 78, 79, 95, 98, 99, 169, 188, 198, 199, 202, 205, 223, 224, 229, 241, 281, 283, 286, 289
Simorgh is also a bird goddess 236
social equality 8, 9, 233, 243

Spirituality 12, 43, 286
stick together as if we have been attached together with Super Glue this makes us immortal 275
Supernatural and artificial thoughts can only pretend unification of humanity but it can never make it happen in real, true or factual scene 213
supernatural god is a thorn in the flesh of any free-minded person 91
supernatural thoughts are those that have connection with an almighty god that owns the ultimate truth 213
superstitious .... XII, 25, 59

T

the almighty god sends us a message that he will not allow making heaven here on this Earth 226
The Conference of the Birds 95, 169
The core is a hidden treasure which invites us for continues research, continuity 37
the essence of humanity 145
The first principle of thinking is to be able to doubt everything we have been taught as beliefs 279
The most falsified thinking in todays modern world is a belief in a thought that just enlightens us 63
the most honourable divine 75
The need for a deity and for obedience to that deity is the ultimate weakness of humanity 41
The one who thinks exists from his own essence 122
the only way to be a religious person is to be hypocrite 103

The only way to the truth is in unity as the fabric of all thoughts, beliefs, and faiths 212
the prolonged life of the goddess culture in Persia 9
There is no one like Jamshid who has such respect for this world 126
There is one democracy, but there are thousands of ways to it ... each way has its own philosophy 263
There is one freedom or democracy, but there are many ways to it 68
The responsibility of Muslim women in the West is also enormous 273
There was no requirement for faith in order to believe 47
The ultimate truth is life VI
the ultimate weakness of humanity 79
The values of humanity also have been stolen from us and given to the God of these religions XVI
Thinking is love of reasoning 120
To come out of religious dogmatic and simplistic thoughts and fall into the trap of a materialistic world is a terrible fate! 53
togetherness and unity is the dean of humanity 201
To the Persians, caring for and nurturing people and nature was the actual prayer to the divine in the root of the culture 223
To the Persians, the divine was the world 59
To the Persians, the truth is hidden and is in darkness, such as caves 57
Truth wins ... evens in defeat 43

U

understanding a problem is a major milestone in solving a problem ... 261

V

Venus .... IV, XII, XIV, 18, 145, 147, 149, 186, 241, 244, 245, 287, 289

W

We are the solution to all of our problems 66
We evolve today to move into tomorrows world 188
We form the divine. The divine forms us 35
we must adore selfishness for the sake of self-confidence 189
when we explore beauty, we are the beauty 147
when we explore meaning, we are the meaning 147
*Who is as bold or brave as to turn his back on religion and all the
 truth and certainties that are known to humanity* 149
*wisdom is the mate of the soul and the principle of government
 in every person* 204
Without unity we are blind 79

X

xenophobia 268

Y

Yoke combines our energy 21
You are the divine 22
you are what you explore 67

You can not be a real scientist and not believing in the cause and effect 162
Youngsters have become accustomed to simplicity and naïveté 10
Youngsters trying to believe in supernatural thoughts and remain static rather than advance dynamically in ideological terms.... 38
You will never know a face unless it is happy 146

Z

Zahhak 126, 127, 201, 204, 286
Zakani 105
Zakariya Razi 158, 159
zealousness 181, 259, 260
zigzag 236
Zohreh .... XIV, 145, 147, 149, 229, 241
Zoroaster 3, 132, 209, 287, 289
Zoroastrian ... 8, 9, 27, 28, 35, 42, 44, 45, 99, 101, 113, 119, 127, 157, 208, 209, 211, 229, 236, 239, 240, 243, 244, 250, 284
Zoroastrianism 3, 64, 113, 196, 250, 256, 287
Zoroastrian takeover of Persia has never been accepted by majority of Persians. 8
Zoroastrian takeover of Persia has never been accepted by Majority of Persians 243
Zunnar 132, 287

This book inspired me to this poem:

Fountains of fire come out of my burning core
Avoid being a beggar, knocking on every door

THE LOST KEY

Dr Soufiani, founder and director of a civil engineering firm in London, is a London University PhD qualified and practising civil and environment engineer. He was researcher at University of London, research assistant at University of East London, and lecturer at Iran University of Science & Technology.

Soufiani's passion about Persian literature has steered him to over ten years of extensive research with a great Persian philosopher, Manuchehr Jamali. Jamali has managed to open up many incredible doors to him in comprehending Persian literature to its true meaning of values, love, unity, and dignity.

Soufiani's understanding of Eastern and Western cultures has given him a great leverage in his exploration of Persian literature in comparison with Western civilization and the lack of democracy in the Middle East. With this book, he highlights Persian literature as an invaluable asset and the lost key in opening the lock of the declining morality in our modern world and the absence of democracy in the Middle East.

The world must sincerely assist in exploration of this nation's literature for the sake of morality. The Middle East must explore and use her own invaluable potential rich literature to rise and fly from her own ashes to establish the ethical society that will give them the tools for building and establishing the foundation of a democratic system.

Many Persian poems have been translated throughout this book to highlight the core values of beautiful Persian romantic and humanistic culture.

Printed in Great Britain
by Amazon.co.uk, Ltd.,
Marston Gate.